HERE'S TO OUR
far-flung
EMPIRE

An account of a Colonial upbringing

Tony Orchard

HERE'S TO OUR
far-flung
EMPIRE

An account of a Colonial upbringing

MEMOIRS
Cirencester

Published by Memoirs

MEMOIRS
PUBLISHING

Memoirs Books

25 Market Place, Cirencester, Gloucestershire, GL7 2NX
info@memoirsbooks.co.uk   www.memoirspublishing.com

ISBN 978-1-909020-25-2

Printed in England

Acknowledgments

Had it not been for World War Two and the 'miracle of Dunkirk' I, along with thousands of other children with parents in the colonies of the then British Empire, would have had an upbringing restricted to boarding schools in Britain, with holidays spent with other folk *in loco parentis*.

However, once out of the box aged just fourteen, I enjoyed a liberating run for the next seventeen years, seeing much of the world and living in three British dominions – if one includes India which, somewhat unfairly, was denied that status due to the prejudices of those times.

Since my experiences were more geographically varied than the majority of such children, several of my extended relatives encouraged me to write them up. That done, it seems like a good idea to collect them into one book.

Therefore, I wish to acknowledge my debts to three groups of folk.

Firstly to my parents for providing me with the best education that they could afford under difficult and detached family conditions.

Secondly, to all those who provided me with a welcome home environment *in loco parentis*, which introduced me to a wider variety of interesting cultural and social experiences, geographically separate, than one would normally have within a single family.

Last but not least, to my son Peter, who provided me with the hardware in the first place to record all these memories, and then soothed my geriatric frustrations with a laptop, though it often behaved in an irrational manner with an apparent mind of its own.

Contents

1.

A Colonial Wedding and Families

I have now reached the ripe old age of eighty plus, and when I look back on my colonial upbringing, which involved no less than seven different groups of people, together with holidays spent with other boys on a farm in South Africa, I think it is about time that I submit it all to paper. My reasons are firstly for the benefit of members of my family, immediate or (more likely) extended, and secondly for anyone else interested in such an upbringing during the final years of the British Empire, before air travel shrank space and time.

I was born in Mombasa, Kenya on 13 June 1926, and christened in the Anglican cathedral, my parents having met and married there a year earlier. My father had been posted from Karachi in 1923 by Shell Oil Co. as assistant to a Mr Bigg-Wither in order to set up a subsidiary operating company in place of Smith McKenzie and Co., who had previously represented the company's interests. This is a familiar risk for any such representative – that as soon as they build up the business to a meaningful size, the parent company decides to establish its own unit, over which it has full control.

My father, G L (Tishy) Orchard, had been in the Royal Horse Artillery in the Great War, during which time he rose from the rank of a lance bombardier to a second lieutenant and served in Salonika and Mesopotamia. On demobilisation he returned to his parents' home in Hoylake, the Wirral, and joined the Cotton Exchange in Liverpool only to be overtaken by the slump in 1920–21. He thus went east to seek his fortune and joined Shell in Karachi, which then was part of British India, for the first of many three-year tours. He clearly enjoyed his bachelor life there, his forte being riding as a gentleman rider – that is, as an amateur, at the races, which were always part of the colonial scene. By all accounts he was a good rider, having learned the hard way in the RHA, and because of his success was not always popular with the professional Australian jockeys, who resented their loss of earnings when an amateur won. At this stage he got the nickname 'Tishy' after a racehorse that was supposed to have crossed its legs over the final jump, and fallen when it was well ahead. Apparently my father was in the habit of leaning up against the bar with a cigarette in one hand, a whisky and soda in the other, and his legs crossed at the heels!

By the time that he arrived in Kenya in 1924 he was on his way, twenty-eight years of age and a good catch in the colonial marriage market. My mother's family had been out there since about 1923 when her father, Sam Watkins, had picked up his family in Southampton and taken them all out to Mombasa, where he had got a job managing a stevedoring company in its main port. Mombasa in those days was somewhat wild and woolly, still an island joined to the mainland by a causeway, and owned by the Omani Sultan of Zanzibar, who leased it to the British. This was clearly the right sort of place for Sam Watkins since he was a character. He had gone to sea in sailing ships 'before the mast', and had worked his way up to being first officer. After marriage he had a home in the Southampton area and between voyages sired four children; his eldest son was sadly killed in the Great War. After retirement from the sea Sam settled down for a while but then got bored and upped sticks, taking his wife and three surviving children. The eldest, always known as Mac, was born in 1900, the elder daughter, Lucie, in 1903, and my mother, Dorothy, in 1907. Lucie and Dorothy were utterly different in character and had both gone to school at the Sacred Heart convent outside Southampton despite being Anglicans. Thus when my mother arrived in Mombasa she was in her late teens, hardly prepared for the traumatic events that ensued in 1924–5.

For reasons that I shall explain in a later chapter, Sam Watkins 'did a runner', to use modern parlance. He suddenly left the colony under a cloud without notice, returned to England and then left for Whangerei, North Island, New Zealand, where he settled for the rest of his life. By this time my mother had become engaged to my father, so that was one daughter off his hands. According to my so-called Aunt 'Tommy' (whose name came from the other Cornish side of our family called Thomas, about whom more later), my father's cousin in England, she received a letter from my father on his engagement, which simply read 'I have found her, and she is wonderful' – so apparently it all started off on the right foot. At the same time Lucie, who had been working as a secretary in the Union Castle Line office in Mombasa, had met 'Jock' Hillcoat, and after their marriage they left for Tanga in the then mandated territory of Tanganyika, where Jock worked for Bird and Co., who owned sisal estates across the country. I cannot recall having met them, although they may have been on leave in England at the same time as my parents when I was very young. But I do recall that when I turned twenty-one they very kindly sent me a set of gold cufflinks and gold collar stud, since in 1947 we still on formal occasions wore separate collars. Mac, the elder son, took himself off to run a cattle ranch on an island on Lake Victoria that was free of tsetse fly until he had saved up enough money to put himself through Cedara Agricultural College outside Pietermaritzberg, Natal, South Africa. He also made his career in the sisal industry in Tanganyika. He was clearly a self-starter, who believed in the dictum 'God helps those who help themselves'.

It is worth recording Mac's homing instinct when he retired to England in the 1960s. He returned with his second wife, Kathleen, a nursing sister whom he had met, his first marriage having gone the way of so many colonial ones years before. Since the family had originated in the Southampton area, which had expanded considerably northwards in the forty years since he had left it as a boy, he and Kathleen found and bought a flat there off the Avenue, in what had become a suburb of the port town. Shortly after taking up residence, Mac went out for a walk around the block and to his surprise found that they were within spitting distance of the local war memorial, on which was inscribed the name of his elder brother, and this was close to their old primary school. When in due course he and Kathleen joined the local golf club, Mac was even more surprised to find that it had been built on land that had been his grandfather's farm!

But back to my parents' wedding. My mother was taken back to England by her mother, who then followed her husband to New Zealand, where she died without seeing any of her children again, with the exception of Mac, who took one of his leaves in the form of a visit there. There is no doubt that life there was very hard on her and that Sam suffered from pangs of remorse for the rest of his days. But that was colonial life for you – one escaped from the humdrum existence in England into the more exciting, and certainly more affluent life in the colonies, but on occasions Tommy Trinder had a point when he remarked, 'Here's to our far-flung Empire, which wasn't flung far enough!' My mother being engaged and determined to get her man returned to Kenya by sea aged eighteen in the care of a chaperone to marry someone twelve years her senior. In view of what goes on aboard passenger ships between the sexes, the presence of a chaperone for an unaccompanied young woman of marriageable age was probably a wise precaution!

They were married in Mombasa's Anglican cathedral (there is also a Roman Catholic one from the days when the Portuguese traded extensively along the East African coast) with Jock Hillcoat 'giving away' my mother. From the photographs it was altogether a grander occasion than they could ever have experienced back in England – as there they were large frogs in a small colonial pond. There are the usual black and white photos of my father looking very dapper in whites, wearing co-respondent shoes and holding a cigarette in a long ivory holder that became his trademark, and my mother perched on a veranda looking relaxed and happy, as well they might have been, compared to life in England.

They lived there for over a year until I was born, and shortly after, they went 'home' to England on leave. The fact that two out of three of the Watkins marriages survived is not a bad average for colonial days. They had the benefit of meeting in the country where they got married, but the usual situation was that a young man, who sometimes had to ask his employer or senior Army officer for permission to marry, came home on leave, lonely and sex-starved, for four to six months. A well-known saying is that every boy should marry the girl next door for social compatibility, but in the case of the colonials, that girl had probably got fed up with waiting and had married someone else. Thus he had only a few months in which to identify the girl and persuade her to throw in her lot with him in some colonial outpost. When I was visiting a very old family friend – in both senses, since she was ninety-three years old in November 2001 – she recounted to my wife, Lene, and me how she had met her future husband on leave from India in London, smart and dapper with a bowler hat and rolled umbrella. The next time that she saw him was on arrival in India, a hot khaki-clad figure, with a dark stain of sweat down the back of his bush jacket! When my parents came to retire from Calcutta some twenty-one years later, the custom was for the local Shell staff to throw a party and for all those present to contribute to a generous gift, which was usually a full set of silver cutlery for the first house that they would own, having spent their career in company 'bungalows'. On that occasion my father apparently got fairly well oiled, and when he rose to make his thanks on behalf of Dorothy and himself, he remarked that as he looked around the table he felt that they should really have struck a medal for them, since he was the only husband present who was returning with the same wife that he had originally brought out! Fortunately the others were similarly relaxed, and Shell had a tradition of second marriages.

Thus my parents returned to their first leave, staying with my paternal grandparents, who lived in a detached corner house at 25 Deneshey Road, Hoylake, the Wirral in Cheshire. My grandfather was a passionate gardener, which was just as well since he did not have too many outlets for any other passions. The main living/dining room was all done up with deep red winged armchairs either side of the fireplace, and a red plush sofa lying the length of the bay window framed by velvet curtains, looking out on to an immaculate back garden, where outdoor life occurred. The 'front room' was full of glass-fronted cabinets containing sets of porcelain and figurines, and it was certainly not for living in. It was 'for best' and I was only allowed in on Sundays when grandpa was having his 'afternoon nap' as he called it, in the living room on the red sofa with the curtains drawn. The front room had lace curtains in the windows that looked on to the garden and Deneshey Road, and that garden was strictly for show.

The lawn was as immaculate as a billiard table, decorated with gnomes and bridges in various pastoral scenes. In the corner by the gate a crop of hollyhocks at least six feet high came up on the sandy soil as regular as clockwork each summer. When it was all looking its best, Grandpa would hover behind the lace curtains of the front room waiting for passers-by to pause and admire – whereupon he would 'just happen' to be going out, his cheerful little face shining with pleasure and lapping up their admiration. Whether he kept a mental record for those whom he had previously taken a bow I know not, but the routine was always the same – surprise, followed by modest acceptance!

Mind you, he needed such an outlet. Both my grandparents were staunch Wesleyans and came from the Penzance area of Cornwall. Their marriage certificate shows that they were married in May 1895 at the Wesleyan chapel there. Grandpa was a bachelor aged twenty-six, while Grandma was a widow aged thirty-three. He was listed as the son of a master builder, while her father had been a tin miner – nothing wrong with that, particularly in Cornwall, but to look at her and to listen to her rather grand voice, one could have concluded that she was the daughter of the Lord Lieutenant. She was tall, dignified, strict and had an aversion against all forms of sin and wickedness, which encompassed all manner of innocent pastimes. She was also sanctimonious and something of a backbiter. Despite being taller than Grandpa and dominating him, nevertheless every day when he returned in the evening from the offices of the Pioneer Life Assurance Company in Liverpool where he was a director, he would sit in the winged chair besides the fireplace, while she brought his carpet slippers to change into and a cup of strong tea.

In the summer of 1926 my father arrived with his nineteen-year-old bride and son of a few months to spend their leave in this cauldron of Wesleyan respectability. According to my mother, her rite of passage was not eased by the fact that at some point Grandma discovered evidence of their lovemaking in the potty under their bed. Consternation and recriminations! Is this the sort of hussy 'who has tempted my Leslie into marriage?' Seven years later Grandma died of advanced breast cancer of which Grandpa was completely oblivious, despite sharing her bed. I can only conclude that their relationship was similar to the story of the upper-crust Englishman, who took an American to his club. The American proffered a cigarette. 'No thanks, tried it once, didn't like it,' replied the Englishman. The American then brought up the subject of golf. 'Tried it once, couldn't take to it,' remarked the Englishman. At a later stage during lunch the Englishman referred to his son. 'Your only son, I presume?' asked the American.

The leave over, my parents left for India, taking me with them for a three-year tour stationed with the Burmah Shell Oil Company in Bombay. Thus I remained there until I was about three and a half, and clearly have no recollections of it, nor stories handed down for that matter.

2.

The First Separation (Years 4–7)

My parents returned from Bombay on their second home leave in the spring of 1930 when I was coming up to four years of age. I can only imagine that once again they were forced to stay with my father's parents under the disapproving eye (so far as my mother was concerned) of my grandmother. Both my parents seemed to share a cordial dislike for her, since I can't recall their ever making a favourable remark about her, and plenty that were the opposite. Or perhaps they lived in fear of her, since she was a tall, intimidating and often disapproving character with a lordly voice. Certainly she could not have read and approved of Alex Comfort's *The Joys of Sex* (assuming that he had written it by then), since any form of even mildly affectionate behaviour between consenting adults brought down her wrath. It fell into the broad category of what she labelled as 'wicked'.

Several years later when I was in the care of my Auntie Tommy, a cousin of my father married to a Church of England vicar in Yorkshire, she described a hoax that she and my father had played on Grandma. It must have been when he returned from the Great War in 1919 and Tommy was also staying at the house in Deneshey Road. One evening Grandma had to go up the road to fetch something when dusk was approaching. There was a gas street lamp outside the house on the corner, and when they judged that Grandma would be returning, my father and aunt donned their coats (and probably hats in those days) and went out, stood in a clinch in the shadow of the lamp and pretended to be a smooching couple. In due course Grandma hove into sight, took one look at them, advanced with her raised umbrella and jabbed Tommy hard in her backside, screaming, 'Get away from my house, you cats, you filthy cats!' When she discovered their identity, like Queen Victoria she was most definitely not amused, and one can only imagine the atmosphere for the next day or so.

My mother was hardly the person to fit comfortably into this atmosphere of severe rectitude and at only twenty-three years of age must have been somewhat intimidated. Certainly Grandma did not approve of her daughter-in-law. When I was in my grandparents' care she regularly referred to Dorothy as a flibberti-gibbet, in phrases such as 'that young lady my Leslie married is nothing but a flibbertigibbet'! I had no idea what this exotic-sounding name meant, but at some stage when I had been staying with them I asked Grandpa, 'What's a flibby gibby, Grandpa?'

His usual friendly, cheerful face at once assumed a hunted look and putting his finger to his lips he said, 'Shush, child, don't ask, not a word to Bessie!' I see that the *Concise OED* defines a flibbertigibbet as 'a gossipy, flighty or restless person (the imitation of chatter)' and to grandma that must have been spot on.

When it came to the end of my parents' leave in September and they were due to return to India I had just turned four, and for whatever reason they decided not to take me with them but to put me into a local school as a boarder, close to my grandparents' house. This was an exceptionally young age even by the standards of India, where children were usually sent 'home' for their education at around seven years of age. When I asked my mother for the reason some years later, she said it had been that my health would not have stood up to the heat of India, but I never really bought that. I suspect the real reason was that like most colonials, particularly those employed by Shell, they were living the life of Riley. My father had opportunities to take his young wife on tour with him, as confirmed in old family photographs, and a brat of my age could not have been left with an ayah. When my brother Tim came along six years after me, although my father was only on a salary, albeit a good one, and with no private income, they hired a red-headed Lancashire girl referred to as Nanny Adams, whom they took out with them for one three-year tour, followed by Sandra and other English girls hired locally in India. So with respect to the looking after of their children, they aped the aristocracy – which they certainly were not.

Hoylake was a small, prosperous residential town stuck out on the westerly tip of the Wirral peninsular of Cheshire, facing out into the bracing breezes that came from the north-west across the Irish Sea. It was essentially a suburb of Liverpool, where those who had made their money in trade lived, probably starting with the West African slave trade and then moving into more legitimate enterprises such as the import of hard wheat for milling from North America, particularly Canada, and then the export of textiles made in Manchester back to Africa. The huge Liver Building on the River Mersey, where the passenger ferries came in from Birkenhead, was a tribute to the vast wealth that had been made through the services of shipping companies such as the Canadian Pacific from Halifax, Nova Scotia and the John Holt Line servicing West African ports. The results of this accumulated wealth could be seen in the substantial houses that lined that side of Meols Drive (pronounced Mells) backing on to Hoylake golf course, which ran for about two miles from Hoylake to West Kirby along the estuary of the River Dee. West Kirby was another commuter town located just around the north-west corner of the Wirral peninsular. Hoylake had one of those seaside links courses where the English Open Golf championship was regularly held, but less frequently now…

Meols was really just an extension of Hoylake on the other Birkenhead side. It was only a brisk walk away, and was made up of residential houses, a railway station and a very large pond, which regularly froze over in winter, strong enough for people to skate and slide over, which gave it a rural appearance. In fact, it was semi-rural. The commuter rail service to Liverpool (although the word 'commuter' had not been invented in those days) was a steam train that started at West Kirby, and was not electrified until around 1936. So in summer when the sash windows of the compartments were down, passengers had to make a quick dive to pull up the windows as the train entered the railway tunnel under the Mersey and clouds of black smoke and specks of soot belched into the compartments. Messy, but fun for small boys.

The school where I was placed was Meols School for Girls and Kindergarten owned by an unmarried lady in her forties, Miss Braithwaite, who lived with her mother on the premises. It was a wide building about three floors high, entered by a flight of steps leading to the front doors. To the left as one entered was Miss Braithwaite's large, comfortable sitting room, full of armchairs, a couch, pouffes for the children to squat on, and a large fireplace with the mantelpiece decorated with the usual bric-a-brac of those times. The modern word 'minimalist' was not part of their vocabulary.

Miss Braithwaite was a lovely lady with a calm friendly face and her hair drawn back into a bun behind her neck. When my mother took me there to board and the penny dropped as to what was happening, I have a vague recollection of throwing a tantrum that rearranged the teacups, but in retrospect I can only say that I could not have fallen into better hands.

Most of the pupils were girls up to about fourteen years of age, but the kindergarten was mixed, and there were a very few older boarders in addition to myself. We shared our own small dormitory at the top of the house, with a separate playroom. This was light and airy in summer but in winter, since the dormitory faced north out to sea, every morning the windows would be visited by a character euphemistically referred to as 'Jack Frost'. In other words, the condensation on the inside of the windows was frozen in the familiar patterns of crystals and whorls, wonderfully decorative particularly when the sun was shining outside, but a sure indication that the inside temperature was sub-zero. During the day in winter these rooms were heated with tall, cylindrical paraffin lamps with a series of holes at the top that could be adjusted with a small lever, but when the wick was turned up to maximise heat, clouds of black smoke would belch out, and the wick would be rapidly turned down again for safety.

Additional warmth could also be achieved by the sheer number of layers of clothes: first 'combinations', followed by a flannel shirt, a long-sleeved pullover and finally a blazer or jacket, all worn above shorts and long woollen socks. Combinations were a single undergarment that included both vest and pants in one. They made one's daily visit to the loo for 'big jobs' a major, slow and chilly exercise. Shorts were kept up with braces and when underpants were worn in warmer weather, the leather straps were threaded through loops in the tops before buttoning on to the trousers. There is no doubt that life in that respect has become a lot easier.

Miss Braithwaite certainly did not believe in the old maxim that 'children were to be seen and not heard'. Her large sitting room was regularly available to us smaller children, particularly at weekends, when she would read and play games with us, usually with some educational content. Sunday teatime was the high point of the week, and since the Great War had only ended about twelve years earlier, I used to get into regular debates with Miss Braithwaite's mother as to whether a submarine fired a torpedo or vice versa. I held to the latter view and we had a small bet on it, until one Christmas came round when Lewis's department store in Liverpool had a grotto, where a mock submarine was made of a large capsule with portholes, mounted on gimbals. We all trooped inside and the door was closed. The capsule rocked and appeared to be sinking into the depths as water sluiced past the ports and it grew darker. When we left after a couple of minutes, there was Mrs Braithwaite waiting to claim her bet. I paid up one sweet.

From the age of five, two things really stick out in my mind. First I caught whooping cough and was ill enough over a period of about five weeks to end up in a wheelchair. Secondly, as one learned to write, the weekly letter on a Sunday to one's parents began with the plaintive cry 'please, what can I say?' and continued for the next thirteen years. The net result is that I tend to send out notes to all and sundry as the thought strikes or I see something that might interest them – so one learned the art of communication. I quickly learned that it was better to stay at the school on a Sunday morning and write, rather than going to my grandparents, where I would be hauled off to the Methodist chapel and have to sit through an excruciating sermon. However, towards the end of my stay there was no dodging this. We would go up the chapel steps, Grandma first in her full regalia, nodding left and right to her friends, followed by Grandpa and myself. This became the seating order so that, come the sermon, Grandpa would exercise remarkable dexterity, taking a tube of Rowntrees clear gums from his left pocket, opening one end with his forefinger and then flipping the sweets into my hand. It is sometimes said that outwardly churchy folk can be pretty sanctimonious and backbiting, and if this is so, then Grandma was true to that type. One Sunday late afternoon I returned from their house to the school, where Miss Braithwaite invited me into her sanctum and asked me how the day had gone. After giving her a rundown of what had transpired I added, 'My grannie says that Miss Braithwaite is such and such and her mother is…'

'That's quite enough Tony, we don't want to hear any more of that,' I was admonished sternly. Which, I suppose, was the first example of my father's less delicate advice many years later when I lived with him in India, to 'keep my mouth shut and my bowels open' – something he must have learned from his Army experience or in the conformist, hierarchical environment of Shell.

Despite my grandparents' reasonable affluence, I have no recollection of their having assistance from either a daily help or a gardener. Grandpa's pride in his garden would have excluded the latter, but Grandma seemed to slave away in the kitchen of her three-bedroom house. There was the usual large kitchen range of those days, where a fire was continually maintained except when she was blacking the stove with whatever the material was. Upstairs there was a bathroom and separate loo, both freezing in winter, and just outside the kitchen door there was another outside loo where the toilet paper consisted of old copies of newspapers, torn up into pieces that would not block the system. Grandpa's regular reading material could not be described as being particularly sophisticated, being mainly 'Tit Bits' and something or other weekly. This probably had something to do with his passion for his garden and his need to get out among his pals down the road. Lest this be construed that he headed for the pub, I should make it clear that of course, in such a strict Wesleyan household, the strongest drink available, only in small glasses, was elderberry wine, and that only for Sunday lunch.

Money also had its 'wicked' side. When I was about six, a mysterious lady turned up and spent a day with them: she was the American widow of Uncle Tom. Exactly who he was I never quite figured out, except that he was about the same age as my father, had been brought up with him by my grandparents. Then, being a bit of a black sheep, he had left for America, where he eventually died of drink – absolute anathema to Grandma! He had also borrowed a fiver from my father, which he never repaid, another source of grievance. However, his widow seemed to be a very nice lady, and as she left she quietly slipped me a one-pound note. Of course I could not keep my trap shut and piped up, 'Look what that nice lady gave me!' Stupid boy! Such a munificent sum was declared as 'wicked' in the hands of one so young and promptly disappeared into the maw of some inaccessible savings box or Post Office book.

If all this makes my grandmother out as being some sort of killjoy, it is probably true, since it is fair to say that no members of the family really warmed to her. And yet I have an enlarged repainted family portrait, about three feet wide by eighteen inches high, of my grandparents with their son, when he was about eighteen years old, all in their Sunday best. She comes across as a good-looking woman with a twinkle in her eye and enormous pride in her family. So perhaps we were all intimidated by her. It must also have been very hard for her to have her only son go off to the war for four years at the age of eighteen, and then within a couple of years after his safe return, with no more than a broken jaw from a mule's kick, see him head off east to earn his living for the rest of her life.

Grandpa's escape route was a couple of hundred yards down the road to the sunken gardens let into the promenade that ran the length of the seafront from Meols to the west end of Hoylake. Steps led down to the area where immaculate bowling greens were laid out alongside a small pavilion. Here he and his pals would assemble in their white ducks, carrying the rubber kneeling mats and containers of bowls. Here he was safe, un-get-at-able, and happy in the company of his friends. There was also a large circular area with a raised bandstand in the centre, where military or other bands would come and play on Sunday afternoons to the audience sitting in collapsible metal chairs. All very decorous.

Further along the promenade towards the centre of town, there was a very large marine swimming pool with high diving boards. It jutted out into the sea from which it took its supply of water for swimming in – unheated of course, so I doubt if the water temperature ever reached above 66° F. The winter storms on that coast could be ferocious. The shore was sandy and very flat leading out into the Dee estuary, so that it was wonderful and safe for shrimping, but one had to walk through yards of decidedly chilly water before it was deep enough to swim in. Small two-man fishing smacks sailed out to sea when the tide came in, to fish offshore. They had to be back in time for the fishermen to beach their boats and then come ashore in their waders. In winter, their boats had to be taken up a ramp inland to avoid being smashed into matchwood by the storms that would roar in over the flat shore to break on to the promenade, regularly gouging great holes out of the concrete and removing the iron railings.

Holidays were blissful, mainly at Easter or in the summer. Christmas was of course spent with my grandparents. Before the end of term, when we helped to decorate Miss Braithwaite's rooms with paper chains and Chinese lanterns, she would tell me to write down on a piece of paper what I would like for Christmas presents, set light to it and watch it waft up the chimney of her sitting room fire. By some amazing method of information transference that I never really understood, at least some of these requests would appear in the empty pillowcase that stood at the foot of my bed on Christmas morning.

I cannot recall my grandparents ever going away for a holiday, not even back to Cornwall. Grandpa would take me up to Liverpool from time to time, or to visit Mr Ormerod, the chairman of the Pioneer Life Assurance Company, his boss and my godfather, out at Southport, but he never got away for a real holiday until Grandma died, when we went with his second wife to Bournemouth. Mr Ormerod was an excellent godfather, always writing to encourage me during my parents' absence, even when I moved down to school in Kent. During the war when I went abroad we lost touch, but as soon as I returned after RN service to go to university, he resumed contact with me. He was a fine, old-fashioned gentleman.

Miss Braithwaite took me at least twice to Anglesey and probably a couple of times to Market Drayton, the birthplace of Robert Clive (of India) in Shropshire. All those days seemed to have been spent in a golden haze like the pictures in Kenneth Graham's illustrated book, *The Golden Age*. Market Drayton was a small rural town in the depths of the Shropshire countryside. I visited it again in the autumn of 2001 and in fact it has not changed a lot, apart from adding the inevitable housing estate on to its edge as well as a German factory for making yoghurt. We used to stay in an archetypal English cottage backing on to a field of wheat. It must have been August since harvesting was going on; horse-drawn binders tied the wheat into sheaves, which were then 'stooked' into upright bundles by the farm workers. These stooks provided ideal cover for a six-year-old to turn into his own house and sit there listening for any of the grown-ups calling for him, and watching the odd field mouse searching around for grain between his knees.

There must also have been a canal nearby, since one of the regular walks was along the towpath, watching the large carthorses pulling by rope the long, decorated barges. When they came to a bridge, the horses would be unhooked and walk around the side to the other end. I assume that the barges were propelled through the tunnels in the traditional way, with the bargemen lying on their backs on the top canopy, 'walking' along the roof to propel the barge along. At any rate, they always came out at the other end and re-hitched the horse to continue their journey. These canals have, of course, now been opened up again for people to spend their holidays in motorised barges, and I read that the experience takes one back into that peaceful, unspoiled and unsophisticated world.

Anglesey is the old Celtic island that lies off the north-west coast of Wales, and from whose port Holyhead the passenger ships leave for Ireland. To reach the island one has to cross the Menai Straits by a most elegant suspension bridge. The first time that we crossed, someone explained to me that when a group of soldiers crossed on foot, they would have to 'break step' to avoid causing the bridge to swing uncomfortably. This question came up every time we crossed thereafter. It was the sort of thing that everyone learned. Therefore it came as more than a surprise when nearly seventy years later in 2000 it appeared that the combined knowledge of Lord Foster (the architect) and Ove Arup (the Danish engineering company) had not anticipated this phenomenon in the design and construction of the Millennium Bridge from the City of London to the South Bank. Weird! And costly – £4 million to rectify their error.

At Holyhead there is a famous lighthouse built offshore on a stack of rocks that one reaches across a narrow footbridge. The sea between the rock and the mainland was a cauldron of swirling currents coming in from the Irish Sea in different directions, causing boiling whirlpools. If anyone got into those in a small boat they would be sucked down like a pea down a waste pipe, I was told, and I believed it. So whenever I walked across, I looked straight ahead and did not linger!

Miss Braithwaite used to rent a cottage near a seaside resort called Rhosneigr on the west side of the island. It was a 'bucket and spade' holiday place with large dunes running down to a wide sandy beach. It was ideal for paddling and shrimping with one of those nets on the end of a stick. I was not taken to church on Sundays but, Wales being a very non-conformist country, the 'Band of Hope' used to set up their red banner between two tall poles dug into the sand. Shades of 'Sister Anna will carry the banner'! So on Sundays we all used to troop down there to sing hymns from sheets that they handed out ('Rock of Ages' comes to mind), in our reedy, unaccompanied voices. Appropriate prayers would be interspersed. On the whole it was more fun than being dragged to the Wesleyan chapel in Hoylake, but there were no Rowntrees clear gums of course. In those pre-war days, all so-called middle-class people employed servants, and Miss Braithwaite had a young local girl to help out in the rented cottage, who sometimes took me for walks. One afternoon as we were crossing the sand dunes, and when hidden from view, she suddenly stopped, lifted up her skirt, pulled down her knickers and saying 'just a minute', squatted. Ever curious I asked, 'Can I look?' to be told, 'Oh, orlright.' So I, too, squatted and a five- or six-year-old child on his haunches can get pretty close to the ground, a worm's eye view, so to speak. What happened next is indelibly imprinted on my mind. She must have been a very hirsute girl, because a stream of steaming water poured out through long black strands of something, before hitting the sand with a splash. The only material that I had seen like it in my young life was what lay clinging to the rocks by the seashore.

'What's that seaweed stuff?' I asked.

She flashed me a sideways glance and said, 'Don't be cheeky!'

Then with a flick of her tail she stood up, pulled up her knickers, grabbed my hand and marched on, instructing me, 'Don't you go telling nobody now!' and until this day I haven't. But she must be in her late eighties by now, if still alive, although why it ever happened only about five minutes after we had left the cottage, I have no idea. Nevertheless, a memorable experience!

In due course, my parents came home on leave in the summer of 1933, when I had just turned seven. What I do clearly recall is their desperate search for digs to stay in. There was no way that they were going to live with my grandparents, so the first month or so was spent in a couple of small terraced houses in Hoylake, where we rented two rooms, one for sleeping and one as a sitting room. These were pretty cramped premises, but in due course they were able to rent one half of Sandhey Farm in Meols, one of those old long buildings that was no longer a farmhouse, which had a large garden in the front. Our part had two bedrooms – a double and a single for me – so we were very comfortable. My father then set about equipping himself with the necessities for a satisfactory leave which, apart from an endless supply of cigarettes (forty to sixty per day), consisted of a new car and a new set of golf clubs from the local sports shop run by an ex-professional – Saddlers Sports in Hoylake High Street, or whatever it was called. The car was a brand new russet-coloured Wolseley, with forward-opening front doors and the registration number OV 4759. I am absolutely sure of that, having reached the age when I can recall such details, but cannot always remember what I have come upstairs for. At any rate, one morning my father and I were walking up the street towards Saddlers Sports, when to my surprise and Tishy's shock we saw his new car, his pride and joy, veering towards us from the opposite direction, across the oncoming traffic, until it pulled up with a screech more or less where we stood transfixed. The driver's door, which by then was next to us facing in the wrong direction, opened to allow my flustered-looking mother to jump out. After a short delay, to allow for passing traffic, and also perhaps to give him time to calm his nerves, the driving instructor got out on the opposite side, came round to Tishy and said, 'I'm sorry sir, but I don't think there is any point in continuing with these lessons!' From then on my mother was a passenger, either of her husband or of the company drivers in India. At the end of their leave in the following January, when my parents had gone to say goodbye to Miss Braithwaite, Tishy turned up with a wad of notes, including some of those lovely crinkly fivers, having sold the car to a butcher for £60. Considering that 1933 must have been well into the depression that had overtaken the country, that was not a bad way to spend a leave.

In August I went into the hospital at West Kirby to have my tonsils and adenoids removed, while my grandmother was in at the same time to die of breast cancer. So Grandpa was left on his own (but not for long), while my parents' leave quite unusually continued over Christmas into the New Year. The next time that I spent Christmas with them was when I was fourteen in India, but that earlier Christmas has stuck in my memory because of the postman on Boxing Day. That of course is meant to be the day when such services are rewarded with a small gift or Christmas 'box'. As far as our postman was concerned, his rewards from his delivery route seemed to have been of a liquid character – what I learned to refer to in the Royal Navy some years later as 'sippers'. By the time that he reached us he was glassy eyed and absolutely reeking, despite which another sherry or whatnot was pressed on him and he was too polite, or too far gone, to refuse. He managed to stagger away from our front door along the side of the house until he reached our neighbour's, at which point he subsided in a heap and took no further interest in the rest of the day. That was also a first as far as I was concerned, and it is probably just as well that Grandma was in her grave by then, and I could not blurt out the awful news to her.

The other problem for colonials on leave, apart from finding suitable accommodation, was to find a suitable boarding school at which to leave their children for the next three years. At seven, I had clearly grown too old for the kindergarten of Meols School. In the autumn I was put into a small boys' school in Hoylake, which proved to be completely unsuitable for boarding, and as a widower, Grandpa could not cope with me in the holidays. Fortunately an alternative was at hand: Dormie House School for boys at 11 Riversdale Road, West Kirby. A Mr Cove owned it, a delightful man who became my guardian, and who allowed me to enter part-way through the school year – that is, in the January winter term, due to the unusual circumstances. There I stayed for the next three years.

Eighteen years on I found myself working in Liverpool, and partly from curiosity and partly from an emotional pull I took the train out to Hoylake and went to Meols School to look up Miss Braithwaite. The new head told me that she had retired, but still lived in the district, having recently moved house. However, I traced her through Directory Enquiries and phoned her. I did not need to explain who I was. There was an instant rapport; the years just rolled back when I went round to have tea with her. I had already decided by then to emigrate to Canada, and after all the business of finding myself a job in a new country and getting settled with a permanent address, after about four months I sent her a card. I received her reply, thanking me for the card, and saying that next time a letter would be better. She was quite right of course, but that was another of the problems of such a varied upbringing – keeping in touch with all the people who helped one along the way in a manner considered appropriate by them, particularly as it happened that at least three of them had no children of their own.

One of life's little regrets.

3.

Formative Years in England (Years 7–10)

West Kirby, where I was left at the Dormie House School in January 1934, was at the north-western tip of the Wirrall peninsular, facing out to the junction of the River Dee estuary with the Irish Sea. But before going into any further detail on that subject, I have to rectify a sin of omission from the last chapter.

In October 1932, my brother Tim was born in Madras and christened in the Anglican cathedral there. Therefore, when our parents came on leave in the summer of 1933, he would have been about eight months old. The problem is that I have absolutely no recollection of his being with them, either at the first two houses where they rented rooms, or later at Sandhey Farm. Normally the arrival of a sibling would make some impression on a brother, but I have no recall of the usual baby noises, feedings, messy nappies and prams, or of his being with us. Furthermore, when our mother took her driving lessons, where was he? One possible answer to this conundrum could be Nanny Adams, the Lancashire girl whom our parents took out with them to India to be Tim's nanny for the next three-year tour until he was four, in addition to the regular Indian ayah. Belt and braces care, so to speak. So the possibility is that Nanny Adams joined them at the start of the leave and looked after Tim in a quiet and inconspicuous manner. The alternative is that he was left in India in the care of some person or institution, which is unlikely but not impossible, as we shall see.

But to get back to the Dormie House School at 11 Riversdale Road, West Kirby. It was owned by a Mr Cove, a delightful man probably in his fifties, who ran it with his wife. It was in a residential road, occupying a largish three-storey house, with an open playground at the back, and some additional buildings for the classrooms. At one side there was a lawn, where minor sports events could take place for the small children, such as sack races, egg and spoon races and short sprints. When we started to play football, we had to walk some distance along the promenade to a field that was either public, or shared with some other school. There were probably about ninety children there, and to my surprise it was still going strong early in the 1990s when I revisited it with my younger son, Tom.

Riversdale Road ran down to the start of the promenade. Going eastwards, one could walk all the way along the sand dunes backing on to Hoylake Golf Club course until one reached the Red Rocks, a wide area of flat sandstone rocks that were a favourite picnic area. Immediately at the foot of Riversdale Road was the beach proper for all the usual activities in summer: paddling, swimming and of course donkey rides. The familiar men riding tricycles, with a large dry ice box on the two front wheels, selling Walls and Eldorado ice creams patrolled the promenade above.

About three-quarters of a mile offshore was Hilbre Island, which one could walk out to between the tides, providing one got the timing right. The Dee estuary was like many of them up there – wide and flat with channels cut into the sand that could fill up with alarming speed when the tide surged in over the flat surface, so that anyone caught on the seaward side of a channel could find themselves in trouble. The safer way of going out to the island, and one much more exciting for small children, was in a horse-drawn cart. When the driver said that it was time to return, it was time to return. The surrounds of the island were pitted with caves in the red sandstone, clearly the previous dens of smugglers, who had built underground passages to the shore that came up we knew not where, but were absolutely sure that they existed somewhere. One could climb up and wander across the top of the island, which was probably a couple of hundred yards in width, and contained some sort of a beacon for passing ships. One could also go out for a day's picnic, which meant being on the island for over six hours to get a clear walk back to shore, and on those occasions there were always schools of porpoises curling their way past.

In the opposite direction the promenade ran for about one to one and a half miles until it ended with Hydro Hotel on the one side, and the marine swimming baths on the seaward side. The Hydro was one of those massive hotels that used to be built in seaside resorts for the solid burghers of Liverpool to come out and take the air. I do not think that there was any water cure as the name implies, but there is no doubt that the air was bracing, very bracing. The dining room was large and imposing, the bedrooms had high ceilings, and the central heating was non-existent. On the seaward side of the promenade was a shallow marine lake, enclosed by a sea wall that one could walk around up to the swimming area, when the tide was at low water or out. It was not too deep, and one could hire rowing boats and probably small sailing boats to take on to it. Every so often in winter, with a massive spring tide, sand from the Dee estuary would be washed over into it and have to be dredged out.

The seawater swimming baths were run by the council. They had the usual changing facilities and the limits of where one could swim were simply marked out by ropes attached to stakes driven into the lake. The deep end went to six feet, and I recall that I swam my first unaided strokes in the summer of my eighth birthday. Needless to say one did not hang about, since it was cold, cold, cold. The only way to avoid hypothermia was to change as quickly as possible and run back to the school.

West Kirby was in fact quite an attractive small town. Its shopping centre was around the railway station. There was a fairly large park with a pond – or maybe a lake would be a better description – around which there were walking paths. The gardens connected what was West Kirby old town, whose houses were in a cottage style, to the new town that sprang up around the rail terminus. At the end of the promenade the road ran out, but footpaths continued up the Dee estuary where there were high firm sand hills, ideal for making kids' impromptu slides. Going east beyond the old village one came to Grange Hill. This was a large open area of sandstone rocks and valleys, mostly covered with heavy gorse through which, either by accident or design, tunnels had been driven, at the right height for small boys to play hide and seek and so on. There was never any danger and one could go up there either alone or in groups, so there was plenty of opportunity to develop one's independence.

The main road out of the town climbed steeply around the edge of Grange Hill and then led away to Caldy, where there was a grammar school, and Thurstaston Hill near Heswall, another area of sandstone and gorse. At least once each summer the gorse overhanging the road cutting would catch fire and suspend traffic until it was extinguished – not that there was all that much traffic in those days. At the top of the hill was the Cottage Loaf Inn, a large thatched building that was a favourite for people to visit for substantial teas. This was on the main road to Chester, the county town at the foot of the Wirral, which was of course founded by the Romans as a border town to keep the Welsh tribes under control, or at least out of Roman England. Just beyond the Cottage Loaf, a road branched right down towards Neston, where the Swiss manufacturer Nestlé established one of their first, if not *the* first, milk and dairy products factory. Cheshire was, and probably still is, one of the major dairy counties in England.

A feature of the roads, which still exists, is that at the major crossroads the fields were protected with metal horizontal railings with four or five bars, the top one curved inwards, and the whole painted white. Where this tradition originated I know not, and when one asks people who live in the area about them, they appear surprised at their existence.

A short distance up the Dee estuary from Neston was the old port of Parkgate, famous for its shrimps, and again a popular spot for families to visit at weekends, since one has to remember that the 1930s were the real start of car ownership for middle-income folk, based on the Austin Seven, made at Cowley near Oxford, and the 'Tin Lizzie' Ford from Dagenham in Essex. The latter led to the excruciating joke among schoolboys, 'What time is it when two Fords pass one another in the road?' The answer: 'Tin past tin!' Indeed it was the time when one could often hear adult's self-righteously criticising those other adults, including their friends of course, who put the ownership of a car before the addition of another child.

Mr and Mrs Cove were a complete contrast. Since my grand-father had been widowed only a few months earlier, he could not cope with me, so the Coves were made my guardians. I still have two separate photos of them from those years, which neatly encapsulate their different personalities. Both were taken when we were on holiday. The first is of Mr Cove, a burly man, leaning out of a cottage window in Coverack, Cornwall, smiling broadly into the camera, with his bald head burned a Cherry Blossom polish tan. The second is of Mrs Cove wearing a hat, sitting erect on the back seat of their Fiat car, with the soft hood rolled back, balancing a saucer in her left hand while about to drink from the cup in her other hand. Her expression was one of mild disapproval with pursed lips, and I am afraid that that is the way she was, although she was always kind and not particularly strict with me. They had no children, and I think that must have been a good part of her problem.

Mr Cove was in charge of the academic side, and his wife of the household. Apart from me there were always one or two other boys boarding from time to time, so she had a resident cook, a local lady who lived at home in the town and used to slip me all sorts of goodies. Not that there was anything inadequate in either the quality or quantity of the food, which in no way compared with the usual muck served up in English boarding schools during that era.

The rest of the staff were mainly young Welsh girls, who came from the other side of the Dee with absolutely no training, and probably no chance of jobs locally, since the economy of north Wales was based on farming and coal mining. They all had two things in common: a universal BO and the potential for a tongue-lashing from Mrs Cove. The former want of personal hygiene they simply could not help, since they arrived with minimum clothes in a cheap case, were housed on the top floor in what was essentially a garret, and had to make do with a bowl and jug of cold water to wash in. I doubt if they were allowed near the bathroom too often, judging by their pong. Being completely untrained, these unfortunates never knew what was expected of them, and consequently received the rough edge of Mrs Cove's tongue. At times it was really so bad that the rest of the staff, such as the cook, would take bets as to how long the new girl would last. After I retired I took a degree through the Open University, where I learned from one of the courses, which included social history, that there were 2 million people in domestic service in Britain in 1939. Given that the population then was about 45 million, that amounts to about four and a half per cent of the total, or say ten per cent of the working population – a misuse of resources, and if the other employers were anything like Mrs C, no wonder there was such a legacy of bitterness from the so-called 'lower classes'. As for bringing their 'followers' into the house, forget it!

By contrast their treatment of 'tramps' – or maybe I should say Mr Cove's treatment of tramps – was completely different. They were great motorists and took me all over England and Wales in their Fiat car, from Llandudno in north Wales to Ely in East Anglia, and from Cheshire in the north to Cornwall in the south-west, although I do not think that we ever got to London. Apart from the 2 million in service, there were probably another one and a half million plus unemployed, particularly in the mining and heavy industry areas. One only has to think of the Jarrow 'hunger' march in the 1930s to London. Thus there were often so-called 'tramps' on the roads as we drove around the country, particularly in the Midlands. They were not 'bums' in the American sense, but men moving around just looking for work. They would often hitch a lift at the roadside, and I never knew Mr Cove fail to tell his driver, of whom more anon, to stop and pick them up. They would be asked where they were going and why, and the answer was usually to such and such a town where they had heard on the grapevine that men were being taken on by such and such a factory. Farm labourers were of course 'tied' to their farmer employers, and lived in 'tied cottages' owned by the farmer, so they could not shop around for other jobs. Most of these men were dressed in a heavy coat or raincoat, even in summer, with their possessions in a small suitcase, and they wore the inevitable cloth cap or tweed hat. They all ended sitting next to me on the back seat, with Mr or Mrs Cove on my other side. Many of them had had to sleep rough beside the road, so they had a damp, river water-like smell from being frequently rained upon. They were all very polite and grateful of course, and Mr Cove was always friendly and encouraging to them. I was to meet their sons on level terms ten years or so later on the lower deck in the RN, and that was another big step in learning how the other half had lived during the 1930s – or maybe 'existed' would be a better word.

The Coves' pride and joy, and their means of getting around the country, was their Fiat car, an open tourer with a soft hood that could be folded back, and heavy-duty celluloid-like windows that slotted into the tops of the doors, which were removed when the hood was down. Since we rarely went over 50 mph this is how we usually travelled in the summer months. There were running boards of course, and the spare wheel was either fixed to the driver's door or was slotted into the mudguard ahead of it. The toolbox also was fastened to the running board, a clear sign of the honesty of those times. Imagine anything being left in the public's vision nowadays! We only ever had one accident. We were bowling along the main road to Chester one day, with most of the adults' weight on the near side, and I was sitting in the offside rear seat. Suddenly there was a crack beneath me, and as I looked out of the window, there was a car wheel running alongside us. I had hardly exclaimed on this (and been told not to be silly) when there was a lurch to the right and we came down on to the car's axle as we ground to a stop. I forget how we got out of that one, but probably an AA man came to our assistance – one of those characters mounted on a motorcycle with sidecar who used to salute any cars that sported their badge. You don't get respect like that nowadays! In the early Thirties cars were either pretty grand or small, affordable ones as mentioned above. The only car at the school better than 'ours' was a Lagonda tourer belonging to Dr Macaffee, whose son was at the school and later took it over. It had one of those long bonnets like a snout, with leather straps to secure the sides, very sexy like garters, probably not equalled until the E-type Jaguar came along in the 1960s.

Mr Cove did not drive himself, possibly because he had a dicky heart, which restricted his exercise, although he was a great one for walking around cathedrals, castles and Roman remains. They therefore had a driver, a Mr Fare, always referred to simply as Fare. He was a great chap, about in his mid-forties, who lived in the old village with his wife, and by then had a grown-up daughter. Even when we went away for several weeks in the summer, he came with us and stayed separately in digs. This was probably just as well from a cost viewpoint because when I look back, I recognise how well we lived. Once a term the Coves would take me into Chester with them as my 'treat'. This involved shopping in the very upmarket shops (posh would be a better word) in the arcades or rows raised above street level, as well as educational sightseeing around the cathedral, the Roman wall that still surrounds the city, and anything else that caught Mr Cove's interest. Lunch would be at the Grosvenor Hotel. Now that really *was* posh, and is even more so now. On one of these visits I bought a gleaming varnished toy yacht, whose sails could be trimmed, and which remained my pride and joy for years. Any town that we visited, which had a pond or lake in its municipal gardens, enabled Mr Fare and me to spend happy hours sailing the yacht. Nor do I recall any ribbing from the other boys over the fact that I received this special attention, which must have been due to the fact that the majority were day boys or, if boarders, had parents in England.

Not too far away on the other side of the Wirral was Port Sunlight, the model, utopian workers' town for the employees of Sunlight soaps, founded by Lord Leverhulme, who later joined up with the Dutch van den Bergs margarine company to become today's Unilever. All the houses were in a cottage style, laid out in tree-lined roads, a far cry from the usual slums of Liverpool and Birkenhead. Probably the main negative as far as the men were concerned was the fact that it was 'dry', with no pubs allowed. It must also have been lacking in today's health and safety regula-tions, because on one school trip by coach, we were told that during the previous week a man working on an overhead girder had slipped off and dropped into a vat of boiling Lifebuoy soap, the brand that became the familiar red-coloured bars. A very nasty way to die.

Industrial accidents and major tragedies were a fairly regular occurrence in those times, particularly in the mining industry. As I mentioned above, north Wales was a centre of the coal mining industry with a very substantial mine at Wrexham on the way from Chester to Snowdonia. It must have been around 1934 when it suffered a massive underground explosion, with many men killed. This was followed by the harrowing pictures in the daily papers of their womenfolk waiting at the pit gates for news of survivors. Apparently this explosion had been so powerful that a motorcyclist passing at the time had been blown off his machine, and whenever we passed that point again I had a mental vision of X marks the spot where he was blown off – or maybe he just fell off through fright. The other feature of that route through Wales to Llandudno on the north-west coast was the presence of a large TB sanatorium, gleaming white, which stood out high on one of the hills above the main road. Tuberculosis was still prevalent and was not to be brought under control until the drugs were developed in World War Two. In fact Nanny Adams, who looked after Tim in India for three years, died of it within a fairly short time of returning to England, so it could be said that he had a narrow escape from infection.

When I look back at the number and range of holidays that I spent with the Coves during those two and a half years, it must have been almost a case of perpetual motion. Short breaks, such as half-terms, were spent either at Betws-y-Coed, an attractive beauty spot of a town on the edge of Snowdonia, surrounded by densely wooded hills, and with a river running through the centre, or at Llandudno, the queen of the north coast facing the isle of Anglesey. The town lies around a sweep of a bay that leads into Colwyn Bay, a slightly less elegant resort to the east. Each town was headed by massive promontories of granite rock, the Great Orme in the case of Llandudno, and the Little Orme for Colwyn Bay. The former was so large that it had a road around its perimeter for sightseers to drive along. These promontories consisted of open, rocky grassland, full of wild flowers adapted to that marine climate, and because of Mr Cove's weak heart it fell upon Mr Fare to take me on exploratory walks over and across them. In fact, he became an unofficial uncle and whenever we were anywhere that required energetic walking, he would step in. I have photos of the two of us on the Great Orme or picnicking by a roadside, and he was always dressed in a rumpled double-breasted suit and a pair of walking shoes – this was long before the age of leisure clothes or footwear. Just across the estuary of the local river to the west was Conwy Castle, everyone's idea of a mediaeval castle, virtually a town within its outer perimeter with castellated battlements, a moat and a drawbridge. Some miles further on the tip of Wales overlooking Anglesey was the even bigger and more threatening Caernarfon Castle. Both of these were built by the Normans first to pacify and then to hold down the fractious Celts, who became the Welsh. There was what the Americans would call a 'squeeze play' with these castles in the west and Chester on the eastern border. In time they probably contributed to any Welsh prejudice versus the English – although the Normans were not English of course, and knocked us about quite a bit too in their inimitable way. So we in turn have transferred our prejudices towards the French.

Llandudno had the usual seaside pier, very close to what must have been a four-star hotel where we stayed. I have a photo of Mr Cove, dressed in a hat and raincoat, standing on the pier behind myself and another boy in our school uniforms, looking every inch the proud father. The only negative that I associate with that seaside town was when a half term coincided with 11 November Remembrance Day. The war memorial was somewhere on the promenade facing out to sea, and we stood there for however long the service lasted, in the teeth of a nor'wester dripping with rain, while the wind whisked our reedy 'Oh God, our help in ages past' into the ether. The only part of me that was not frozen was my hand, firmly gripped by Mr Cove's, and I wondered what good our actions were doing the dead.

I don't know who paid the hotel bills, whether they were charged up to my parents or not, because when we visited Cheltenham, that grande dame of the Cotswolds, retirement home of choleric colonels and Anglo-Indian (in the non-Eurasian sense) colonials, we stayed at the Queen's Hotel, and when in Torquay on another occasion, at the Imperial no less. Not that I felt particularly privileged; it just seemed to be par for the course. The Cotswolds were then the heart of rural England, prosperous even in the 1930s, but not the tourist honeypot that they have become. Foxhunting was still a familiar part of the local life, and all the gift shops sold carved wooden models of horses in full flight with their riders in pink habit, pursuing their prey. No chance of such souvenirs now. Since then a bill has been introduced in Parliament to ban such rural sports or pest control – depending on one's point of view – with little change in the actual situation on the ground. Cheltenham was within easy reach of castles such as Ludlow, again on the Welsh border, a really spooky but well-preserved ruin, high above the bend of a river, as well as the massive and well-preserved one at Warwick, with its huge battlements and almost unrivalled collection of armour and weaponry. This has now become a major tourist attraction.

For spiritual tourism we had Worcester and Gloucester cathedrals within reach, and somehow Mr Cove took us across the country to visit Lincoln and Ely cathedrals. Lincoln was one of the five main centres of occupation during the 'Danelaw' of the Danish period in East Anglia, and like York has several streets, whose name ends in 'gate', which comes from the Danish for a narrow road. When William the Conqueror came along he instructed that a cathedral be built there on a hill overlooking the flat expanse of the surrounding countryside, which was started in 1192 and is the third largest after York Minster and St Paul's Cathedral. But the Scandinavian connection did not die, because a couple of centuries later the Norwegians decided to build a Gothic cathedral in their old Norse capital of Trondheim. They took the Lincoln design as their template, and brought artisans over from England to build it. My wife, Lene, and I visited it for a weekend. Lincoln has two features that I recall. It has the most wonderful chapter house supported by a single central pillar, with fluted stone ribs spreading outwards in a circle. On one of the columns in the nave, an artisan had carved a small gargoyle, sitting cross-legged high up on the pillar, the so-called 'Lincoln Imp'. It really has to be brought to one's attention to see it.

Ely at that time was just a large village, or a small town, on the edge of the Fens about twelve miles from Cambridge, which was then almost purely a university city. Cambridge is now a scientific centre as well, so Ely has become almost a residential suburb of its larger sister. St Etheldreda, Queen of Northumbria, founded its cathedral in 673. During the Norman period it was substantially rebuilt, but in 1322 the central tower collapsed while under construction. However, to use modern business jargon, a problem was turned into an opportunity, and the gaping hole was replaced with a massive octagonal tower, seventy-two feet in diameter, and the whole crowned with a lantern roof. Despite his heart, Mr Cove was determined to get to the top of all this, all 179 steps I was told, dark and spirally wound. I recall being so scared as we climbed ever upwards that I went up the last part on all fours and stayed so close to Mr Cove that I got a bloody nose from his heel coming up into my face. Nevertheless, it was an achievement, and a wonderful view from the top – if you like flat fens that is.

We actually stayed in Cambridge at the Garden House Hotel on the edge of the 'backs', another comfortable watering hole that still thrives. Cambridge has a lot going for it in architectural terms since, unlike Oxford, which is mainly built out of Cotswold stone, it is a mixture of Gothic (as in King's College Chapel), neoclassical and Georgian. Not many tourists to this country head for that part of the world, preferring to visit the better-known places west of London. An example of this is that about thirty years ago I was flying back from a business trip to Milan and found myself sitting next to a retired American couple, who were ending their tour of the Continent with a three-day coach tour in England. When I asked them, 'Where will you be going? Windsor, Oxford and Stratford-upon-Avon?' they looked at me in astonishment and replied, 'Yes, how in the world did you know that?'

The other memorable holidays were a couple of summers in Devon and Cornwall. In 1934, the huge 'J' class yachts decided to race a triangular course in Torbay. I don't think that it was an official part of the America's Cup competition, since that would have been sailed where the Cup was held – in America. Nevertheless, they were all there, the *Royal Sovereign*, the *Endeavour*, built by Thomas Sopwith to try to regain the Cup, the *Velsheda*, a lovely creamy white yacht, which is still available for hire (as is the *Endeavour*), as well as the *Astra*. The latter had a green hull and varnished wooden mast, and was the only one that did not meet the overall measurements of the 'J' class. So we spent the afternoons sitting on the headland watching them tacking and running between Torquay and the old fishing port of Brixham to the west. They were a sight for sore eyes, particularly when a three-masted old tea clipper sailed in and anchored offshore.

It probably took two to three days to motor down there from West Kirby at our leisurely pace before the days of motorways. As one enters the county of Somerset from the north in the region of Bridgwater, rain drains off the Quantock Hills and also runs in from a large estuary to form the so-called Somerset Levels. These are a large, flat, marshy area, criss-crossed by wide dikes that are controlled by gates like locks that raise or lower the water level. It was in this area that the Anglo-Saxons finally trapped the Danish army, and defeated it. At any rate, we were driving through this after lunch one day when what later turned out to be a butcher's van approached us at high speed and out of control at a point where the main road took an S-bend around a series of dikes. It was clearly going too fast, heeled over on to two wheels and shot down a bank into deep water to lie on its side. We stopped; Mr Fare jumped out, waded in and pulled the driver out through the front passenger door. He was cut about the head a bit, but he was laid face down on the bank, while Mr Fare pumped the small of his back. Vast quantities of liquid gushed from his mouth. Mr Cove looked concerned. 'He seems to have swallowed an awful lot of ditch water in such a short time.'

'Yes,' Mr Fare replied drily, 'beer-smelling ditch water!'

I don't know how that was sorted out, the AA again I expect (the motoring organisation that is, not Alcoholics Anonymous).

Probably our longest and certainly most memorable holiday was at Coverack, an archetypal Cornish fishing village on the east and therefore rockier side of the Lizard Peninsular. This is a remarkable small area, varying from the lushness of the Helford River in the north, to the 180-foot serpentine cliffs of Lizard Point in the south, the most southerly point in England. In the centre are the Goonhilly Downs, a large, flat moor with an earth-satellite station in the centre. Fortunately all this area was taken over by the National Trust after World War Two, so it has remained the same. The cottage that we rented, 'Tregisky', is still there, overlooking the bay facing east out over the Mannacle Rocks. It had a long, sloping garden full of semi-tropical palm, aloe and other such trees. There were no mains gas or electricity, but there was a system whereby to get what was probably gas,

Mr Cove and I had to wind up a heavy weight, using a long handle, and when after a few days the weight fell, it had to be wound up again. I have no idea what it was or the principle on which it worked, nor have I been able to find anyone who can suggest what it was.

In those days before the Common European Fishing Policy ruined our waters, the seas around Cornwall were jumping with mackerel. We would rent a dingy, which Mr Cove would row out into the bay, where we would sit and fish with several hooks attached to each line. It did not take much skill to pull them in. On August Bank Holiday there was a fair and regatta for the locals and holiday visitors. Competitions included diving down off the harbour mole into eight feet or so of water to retrieve plates scattered around the bottom, and bring them ashore clutched to the swimmer's chest without spilling them, and the traditional pillow fight between two sitting on a greasy boom over the water. Mr Fare, in the meantime, was in his element playing cricket with the locals and visitors, bowling right arm round the wicket. So a good time was had by all.

On the opposite side of the peninsular to Coverack was Mullion Cove, another typical Cornish village. The harbour was separated from the beach by a cave through the rocks about fifteen yards long, so one can only approach the beach when the tide allows, and return before the cave fills up on the high tide. There is also a magnificent walk along the cliffs from Mullion to Kynance Cove, near Lizard Point, which is now part of the official coastal path that runs for about 600 miles around Devon and Cornwall. Some time ago I took Lene down there for a holiday, and as we walked back from Mullion harbour to the car park, we came to a sentry box where a woman was sitting, renting out boats. Her skin was burned red-brown, she had upper arms like hams, and her wild brown hair was bleached in streaks. She took one look at Lene, recognised a difference, and our exchange went something like this, in an accent thicker than clotted cream.

'You bain't be from around 'ere, be you, my 'andsome?'

'No,' replies Lene.

'Where you from then?' she asks.

'From the north,' replies Lene.

'How faarr north?'

'Very far,' advises Lene.

Pause for some serious thought. Then: 'Fur'n Exeter?'

I decided to take a hand. 'She's from Denmark.'

Another pause. 'That be up Norway way, ain't it?'

We agreed on that. On further questioning she told me that she had been a Wren in Devonport during the war. If that were true, I would say that she had slipped a few notches down the social scale. Wrens were mostly slightly superior gels. She looked more like the ladies who used to sit in the corner of the pubs, sipping their port and lemons, waiting for a lonely sailor.

Whatever she was, she was the purest, original West Country article.

Thus I owe an enormous debt to the Coves, particularly Mr Cove, and Mr Fare for that matter. They were the people who introduced me to great swathes of the north Wales and English countryside, and helped me to develop a lasting affection for it. With Mr Cove I had a wonderful guide and running commentary on our historical monuments, cathedrals and simple but varied holiday pleasures. Many look back fondly to the halcyon days of holidays in the 1930s for those fortunate enough to have the money for them, and I certainly do.

My time with them was always going to come to an end, but it was unfortunate in the way that it happened. My parents had come home on leave in the spring of 1936, and Grandpa died suddenly shortly after their return. That gave my father the chance to cut his roots with the north of England, because most of the staff in Shell either came from the south or were Scots. As I said in the first chapter, home leave put a lot of pressure on people, whether to find a wife, sort out the children's education or who was going to look after them during holidays in the next tour, and it is quite possible that my father was not able to give the normal term's notice for my leaving Dormie House, or would not pay a term's fees in lieu. My parents came to collect me a couple of days after term's end and on the appointed morning Mr Cove told me that his wife did not wish to meet my parents, and that I was to wait at the gate with my suitcase. When they rolled up in a brand new, blue Morris 14, my mother got out and came to the gate, telling me that she would just go to the door and say goodbye. When I told her that the Coves did not wish to see them, and had to repeat it, she went to tell Tishy who was sitting in the driver's seat like some pre-Copernican pope, expecting the universe to revolve around him. 'Don't be silly,' he instructed her, 'just go and ring the bell.' No answer, of course. So we drove off with my parents protesting the extraordinary behaviour of the Coves, followed by my response from the back seat, that if anyone's behaviour was extraordinary, it was theirs. The Coves had looked after me as their own for three years, and he, Tishy, did not even have the courtesy to get out of the car. To say that this went down like a lead balloon would be a very major understatement, and so began the tense filial relationship between father and elder son that one sometimes reads about.

Sixteen years later I found myself back in Liverpool in my first job, and took the train out to West Kirby. By then Mr Cove was widowed and had retired and sold the school to Dr Macaffee's son. He was delighted to see me again and to hear about what had happened in the interval since I left, which had included going around the world a couple of times. When I decided to emigrate to Canada in 1952 he gave me the six volumes of Churchill's history of the Second World War. So all was well that ended well, and we parted friends for the second and last time.

In the meantime, what of Grandpa while I was at Dormie House School? After Grandma died in 1933 he lived alone in the same house and I did not see him, but since he had been waited on hand and foot, literally, he must have found it very difficult to look after himself. There were no pre-cooked meals from Tesco in those days that one just bungs into the oven at 200°C for thirty-five minutes. Across the road lived a schoolteacher called Ada Edgerton who after a short period of mourning became Grandpa's second wife. I have to say that she appeared to bring much happiness into the old boy's life, and when my Sunday visits to their house resumed, often with another boy taken along, they were free of the previous crushing religious significance. We even all went on holiday together to Bournemouth, which for them was probably their honeymoon. It was the first time that I can recall that he ever went away; he had not even gone back to Cornwall, as one might have expected. A photo shows the three of us walking along the promenade below the cliffs dressed in winter clothing and all looking very happy.

I can only think of two flies in the ointment. The first was that they acquired a wire-haired terrier called Pickles that would fight anything and everything. When I was sent out to take it for walks all dolled up in my school uniform, Grandpa insisted that I took one of his varnished walking sticks to fend off other dogs, although the reverse was required – that is, to restrain Pickles from attacking them. After being jeered on a couple of occasions by the local lads as a toffee-nosed little prep school boy with a fancy walking stick, I stuck the end down a grating in the gutter and snapped it off to a length that could be concealed under my raincoat. Aunt Ada understood well, and pacified Grandpa.

The other minor burden was that Grandma, virtually on her deathbed, had decided that I was to be given lessons in playing the violin, just as 'her dear Leslie' (my father) had played it in the Army during the Great War. Since she had put money aside for this forlorn attempt, there was no avoiding it. By the third year at Dormie House I was just about able to saw my way through the 'Londonderry Air' and 'Melody in F', *con* absolutely no *brio*. So an upstairs room was rented in West Kirby one evening, and Grandpa's elderly friends and my godfather (his chairman in the Pioneer Life Assurance Company, as mentioned) all came along and sat in straight-backed chairs around the wall, applauding my atrocious efforts as if I were Yehudi Menuhin. Why the floor did not just open up and swallow me I don't know, because dammit! I prayed hard enough for it to happen. Final release from the torment came when I went for an examination at Rushworth and Draper in Liverpool. The pass mark was 100 out of a possible 150, and I was given 99, and that was probably a gross exaggeration, a kinder way of saying 66 or 33. The net result was that when I was sent to my next school in Kent that September, violin lessons were dropped and, on my father's instructions, replaced with boxing. A bit of a contrast, really.

But what of my brother Tim, who in the summer of 1936

would have been rising four years old? There was absolutely no sign of him, nor, as far as I can recall, any mention of him. In August my parents and I went over by ferry to Ireland with our new car, and drove right across to County Clare in the south-west, not far from Killarney. There Tishy played golf, one of the obsessions of his life, and my mother and I fished in a local lake and small river with a new greenheart rod. Clearly one needs more than an expensive rod and some flies to catch fish success-fully, because in the two weeks our total haul amounted to one fish, about six inches long, whose scales were of a green and orange hue, that did not look too edible. So we left it, but we had a lot of fun together in the meantime.

Tim may have been staying again with Nanny Adams at her home near Liverpool. While in India, he recalls spending several periods at a convent school in Kotagiri, in the Nilgiri Hills, which was not too far from Ootacamund, the 'snooty Ooty' of colonial fame, where the British overseas lived up to their motto, 'When in Rome, do exactly as you would do at home'. However, when he was there, Tim must have been well looked after, because years later when he was a tea planter in Ooty in the early 1960s he went back to look up the mother superior and bring her up to date with what had happened to him in the meantime.

So Tim had his 'Miss Braithwaite' too.

4.

A Pukka Southern School (Years 10–13)

Thus my six years in the Wirrall, Cheshire came to an end with the death of my grandfather, and since my father had found a base for us that became more or less a home from home for the family when they were on leave from India. This was at the West Kent Hotel at Bickley, Kent, between Bromley and Chislehurst, which adjoined the golf club of the same name, through which Tishy had come across some sons of a member called Holdsworth. These he adjudged to be 'the right type'. There were four brothers, all of whom attended as day boys at a local prep school called Bickley Hall. Tragically two of them were killed as pilots in the RAF. I had been scheduled to go on to a school called the Lees in West Kirby. It had a very good reputation, since whenever I have mentioned that I spent my early years in that area to people who knew of it, their invariable comment is, 'Oh, were you a Lees boy then?' As far as I know it has closed down now, but Dormie House continued to thrive under the headmastership of the son of Dr Macaffee, who was a pupil there at the same time as I was. No doubt he has retired by now. I was due to have my Cheshire accent erased from my speech, and to become a proper little Home Counties boy.

However, it is good to know that in this new century, some sixty-five years on, folk still hang on to their regional accents. A couple of years ago I was waiting outside our local sub-post office, exchanging the usual pleasantries with an old chap wearing a conventional men's cap, who spoke with a northern accent. Because it was quite soft I asked him if he came from Cheshire.

'Oh no,' he replied, 'I'm from York-shire' (pronounced as two words).

'I'm sorry if I insulted you by asking if you hailed from Cheshire,' I went on.

'No, you didn't insult me at all by that,' he assured me.

'Supposing I had enquired if you came from Lancashire?' I asked.

'That would have done it!' he replied.

And so after the holiday in Ireland I headed south for the first time in early September 1936 to stay at the West Kent Hotel with my parents and Tim. Confirming what I thought in the last chapter, Tim must have been parked with someone in England during our holiday, because when I was going through a box of old family photos, I came across a photo of Tim, Tishy and me taken on the entrance steps to the hotel. Tim and I looked to be about the ages of four and ten respectively. The hotel also had a small lodge at the entrance to the drive, with a bedroom that Tim and I shared, so we had our own private quarters.

In short order I was kitted out with the required number of clothes and other items on the list from the school shop, Daniel Niel behind Selfridges, and my mother did what every middle-class mother did in those days, sewed in the Cash's name tapes. This became a sort of rite of passage. At the beginning of September I was taken to the school with my trunk, introduced to the headmaster and owner, Mr Bernie Farnfield and his wife Dorothy, and assigned to a dormitory. Two weeks later my parents left for India with Tim by a P&O ship from Tilbury docks, and that was the start of my four-year stay at Bickley Hall.

Bickley Hall was an archetypal prep school in the London area, and competed in both sport and academic records with other similar schools including St Hughes just down the road, Colet Court, Dulwich Junior School and the same for Sevenoaks. I cannot think of a better description of its ethos and what it was like to be there than the Hogwarts School of Harry Potter fame. In fact, I find it almost incredible that fifty years after Anthony Crosland, the Labour Minister for Education, and his sidekick Shirley Williams did their best to kill off private schools, including the former's infamous remark as to what he would like to do with grammar schools, a single mother can write a bestseller for children that glorifies such prep school life. Bickley Hall had it all: houses (Grey and Cerise after the school colours), a Latin motto, *in Domino confido* (in the Lord I trust), dormitories named after

British heroes like Scott, Byers, Shackleton and so on, a school chapel of its own, emphasis on the team spirit and conformity ('play up, play up and play the game'), and last but not least the sine qua non for such establishments, bloody awful food.

The actual school was a large late Victorian or Edwardian building, built on a raised bank above the surrounding playing fields and woods, with arched cellars beneath it, that proved to be most useful when during World War Two they took the risk of staying put rather than evacuating to a safer rural area. The cellars were shored up against bombs in the early part, and later on against the V1 'doodlebugs', on whose flight path to central London the school lay. The school grounds were entered off the Bickley Park Road, just above Chislehurst station, with a lodge at the entrance in which lived the Classics master, 'Solly', and his wife. His name had been anglicised from Solomon to Selwyn. He was a brilliant, demanding teacher, with a tendency to sarcasm that he would apologise for when he had reduced any boy to tears, but he was the master that one would always remember, and he made Latin my best subject throughout the rest of my school career.

The total grounds must have covered twenty acres that included two pitches for football in the autumn term, and Rugby in the winter, with an immaculate cricket square between them. Behind the school building there were woods leading to an old courtyard and clock house area, where some of the junior classes were located, a large gymnasium with a stage for plays, and the school chapel built in an old stable. Next to it was a large rose garden that was Mrs Bernie's pride and joy, full of all the old-fashioned musk and other roses that have now been driven off the market by hybrids. There was even an enclosed twenty-five-yard heated swimming pool with changing rooms that opened in June for the summer term, and then stayed open through the summer for the surrounding residents.

One final item was a small, two-roomed cottage next to the entrance to the clock house where a Mrs Hunt lived on her own. She must have been in her sixties, but who she was or why she was there I know not. She dressed like the proverbial bag lady in layers of shapeless clothes, and clearly had no access to washing facilities. Occasionally one caught up with her struggling on her flat, splayed feet back to the school carrying her basket up St George's Road from the 227 bus stop, and it was expected of anyone to give her a hand. That's when one discovered that she had no washing facilities to speak of.

The Farnfields were from a famous sporting family. Mr Bernie and his brother Mr Archie had originally jointly owned the school, but the latter had died before I arrived. With several other brothers and cousins they had more or less made up a soccer and cricket team, and many of them played for the famous amateur team of those days, the Corinthians. Those were very much the days of the gifted amateurs, who were trained to go out and run an Empire with a Bible in one hand and a cricket bat in the other. As far as the latter is concerned one can only say that they succeeded brilliantly with the teams of the three Indian subcontinental countries, who now regularly beat their mentors. The Empire strikes back with a vengeance! With the Farnfield connections we also had visits to the school from players of the Australian Test cricket teams that in those days took six weeks to sail from their country to ours. I am afraid that any inspiration that they gave out was lost on me, since I gave up playing the game at the earliest available opportunity after leaving, which was two years later in South Africa.

Joining a new school in midstream is never particularly easy, especially when one is moved from one end of the country to the other without one's mates. At the end of the first Christmas term the school play was put on in the gymnasium cum assembly hall complete with stage. The parents would turn up dressed to the nines, the fathers in three-piece suits and the mothers with hats and grinning fox fur stoles around their shoulders. The play was *Treasure Island* and for some reason I was given a part that was so minor that it was not really rehearsed out loud in the dress rehearsal. I was one of the loyal members of the crew called something like Redfern, and when the pirates attempted to reboard the ship I had to jump on to the top of the gangway with a cocked musket and repel them. This I did and yelled in a broad Cheshire accent 'staaand baack there, or I'll fie-yer!' The audience erupted, none of them clearly ever having been north of the proverbial Watford, and I was left to ponder on the reasons for their reaction to such an innocuous sentence.

The changeover from violin lessons to boxing was even more traumatic. These took place in the gym on Thursday afternoons, and the gloves were battered, mostly unmatched ones with tattered leather backs, except for when we had boxing matches between houses or against other schools, when they would produce reasonable sets. Every year we would play one football match and have one boxing competition going through the weights against the East End boys from the Bermondsey or West Ham Boys Club, from that part of London's docklands south of the river between Tower Bridge and the Isle of Dogs. This was all part of the well-known efforts to bridge the social gap between private school boys and underprivileged lads. What it really achieved was to demonstrate the latter's utter superiority in the chosen sports, although they had access to a wider base to choose from. When it came to the football records for the term playing against other schools, itemising 'played so many, won such and such, and lost whatever', the match versus the Boys' Club, was not included. The result was invariably eight goals to one, or ten to two in their favour, since they had learned their football kicking a tin can around the environs of Tooley Street, often with their bare feet.

At the end of the second year I was put into the team to box against them. This area of London produced the future Alan Minters of boxing or the infamous present-day supporters of Millwall football club. A soft eleven-year-old prep school boy was put into the ring with an undersized but streetwise fourteen-year-old. It was no contest and stopped in the first round. However, I must have learned something from that experience, even if it was a warped version of the Christian premise that 'it's better to give than to receive' (that is, in boxing, points could be scored for aggression or leading the fight) since two years later I was made Captain of Boxing. The best part of those meetings was the tea afterwards when we all sat down in the dining hall with our opponents to huge plates of bangers and mash. Those kids really got stuck in, and cleaned the last scrap from their plates. Only in the last couple of years have I come across sausages which taste as good as those, and they are sold under the 'Porkinson's' brand. I thought of it about ten years later in the Navy, when one day I was coming alongside our ship in a launch and hooked on to the boom. The stoker and I then had to shin up a couple of ropes hanging down, which I could do with ease, while he struggled. 'It's all right for you mate,' he said, 'You was brought up on proper food while we had bread and scrape [dripping] half the time.' Funnily enough dripping on toast had been quite a treat for us – like tripe and onions cooked in milk when I spent holidays in Yorkshire.

There were very few other boys at the school with parents abroad. I can only think of the Vernede family, whose parents were on a tea estate in Assam. The younger St John made his name with a monumental boxing bout against one of the Bermondsey boys, where there was blood from their noses everywhere, but he prevailed. The system then was that each term had a half-term long weekend in the middle, plus one or two exeats on Sundays. Even if the boys' homes were nearby in the London area, that was the only time that the boarders, who were the majority, could get out. So we colonials depended on someone asking us home for the day or the weekend, and it usually happened. The furthest afield that I went was to Denham, west of Uxbridge, and not too far from where I live now. If one did not get out, then it was a drag, but fortunately an infrequent one. Once in a while a friend of my parents from India would turn up to see how things were, and as they took their leave by the gate into St George's Road they would slip me a one-pound note. Such were the compensations for parental absence.

In the meantime, my parents were in Madras, from where one received the weekly letter that took two to three weeks to arrive, depending on whether the mail took the short cut by train from Marseilles or not. These letters were often accompanied by small black-and-white photos of life out there. They lived in a large so-called bungalow set in spacious grounds, since, as I was to discover later, Shell were among the most generous of employers for all levels of their staff. Dogs featured prominently among the photos. First there was an Irish Setter called Rory, but the constant heat of Madras was not really suitable for such a breed, and he was replaced by several generations of Sydney Silkies, small dogs like a Yorkie, who no doubt yapped at the heels of the locals that they did not know. Beach parties and picnics seemed to be a frequent way of socialising, and I have inherited a box of photos with one that shows Dorothy and Tishy lying together in the shallows in a passionate clinch that anticipated Bert Lancaster and Deborah Kerr in 'From Here to Eternity' by about seven years. They should have collected royalties on it! They were clearly very happy together in their younger days.

The bungalow was in fact a house with an upper floor surrounded by a wide veranda for coolness and shade. Tim was at the convent school at Kotagiri, and when at home was looked after by an ayah and a new nanny called Sandra, who could have been out from England, or a local so-called 'country-born' girl, using that awful term that referred to those of British parentage, who were born and educated in India, rather than sent 'home' to school. In the pecking order of the Raj they were a caste below the expatriates, but above the Anglo-Indians. According to Tim, the family had the use of two cars, a Humber and a Buick. The oil business in India at that time was dominated by the Burmah Shell Oil Company and the American Standard Vacuum Oil Company. (Why there was an 'h' in Burmah I never found out, except possibly that was how the Brits pronounced Pune as Poonah.) Both companies carried a lot of clout locally, so their expatriate management staff would be invited to celebrations within the princely states. Thus every so often I would receive a coloured postcard of the Maharajah of Mysore's palace, when it was my parents' turn to represent the company at his durbar, housed in the elaborate tented camps of India.

As has been well documented, life under the Raj involved the men working throughout the year wherever they were based, while during the monsoon months their wives went up to the local hill stations such as Ootacamund for Madras, or Simla for Delhi, to indulge themselves in all the social activities described so vividly by Rudyard Kipling in *Plain Tales from the Hills*. But in the summer of 1938 my mother decided that she wished to go one better and do the summer season in London, and my father paid her fare and sent her off to stay with the mother of one of her girlfriends, a Mrs Sharpe who lived in a tall terraced house in a road between Shepherds Bush and Kensington. Tishy took the precaution of asking an older bachelor friend, Sir Ernest M., who was on leave at the same time, to keep an eye on her. Thus was I introduced to oysters when on my twelfth birthday he took us to the famous fish restaurant, Scott's, which was then on Piccadilly Circus overlooking the statue of Eros. It has moved now to somewhere close to Grosvenor Square. I wrote in the visitors, book, 'Had my first oysters and enjoyed them very much.' Not bad for a twelve-year-old in those days.

During that summer term my mother lived at the Tiger's Head, a pub on Chislehurst Common. She did the usual things that other parents did, namely visit the school on Saturday afternoons when there was usually a cricket match in play, to see their sons. After the end of term she headed for the bright lights of London with me in tow, staying with Mrs Sharpe. Looking back I think it must have been a case not so much of the seven-year itch as the thirteen-year itch, since she had married in Mombasa at the age of eighteen in 1925. There was a milliner's shop in Old Bond Street on the west side that we used to visit fairly regularly, run by a Jewish family called Swerlings. The young assistant seemed to take great interest in Dorothy's social goings on, kitting her out for whatever was the 'next excitement' – the races, dinner or the theatre – since there were always stray chaps home on leave looking for someone to take out. However, Mrs Sharpe ran a tight ship, and I noticed that whenever her charge was out on the tiles of an evening, she stayed up until she returned. Mrs Sharpe had a son, Alec, who had just gone through a messy divorce and was available to take me around the sights of London, to sail my yacht on the round pond in Kensington Gardens, on visits to the Tower, or best of all to Hamleys toy store in Regent Street, which appears to have gone from strength to strength, and continues to serve the children of all ages. When one looks back it is extraordinary how formally children, particularly from private schools, were dressed in those days, and expensively too. One afternoon Dorothy and I were window-shopping down Oxford Street in the middle of August. The weather was hot and sultry as it can be before a thunderstorm, and I was dressed in a Harris tweed suit with long stockings for God's sake. The perspiration just ran off my face. Looking at me my mother remarked that she could not imagine that I could stand up to the climate of India, which was probably an attempt to convince herself that they had done the right thing in leaving me here. Little did we know that within two years I would be in India, and took to the heat and sun like a sunflower in Provence.

With the beginning of September, it was back to Bickley Hall and its ring fence for the next thirteen weeks, the same faces morning, noon and night, the same routine and school discipline. 'How d'ya get them back on the farm, now that they've seen Paree?' Schools located in the middle of towns such as Harrow, Eton or Winchester have the advantage that the pupils can mingle with the world 'outside', to use the term often expressed by long-term servicemen in the Armed Forces. My mother sailed back to India, and after this interlude I went back to spending my holidays in a Yorkshire vicarage.

The Reverend Claud Stephenson was a Church of England vicar in the West Riding of Yorkshire, and was married to a Cornish cousin of my father, called Florence or Flossie. However, because she was of the Thomas family she was always 'Auntie Tommy' to me. Uncle Claud originally came from Lancashire, but his Yorkshire parishioners did not appear to hold this against him in any way! He had been a padre in the Great War as a young man, and had therefore seen many terrible things, as had Tommy, who had been a nurse in France. I first met them briefly when I was about six years old, when Grandpa put me on a coach in Liverpool to go across the Pennines to Leeds, where Claud met me. A couple of ladies on the bus were asked to keep an eye on me and I rewarded them by bending their ears with my chatter for the whole way. Innocent, trusting days. I doubt if six-year-olds are allowed such freedom now. Claud and Tommy lived in a vicarage in the parish of St Peter's church, somewhere near the quaintly named town of Heckmondwyke. It was a brief stay, perhaps a half-term or part of the Easter holidays from Meols School, but it was the start of a very close, almost paternal relationship. Therefore when I started at Bickley Hall in the autumn term of 1936, these two were about the only relatives I had in this country, and again they were childless.

The journey up to Yorkshire at the end of each term was made by train, first to Victoria Station, then bus across London lugging my suitcase of clothes, and another long distance train to Leeds from probably Euston Station. By this time they had moved to another parish at Staincliffe, up the top of the long, steep hill above Dewsbury, the centre of the woollen industry in the West Riding of Yorkshire. Living in the vicarage in those days, one met folk of all levels of the local society, who invariably called Claud 'vicar'. As one would expect they were down to earth and all spoke with a similar Yorkshire accent, whether mill owner or mill worker. The one thing that was not allowed was to have 'side', which amounted to conceit, swank, putting on airs and graces, particularly a 'soothern' version of the latter. In those days, before the advent of leisure clothes, I would be dressed in grey flannel shorts and jacket or a pullover, with long grey socks with cerise tops, denoting our school colours. So fading into the background was not an option, and 'no side' it had to be to survive.

Claud and Tommy lived in a typical large, stone C of E vicarage in a road off the main road, with about a quarter-acre garden, between the church and the C of E primary school. There was the usual vast kitchen with a large black iron range, where life would be lived in the winter since there was no central heating other than to the bathroom, and it was perishing. Claud would light a fire in a living room with a large bay window looking over the sloping lawn at the back, but that took a while to warm up. He also had his study, to which he would repair to prepare his Sunday sermons. In most winters there was heavy snow, enough for me to make a giant snowball about 4'6" high by starting small and just rolling it around.

Claud was a genuinely good man, about 5'9" tall, rotund, with a full mouth and a jovial, mock-pompous manner. Although I was in the choir at school he never suggested that I joined his in the church, which as far as I was concerned would have been the kiss of death with the local tykes. He and Tommy were clearly not even affluent, just reasonably well off, but I never saw them turn away one of the down-and-outs, who occasionally called at the back door, without giving them something, some small money or more often food. They had friends among the local mill owners, particular Albert and Vera Stockdale, and despite his relative wealth Albert would still come round for a meal wearing a collarless shirt with a gold-coloured stud at the neck. However, socially it was still a case of 'Room at the Top' with the mill owners living in large houses at the top of the hill and the workers in their terraced houses down the bottom. The one common feature of those cottages was the state of their doorsteps, which were made of a light-coloured stone. A Yorkshire housewife was expected to get down on her hands and knees and holystone (scour) that doorstep until it shone. Anyone who did not was regarded as a failure as a wife, bordering on being a slut, and probably got a bloody good hiding from her old man, to use the vernacular.

My uncle's mill owner friends, like the Stockdales, were well aware of Claud's financial circumstances and allowed Tommy to go to the mill and buy material for dresses or curtains at cost price. Since they had no children of their own they kept an Irish setter called Judy, who was my reason for roaming the local area, since I did not have much opportunity to make holiday friends among the locals. There was only one that I got to know at all, called Brian. He was the pride and joy of his Yorkshire mum, who used to bang on about 'ow-er Bri-yan this', and 'ow-er Bri-yan that', which I have to confess I found somewhat irritating. Nevertheless, he was company.

Claud and Tommy must have been in their late forties when I was staying with them. Auntie Tommy was a lovely lady, with long thick hair drawn into some sort of a bun at the back of her head. We used to talk, talk, talk together in the kitchen for hours – and I mean *hours* – when she used to fill me in on all the details of the family down in Cornwall, where my grandparents had come from, but with whom I was not to come into contact until 1946–7: an uncle Peter, aunt Mitchie and Martha, their daughter, as well as the Thomas family, who had been tin miners until that collapsed, then smallholders and livestock dealers, and to whom she was related.

I think that I can also date my habit of snoring loudly to that kitchen. One day Claud and I were mock wrestling in it, and he did not realise that his thirteen stone or more was too much for my seven stone or thereabouts. So a light shove from him propelled me backwards on to the sharp corner of the kitchen dresser. I felt a sharp pain in my kidney, blacked out and fell face downwards on to the stone-flagged floor, and spreadeagled my nose across my face. The end result was that when I used to wake up in the dormitory at Hilton in South Africa, my bed was often surrounded by slippers, shoes, or whatever came to hand for a missile by the morning.

Some time before I left Bickley Hall, Claud and Tommy were moved to another parish at Woodkirk, near Morley on the way to Leeds, and not too far from Batley. This was probably no more than ten or fifteen miles from Dewsbury, but it was coal-mining country, with a different type of parishioner, and more open countryside around for walks, somewhat scarred with the familiar slag heaps. It was the same type of stone vicarage, equally cold in winter, but with a much larger, attractive garden, with parts for flowers and the rest a kitchen garden. Claud seemed to have got a leg up financially by this move, since he was able to join (or at any rate play at) a golf club near Leeds, to which we went by bus, since they still had no car. Claud also developed the habit of getting up first to light the fires and brew up the most fantastic café au lait for breakfast that I have ever tasted. The main road from Batley to Morley took an S-turn as it passed the vicarage, and immediately opposite was a pub. At the weekend he would nip across the road with an enamel jug and fill it up with beer for our lunch. Come to think of it, that must have been about five years later when I stayed with them on my return from South Africa, since I was well under age while at Bickley. Nevertheless, the people were the same: miners, who called a spade a bloody shovel. One day Claud was going on his parish rounds when he met a miner's wife with one of her sons in tow, aged around ten years.

'Good morning, Mrs Bloggs,' says Claud, 'and how are you today?'

'I'm very well, thank you vicar.'

Claud observes the boy and asks, 'Is that your little lad?'

'Aye, that's ow-er Willie, vicar,' she replies. ' 'Aven't you met 'im before?'

'I don't think I have,' says Claud.

Turning to her son, who was scuffing something around in the gutter, Mrs Bloggs instructs him to 'say 'ow-do t'vicar'.

The child continues to scuff around in the gutter with his head lowered. 'Did you 'ear me?' asks his mother. 'I said, say 'ow-do t'vicar.'

Still no response, at which a hand shot out attached to an arm like a ham, grabbed Willie by the scruff of the neck, jerked him onto the pavement, and with a roar instructed him, 'Willie, I said coom 'ere, yer little booger, and say 'ow-do t' bloody vicar!'

Willie did as he was told and probably got the strap when he got home again. No doubt he grew up to be an honest, down-to-earth Yorkshire type.

Claud just took it all in his stride and had an excellent relationship with his parishioners. He knew their family ups and downs, he knew which of the brides that he married should not have been dressed in white (in those days at least) since the vicarage overlooked the graveyard (a favourite courting spot) and which were shotgun weddings. The parishioners used to bring us terrific rhubarb in season, grown under black glass or inverted dustbins, because for some reason the soil there was peculiarly suited to that crop. Perhaps it was due to the coal dust in the soil. But it is all change now. When the West Riding was going through one of its periodic textile crises in the 1970s, the mill owners or textile companies, instead of investing in new plants to improve productivity, as happened in Finland or Germany, resorted to one of the curses of the old Empire, and brought in cheap labour from the Indian subcontinent. Thus old towns like Dewsbury and Bradford have imported their own race problems for present and future generations to resolve.

Batley had a short renaissance in the 1970s when the so-called Batley Working Men's Club was the venue for some terrific entertainment for the miners and their families from the likes of Shirley Bassey strutting her stuff. But it was all swept away in the national miners' strike and pit closures of the 1980s.

In the spring of 1939 my parents came home on leave bringing Tim, now six and a half years old, to join me at Bickley Hall. More or less immediately they headed off to spend the month of

June in Scotland so that Tishy could indulge his obsession with golf in the Pitlochry area, while his wife twiddled her thumbs or knitted. But Tim's arrival at the school was memorable. He was a small chap with big, blue eyes and curly fair hair. We were all in the headmaster's sitting room while introductions were being made, until around 6 p.m. another young boy was sent for from Tim's dormitory to act as his 'shepherd', or whatever they were called, to show the new boy around until he found his feet. Tim had clearly spent a considerable amount of his young years in the hearing of adults in India, because when Mr Bernie turned to him and said, 'Well, Tim, I think it is time that you went off to your dormitory now,' Tim replied, 'Right-ho, old boy!' and trotted off. Mr Bernie thought it was a huge joke, but Tim had to be gradually weaned from adult-speak in his own interests with the other boys.

The West Kent Hotel became our home from home during that summer of 1939, right up to the declaration of war against Germany. The actual building was on a slight mound with lawns and gardens flowing away from all around it. There was a squash club, tennis courts and an open-air swimming pool, since it was also a country club. A path led down through a spinney to the road to Petts Wood, which was then a village, and there was a very large, walled kitchen garden, a real old-fashioned one with an arc of hazel trees around one side. There is no doubt that we lived well. At one stage during that summer our cousin Ann Hillcoat came to stay for a week during the holidays from her convent school. She was within three months of my age, which was then thirteen, and this was the first time that I met her, but not the last, as a later chapter will reveal. I have one abiding memory of her, apart from a photo in her school uniform, looking a bit tentative. Somewhere, perhaps in the kitchen garden, I had climbed on to a wall and was walking along the top looking over the other side. At one stage I felt that I was standing on something soft, and on looking down saw that it was Ann's hand as she was trying to climb up. That girl did not make a squeak of protest, so she was 'all right' by my standards!

Attached to the hotel was the West Kent Golf Club, the main reason for our staying there, and where Tishy had temporary membership. In the late summer evenings we would go out on the course, he to play and me to caddy – golf trolleys not having been invented in those days, and caddies not being available at that hour. This is where I first learned to 'box the compass'. As he addressed the ball, assuming that he was facing due north, I had to stand mute and still at north-east by north – not north-north-east, you understand, nor even north-east by east, but specifically at north-east by north. Between strokes there followed advice on my future, questions about what I wanted to do, and exhortations that I must 'get on'.

The one person that I must not end up like was Uncle Claud, for whom he had hardly a good word to say in his favour. Nevertheless this was the man into whose care Tishy had entrusted me for the past three years, when no one else was available, and without whose avuncular hospitality I would have been consigned to boring holiday homes, a mere extension of school life. In the mid-1960s, when I was married with two sons, a French poodle and a Danish mother-in-law called Eva, I took them all up to the Lake District to show them something new of England and do a bit of hill walking. On our way back south we stopped in West Kirby, to which town of all coincidental places Claud had retired with his second wife, Aunt Tommy having died of cancer some years previously. Since we were staying in the town, we had supper with them after which we had time to stay on and chat in a relaxed manner. When we returned home, Eva asked me what my relationship was with that man Claud, because 'you were talking together like a father and son'. Exactly.

The war clouds built up inexorably during that summer, despite which we went off as a family for a traditional bucket-and-spade seaside holiday at Minnis Bay, near Birchington on the tip of Kent jutting into the Thames estuary. There were rock pools, the fish was delicious, we visited Margate, where there was a vast fun fair called 'Dreamland' or something like that, and a large seawater swimming pool. We also drove around the Kent countryside to the North Foreland, where there was a lighthouse as well as a golf course, since Tishy had invested again in a Morris 14 for the duration of their leave. There is absolutely no doubt that Shell provided their employees and their families with a high standard of living. We returned to the West Kent Hotel towards the end of August in time to be there for the declaration of war on Sunday, 3 September. Like the rest of the population we were all glued to the radio to listen to Chamberlain announcing in that droning voice that as of 11 a.m. no reply had been received back from Germany to our ultimatum, and therefore a state of war existed.

The received wisdom then was that such a declaration would be followed immediately with mass bombing raids on the south of England, so we set to filling sandbags and laid them over the half-sunken windows of the cellar, where the bar was located, as well as the table tennis and the billiards tables. Within a few minutes a false air raid alarm went off, and then as we all know the 'phoney war' began and very little happened for weeks, if not months. There was a couple staying there whose son was in the RAF Volunteer Reserve based at Biggin Hill air station as a fighter pilot, just a few miles down the road. Every so often he would pop back in his open Morris 8 to have a meal with his parents or stay the night, and it was all very amateurish compared to what was happening in Poland.

And so Tim and I went back to Bickley Hall, and towards the end of September or early October our parents boarded the P&O liner at Tilbury docks to return to India for three years. Nobody believed that the war would go on for that long, but no one really had the faintest idea of what was ahead of us.

5.

Dunkirk: Reverse Evacuation to India (Years 14–15)

September 1939, therefore, saw our parents return to India for another three-year tour, this time in the Calcutta office, the outbreak of the Second World War on the international scene, and as far as Tim and I were concerned, his first year at Bickley Hall and my fourth and last year there.

The anticipated mass bombing did not materialise and after some leaflet raids over the German cities to tell them what a silly lot they were to take on the might of the British Empire, our divisions that had been sent across to the front between France and Germany settled down to what has been described as the 'phoney war', as the popular song went, we were going 'to hang out the washing on the Siegfried Line'; London theatres were taken over by the Lambeth Walk, and when the real fighting started it would be a cakewalk, or so we were told, since German soldiers were automatons, who could not think for themselves, but only respond to orders from above. Knock off their officers and the rest would not know what to do.

Since Bickley Hall was a gung-ho sort of place, we had *Daily Telegraph* maps pinned up in the senior classroom so that we could follow what little action there was on the Western Front, with comments from reporters such as Sefton Delmer, who was shown wearing his trilby hat at a rakish angle. Everyone wore headgear in those days – proper hats that is, not baseball caps or cloth caps, and archive film now screened on the History Channel shows Berliners in the ruins of their city in 1945, helping to clear the rubble, in coats and formal hats.

Some of our masters must have gone off to the services (although conscription was not introduced in the first phase), since we acquired a new, tall, gangling master, whose stock in trade was a length of rope with a knot at the end. He may have had some sort of a religious mania since he called it Matthew and carried it with him at all times, so that he could inflict instant chastisement on any errant boy. No one seemed to turn a hair at this, although it was different from the usual form of ultimate punishment, which consisted of being told to present oneself at some future time at a master's study for so many of the best. A couple of swipes from 'Matthew' were preferable really, since one did not have the anticipatory waiting period. One can only imagine the furore that such a weapon would cause in any classroom nowadays! The rest of the standards were not allowed to fall; for example, we still had to dress formally for the Sunday services in the chapel made out of a section of the old clock house. The smaller boys – that is probably up to the age of eleven – had to wear Eton suits. These included the short jackets commonly known as 'bum freezers', with the large, starched Eton collars that required studs front and back. The older boys wore Marlborough or full-length jackets, but still with Eton collars. Quite an expense for the parents for the sake of one hour each week of term time. But those were the standards.

I have no recollection as to how or where Tim and I spent that first Christmas holiday, the first time that we had ever been together at school. If we went up to one of the Yorkshire vicarages with Claud and Auntie Tommy I cannot recall it, but I presume that we did. That first winter of the war in 1940 was a bitterly cold one, with deep snow for the south of England over many weeks. There were frosts hard enough to freeze the local ponds up on Chislehurst Common, where we were sent in the afternoons instead of the usual organised games, to slide around on the ice. Photos in the newspapers showed our soldiers stuck in their trenches or as part of the Maginot Line, cold, fed up and far from home to paraphrase the impolite Service slang, and all the women of Britain were urged to knit them mittens or squares that could be made up into blankets. Good patriotic stuff while we waited complacently for the real war to begin, little realising that then the roof would fall in.

When it came to the Easter holidays, for whatever reason the Stephensons could not have us. Perhaps they were moving from one vicarage at Staincliffe to the other at Woodkirk. We found ourselves in a so-called 'holiday home' in Bexhill-on-Sea on the south coast near Hastings. There must have been scores of these establishments around the country where children whose parents were abroad were farmed out. If this was a fair example of them, they were not to be recommended. Tim was placed in the junior section and I in the senior, with boys and girls from about thirteen to seventeen years of age. It was run by a couple who simply provided the basics of board, food and lodging, then left us to get on with it. Walking along the promenade was about the most exiting thing to do. Rudyard Kipling of course wrote his classic story *Baa Baa Black Sheep* about his extended experiences in such a home, which was even made into a play. This place in Bexhill was nothing like that; it was just boring, an extension of school communal living into one's holidays without one's mates to spend it with. If other children had a steady holiday diet of that, as I am sure many of them did, I can only sympathise with them. Fortunately for Tim and me, it was the first and last time we experienced it before the major events of the war in that summer of 1940 completely changed the direction of our lives.

So the spring of 1940 arrived with the German Blitzkrieg around the static Maginot Line, the invasions of Belgium and the Netherlands, and the retreat of the British Expeditionary Force to the evacuation point at Dunkirk. Newspapers were full of pictures of French and Belgian people fleeing with all that they could carry on horse-drawn wagons or handcarts. We read about the terrifying effect of Stuka dive-bombers on armed and unarmed alike, and the speed of the German Panzer divisions. The school had a specific interest in that one of the Vernede brothers, sons of a tea planter in Assam, who was in the Artists' Rifles, and made a last but fruitless stand at Calais. I don't think he survived.

And yet it was a wonderful, hot summer, with June nights so humid that we used to lean out of the dormitory windows until late at night listening to the screech owls in the woods. The excitement must have stirred the stag beetles into an amorous frenzy because they seemed to appear in their hundreds from nowhere – those prehistoric-looking beetles with heavy curved pincers growing from the front of their heads. I regret to say that we used to place them head to head to encourage them to lock horns and wrestle. Sadly they are virtually no more, due to insecticides. It was also a particularly good June for dragonflies with their brilliant colours, swooping over the ponds in Mrs Bernie's walled garden. They seem to be making a bit of a comeback. But for those of us leaving that term, it was the time for swotting for the Common Entrance or scholarship exams that we would take for entrance to whatever public school we were down for. In my case, it was Aldenham near Watford, for the inconsequential reason that it was a 'football' school, and football along with boxing were my best sports.

Despite the evacuation of the British Expeditionary Force from Dunkirk in the middle of June, with photos in the press of soldiers waiting on the beaches and returning to London from Dover by train, with stops for cups of tea from the ladies of the Women's' Voluntary Services (WVS), life for us went on as usual. One Saturday afternoon we were playing cricket against another school, perhaps Colett Court, where two returned soldiers were invited in and sat on the boundary, regaling us with stories of the cruelties of the Germans. It must all have seemed unreal to them, one week being bombed on a beach and the next sitting on a green field watching a boys' game.

Term finally came to an end in July. We took our farewells of those we had known, played with or fought against on occasion, and that was it. Tim and I remained in the empty shell of the school on our own in limbo for a couple of weeks, to await events. Dunkirk proved to be the key that changed the lives of all of us children with parents in India and the other colonial outposts. Parents could have been away from their children for anything up to three years, and now the war was on for real. There was never any thought that Britain might lose, only that it might take a bit longer than expected. So the decision was taken to evacuate to join our parents, some to return to family life only recently curtailed, others such as myself to sample it properly for the first time in memory. We were taken to buy clothes for the trip, and I am sure that the staff had no idea how long it would be, but Tim and I were each equipped with two pairs of Aertex shirts and two pairs of blue gym shorts for what proved to be a six-week voyage around the Cape to Bombay. Oh, and £5 pocket money between us. We were to join the SS *Strathmore*, one of the prides of the P&O fleet waiting to sail from Liverpool – around 4 August from memory. Dennis Pratten, the French master, and his wife, Peggy, took Tim and me up to stay in a hotel in Russell Square, London, before putting us on to the 'boat train' for Liverpool the next morning. Where Mr Bernie was, I cannot recall.

So we boarded the *Strathmore* in her dock at Liverpool, painted overall in varied stripes of grey, no longer in her usual P&O livery of cream hull and yellow funnel. There is a wonderful scale model of her in the P&O collection at the National Maritime Museum at Greenwich. Our worldly possessions were packed into those green trunks encircled with three wooden bands for strength, with a tray in the top for smaller, lighter items of clothing. The cabin crew took over once our cabin numbers had been identified at the purser's office, and Tim and I were shepherded into a first-class single cabin *each*, back to back on the same deck where cabins were far enough above the waterline to have portholes. Each was fitted out with a single bed rather than a bunk, an armchair to sit in and a washbasin. Thus we entered the world of Shell, who always travelled first class and still do, as far as I know. By the end of the war, when some of our school friends returned to the UK such single cabins would have slept four, and the doubles eight. That first night on board there was apparently an air raid on Liverpool docks and the alarms had sounded, but Tim and I slept through the lot in our new-found luxury quarters.

As far as I can recall we left Liverpool in a convoy and sailed around the north of Ireland. Early on the first morning at sea we were assigned to our lifeboat stations, and were assembled for drill. This consisted of being told how the boats would be lowered from the davits by members of the crew, and when they came level with our deck we were to step in. Just like that! We were also issued with those old, heavy cork-block lifebelts, and shown how to put them over our heads and then tie the tapes around the waist. And just remember one other thing. If you miss the lifeboat and have to jump for it over the side, grip the front cork blocks and pull down hard, otherwise when you hit the water they would bob up and break your neck! A cheerful but memorable message as these lines prove.

Thus it was now time to explore the wonderful world of P&O. There must have been several hundred mostly unaccompanied girls and boys on board, between the ages of seven to seventeen years of age. There were also some families travelling with small children, and some nurses with white uniforms and head cowls to look after the very small ones. P&O ships had a hierarchy like everything connected with the Raj. At the top were the captain, deck officers and the purser – all British, as was the head steward of the first-class dining saloon. There were three classes of passengers: first, second and steerage. Some of the open decks – perhaps even the boat deck – had metal railings across them to divide the second from the first class. Right in the stern below the water line were the steerage-class dormitories, immediately above the twin propellers, so that the occupants were lulled to sleep with the thump, thump, thump of their revolutions. On our voyage, steerage was occupied with RN sailors going out to pick up ships in Trincomalee – Ceylon as it was then called. The cabin staff were Goanese or Portuguese Eurasians, very friendly and helpful. The engine room crew were British, probably with a bias towards Scots, and the deck crew were Lascars or Indian sailors.

The morning routine started early. At around 6.30 a.m. the Lascars would pad along the decks in their bare feet, fitting the hoses to the seawater supply points for hosing down the decks, scrubbing them and squeegee-ing them dry. Breakfast was then served up to about 10 a.m. followed by cups of Bovril that were brought round to those passengers who were sitting in deckchairs under a blanket on the boat deck until we got into warmer climes. But that, as far as I can recall, only eliminated the blankets, not the need for Bovril. There were staterooms, other smaller rooms where films were put on, a swimming pool and shops at the foot of a sweeping stairway before going down to the cabins. The cabins led off long corridors with cross runs, so that it took a little time to orient oneself. Throughout the ship there was that steady hum of engines and motors, and the smell of seawater mixed with oil that modern, sanitised cruise vessels seem to have lost. But the holy of holies was the first-class dining saloon. Entering there for the first time was like walking into Harrods's food hall. Rationing in Britain had hardly started, but compared to boarding school nosh this was of an entirely different order. To think that every three years our parents experienced six weeks of this living on their way to and from the UK and India! In retrospect this was probably when doubts crept into one's mind over their claims of the sacrifices they made by having to make their living in India. Temporary exile from one's own country maybe, but not material sacrifices. Lording it over this establishment was the head steward, dressed in a splendid uniform of a jacket, with either lapel or shoulder decorations in blue and gold, hair parted down the middle, radiating hospitality. If the captain was God on such a ship, this character was at least St Peter and we called him 'sir' as we would anyone else in authority.

There were two other brothers on board, whose father worked for Burmah Shell in Madras, Tony Johnstone, who was just fourteen as I was, and his brother David aged ten, or three years older than Tim. The head waiter took us to our table for four, which we shared for the rest of the voyage. For a couple of weeks we simply selected from the menu until one of us asked him how much we were allowed to eat. 'As much as you like, boys,' came the generous reply from the All Highest. So we took him at his word. Starting with the soup, usually mulligatawny (a curry-flavoured soup), we proceeded through fish, a roast (beef, lamb or pork), followed by curry and rice with all the trimmings and that new discovery, mango chutney, then some trifle; the whole was rounded off with cheese and biscuits. After about three days of this the head steward came by our table, casually enquired if everything was all right and if we were getting enough to eat. To both of his questions we gave him our heartfelt assurance. He then wandered on, but after a few steps turned round, came back to our table and asked if we understood the arrangements for payment for the voyage? When we shook our heads he said, 'Well, the passage has been paid for by your parents or their company, but as for what you eat, we keep a record and the bill will be sent to your parents at the end of the voyage.' With that he strolled off. Consternation, disbelief, followed by some rapid, anxious enquiries around the few adults among the passengers for reassurance. But that was the last time we 'ate the menu'.

After a few days we found ourselves out in the Atlantic without another ship in sight. The *Strathmore* could steam at fifteen knots or seventeen miles per hour, so she did not need to be held back by a convoy, and could outpace any submerged submarine, making a zigzag course to avoid becoming an easy target. We must have sailed right across towards South America before heading back east to Cape Town, which was reached just short of three weeks after leaving Liverpool.

As we approached the equator it warmed up, and it was time to discard our school clothes of grey flannel shorts, shirt and long socks for the two sets of tropical gear that the Prattens had bought for us. This raised the question of laundry, which had to be done at least every two days, if not every day, if we were not to become smelly. In among the hordes of young, cheerful girls on board I had met a freckle-faced, auburn-haired Scottish girl called Margaret, with whom it turned out I shared a fourteenth birthday to the day. On such flimsy coincidences do shipboard friendships start, particularly when it had the practical advantage that she offered to help with our 'dhobi-ing' (laundry). So each day she took over the Aertex shirts, while I washed Tim's and my pants, tying them to the ceiling air vents to dry. However, this became too much of a good thing, so we had to spend some of our £5 allowance on extra sets of tropical clothes. I never did hear what happened to Margaret whatever her family name was, since she went on from India to join her parents in Singapore, and they of course were overwhelmed by the Japanese 17 months later.

To get back to that £5. Since I was almost exactly twice Tim's age I allocated myself half a crown and him 1s 3d per week for pocket money, confectionery, ices, etc. We also had to buy our own seawater soap, which was not provided. In my defence I claim that any older brother would have made the same allocation. So what with that and the extra clothes we were rapidly running through our funds as we approached Cape Town. The day prior to our arrival, the passengers' notice board indicated that there were coach trips to be had touring all the famous landmarks such as the Lion's Head, the Twelve Apostles along the drive to the Cape Point, the Prime Minister's house, Groote Schuur, built by Cecil Rhodes and so on, at a cost of 10s/- per head. Clearly this was too good to miss, but not to be afforded. So I went to the purser and asked him if he could identify any passenger that worked for Burmah Shell. There indeed was a Mr Donaldson, and when I knew that he would be dressing for dinner, since even in the heat of a closed-up, blacked-out ship that convention was still enforced, I went to his cabin and knocked on the door. Sure enough, when he answered, he was attaching a bow tie to a dicky front, and since the purser had introduced me to the convention of an IOU for a loan, I blurted out who Tim and I were, our father's position in the same company, and our need for extra funds. Without hesitation he turned to his wallet or a drawer, drew out one of those crisp, crinkly white old fivers, and handed it to me with a smile and a wish that we would enjoy ourselves. He got the IOU in return, and that was my first experience of highish finance. Such things are relative after all.

After a couple of days in Cape Town we set sail to round Cape Agulhas, which as everyone should know is the southernmost point of Africa, and where one leaves the dark-green waters of the Atlantic for the aquamarine colours of the Indian Ocean. There really is a noticeable difference, as one can also see at the junction of the Atlantic and the Caribbean when one stands on a high point at the east end of the island of Tobago. The nights spent on the open deck to get away from the heat of the blacked-out and sweltering interior were memorable. A black, warm velvet cloak seemed to envelop our shoulders as we leaned over the guard rails hour after hour, watching the bubbling, sparkling phosphorescent wake, starting with the bow wave before gliding down the side to form a broad, silver wake streaming out behind us. This must be a phenomenon of tropical sea temperatures since I was to observe it four years later when sailing across the Pacific Ocean. Shipboard life on a voyage as long as this one takes on a routine for the passengers as well as the crew. Eating always gets a high priority as well as keeping amused and exercised with deck games – deck quoits, shuffleboard. There were Housie Housie sessions for the adults, and for the children in first class at least the swimming pool, permanent or canvas, became a focal meeting point to get to know better that phenomenon that we had been denied in our previous school lives: children of the opposite sex. Our parents can only be grateful that this six-week voyage took place in the repressed or innocent 1940s, when children were still allowed a childhood, rather than at the end of the century, when a high proportion of the girls would probably have walked down the gang plank at Bombay in the early stages of juvenile pregnancy. There was also the inevitable amateur concert party in which we all had to play a part. The Johnstone/Orchard quartet rose to the occasion with the only song that came to mind, namely 'There's a hole in my bucket, dear Liza, dear Liza' etc., which to our surprise was rewarded with enthusiastic applause from the assembled adults. A benign spirit towards us seemed to prevail.

At the same time there was a man in his forties on board, who fitted to a T the character in one of Somerset Maugham's short stories called 'The Know-All'. He was hail-fellow-well-met, threw money around buying drinks, knew everything and had met everyone, and was generally a bit of a pain. I cannot remember if he was in first or second class – probably first since we used to see him – but what we did not know was that he spent a considerable amount of his time hobnobbing with the RN sailors in steerage, buying them drinks, chatting them up and generally acting the 'good egg' to sailors on a few shillings a day. As we made our way north up the east coast of Africa, people began to ask who was this chap, who was always on the move, talking, questioning, greeting any sally with roars of hearty laughter and then moving on. As soon as we sailed into Mombasa we got our answer. No sooner had we berthed alongside the quay than a couple of men came up the gangway, sought him out wherever he was, and Mr Know-All went ashore under arrest. Great excitement – our very own spy. Of course, we had suspected it all along. *Of course* we had! The general consensus was that he had been chatting up the RN sailors to get the names and locations of the ships they were being drafted to, presumably for the benefit of German submarines about to operate in the Indian Ocean.

There was nothing much to go ashore for in Mombasa. I am not sure whether by then it was part of the mainland, or if it was still an island joined by a causeway, as it had been when my parents lived there in the 1920s. But the tarpaulins were taken off the hatches, which were opened, the derricks were swung out with their ropes and nets for removing the cargo or taking more on board, and we were entertained by the African labourers chanting in unison as they hauled on ropes or lifted loads. The invention of the cargo container may have restricted pilfering, but it has made dock life a lot less interesting. We then sailed off on the last leg across the Arabian Sea to Bombay, and this was the stage where Tim's money either ran out, or ice creams assumed a higher priority than a haircut. He secured a pair of scissors from someone and simply chopped off his curly locks in a straight line across the front of his head. On arrival it was referred to as his prison haircut, whereas he had in fact executed an early example of what became the accepted American crew cut.

It has become a truism to say that absolutely nothing prepares one for one's first arrival in India, and this is emphasised at collecting points such as quaysides or main railway stations. It is the sheer press of people and their variety of dress and appearance, the colours of the ladies in their sarees, the noise, the wandering cows that seemed to get priority, the seething bustle that somehow never quite reaches gridlock, and last but not least the refuse casually dumped anywhere and everywhere with the inevitable smells of food and excrement. Either you love it or run a mile, never to return. We lined the rails in one great excited scrum high above the dockside, trying to identify our parents, who tended to be in separate groups, some alone, others with a bearer in tow to help. Somewhere in among the parents we identified our mother with a porter or two to carry our trunks and the bedding rolls that she had had to bring for our train journey to Calcutta, and we set off for the Victoria Rail Terminus, that huge gothic, Indo-Saracenic memorial to Victorian architecture, with which Bombay is still replete. It simply must have owed part of its design to the St Pancras Chambers in the Euston Road, London, since it was built only a few years after the latter.

To paraphrase Dr Samuel Johnson's well-known aphorism, 'he who is tired of Indian mainline railway stations is tired of life', and they have maintained their fascination. Victoria Terminus in

1940 was still essentially the same in atmosphere as Sealdah station in Calcutta, or Delhi in 1998, with the exception that in the cold weather, steam from the engines no longer blends with the early morning mist that trails across the various recumbent bodies on the benches, wound up in their cotton shrouds. In the current ongoing debate concerning the legacies of the British Raj, the construction of the Indian rail system (the second longest in the world, with its three or four gauges from main lines to hill station railways), must come close to the top of the list of positive benefits. Their trains do not always run to time, of course – one would not expect them to do so over such great distances and varied terrain. My favourite story on this subject relates to the longest line that runs from somewhere in the south 2,400 miles north to Delhi or beyond. There was once an Englishman who used to board this train from time to time somewhere along its route – let us say at Hyderabad. On one occasion when the train was due in at 23.30 hours he decided to anticipate its arrival to be ready and went to the station half an hour early at 23.00. To his surprise, as he arrived, the train steamed in. He turned to another passenger on the platform and said, 'I'm amazed. In all the times that I have caught this train, I have never known it to be early.' 'It's not,' replied the other passenger. 'This is yesterday's train, it's twenty-three and a half hours late!'

Nevertheless, joining a train is still the same experience. All is crowds, chaos and noise. Emaciated porters with spindly legs, that look as if they could be snapped like matchsticks, compete for your custom. The winner puts your worldly possessions on his head and scurries off into the scrum of persons. Every time you think that will be the last that you will see of your worldly goods, but every time when you catch up with him, there he is waiting exactly outside your pre-booked compartment. They must have some sort of satellite direction finding system. It was still the same in 1998 when I returned to Calcutta with Lene to tour north-east India by train. Our Bengali tour guide took us to Sealdah station for the night train to Darjeeling. Beating off the rest of the coolies (as he called them, meaning unskilled native labourers; I would not dare to do so in these politically correct days) he selected a fairly robust-looking one and forced him to carry two eighteen-kilo cases on his head, as well as Lene's bulky soft bag under his arm. Poor bastard! I made sure that I slipped him a good additional tip to the guide's, and that the guide did not see my doing so!

In the 1940s a first-class compartment had four green leather bunks, two of which could be fastened up with straps. There was thus plenty of space to move around in by day, and there was a washroom and loo attached. Near the door a large block of ice was deposited into a tray to provide cooling, and was renewed as the journey went on. The windows had three barriers: glass, a fine meshed metal layer against the mosquitoes, and a blind to shut out the station and other lights at night. But nothing could shut out the noise: food sellers, char *wallahs*, people calling after porters, the steam hissing from the engine.

Meals were taken at the station restaurants. At the station where you had breakfast, you would be given the menu to choose lunch wherever the train was due to stop, and the same for dinner. If the service was slow, then there was a mad rush to get through it all and back on to the train before it pulled out. Breakfasts were a new experience. Apart from bacon and some-what rubbery eggs, I was introduced to pawpaw or papaya for the first time, the somewhat rich taste made more palatable with the contents of a lime squeezed over it. The other two meals had a pattern that I would describe as British colonial. The choice of soups was usually mulligatawny, that makeover of yesterday's curry, or a pea or lentil soup. The main course was frequently a curry or some sort of chicken, followed by those great icons, steamed sponge pudding with golden syrup or spotted dick. Never mind if the temperature was 102° in the shade, that was the menu carried by our Empire builders to the farthest corners of the earth. Pea soup and steamed sponge pudding still appeared on hotel menus in colonies as far separated as Jamaica and Kenya that I visited in the 1950s.

The journey from Bombay to Calcutta took three nights and two days of steady 'clackety-clack' for mile after mile over the rails. We had arrived at Bombay around 15 September when the monsoon was virtually over and the countryside was well watered, so that the vivid green of the paddy fields contrasted with the red-brown lateritic earth of the Indian plains. One rural village after the other, usually ringed with a thorn fence, hove into view from our carriage windows, and where the track ran close enough to a village, children raced out to wave our smoking monster on its way. Fifty years later, when I repeated such a journey, those villages looked much the same, with the difference that many had sprouted a satellite dish above their mud huts, which put their people in touch with the great wide world beyond. And what did they watch? According to a young schoolgirl that we met in Darjeeling, her favourite viewing was *Baywatch*! I will always recall that first experience across the face of India not as a mundane rail journey, but more like a flight on a Persian rug that wafted us from west to east, with noises and odours thrown in for good measure.

Howrah station in Calcutta is another of the great experiences, with its adjoining massive iron bridge that links it with Calcutta proper on the other side of the Hooghly River. There to meet us was our father with car and driver, to take us back to our company flat in Raja Santosh Road in Alipore, one of the more prosperous suburbs where the Westerners lived. We had the usual clutch of servants that were part of the caste system of division of labour, which as a by-product gave additional employment. We had a butler from Madras, who had been with my parents for eight years before they came to Calcutta. He was a really nice chap, must have been in his late forties, and had a somewhat straggly moustache and a worried look. He had left his family back in Madras and probably got back to see them no more often than once per year. The bearer or *kitmagar*, helped at table, set out Tishy's clothes and generally helped the butler. There was a cook, who had his family on site in the servants' quarters; a *masalchi* who, so far as I can remember, helped the cook with the messy jobs and washing up; an ayah, a dear old hill lady who helped our mother with clothes, laundry, sewing and whatnot; the *jemadah* or sweeper, who also took the dogs for walks; the *mali* or gardener; the *chowkidar* or watchman shared with other flats, usually a Pathan or one of the other wild and woolly tribesmen from the north-west and certainly not a Bengali, and of course there was the abovementioned driver provided by Shell for the company car.

Did our parents live well? No doubt about it. Was dealing with servant problems one of the main occupations of a memsahib's life? Of course. With such a mix of castes, division of responsibilities, races such as Madrasis (who spoke Tamil, a south Indian language), Bengalis (who spoke Bengali, which is not similar to Hindi), the *chowkidar*, who spoke Urdu – assuming he would deign to speak to mere plains people – not to forget the employers who only spoke a smattering of 'Kitchen Hindustani', there was plenty of cause for servant trouble. Hindustani was a corruption of Hindi that virtually only dealt in the imperative tense. Do this, come here, drive slowly (*aste, aste* driver!) whisky *lao* (bring), or the cry '*Koi hai?*' after which expatriate men were nicknamed, meaning 'is there any one there?' and if so, come quickly or *ek dum* (at once). It did not leave much room for please, thank you or philosophical discussion, although *achcha* or *bahut achcha* was the equivalent of 'thank you very much' and was often used. Relations with servants were on the whole good, but they were the main interface with the native peoples, at least for the 'box *wallahs*' in cities.

Calcutta in those days was still a fine city of about 2 million, with many advantages. In the first place, Bengal has a cold weather season running from about the end of October to March, when life is very liveable, and in fact mornings could be distinctly chilly, particularly for the wretched poor camped out on the pavements. Secondly, the bungalows or flats had flush toilets, rather than the 'thunder boxes' of Madras, which reduced the dysentery levels. Thirdly and most importantly, there was the Maidan, the vast open grassy space in the centre that acts as a lung, rather like Hyde Park in London, even if its original raison d'être had been as a clear field of fire for the guns of Fort William against the native area in the late eighteenth century. The Maidan has been preserved, and when we were there in February 1998 there was a huge tented camp for the English book fair that pulled in 250,000 people per day over a week with a heavy presence from publishers of IT material! Calcutta also had its racecourse, is where the Rugby Union Calcutta Cup originated, the Victoria Memorial, Lord Curzon's answer to the Taj Mahal, the old Viceregal Lodge, where the Viceroy lived and ruled until the capital was moved to Delhi in 1912. In other words, although younger than New York, it was in many ways a European city set down in the middle of Bengal, since the trader Job Charnock first got permission from the Moghul Emperor to found it in 1690, as a reward for marrying a Hindu widow, thus saving her from the terrible death of *suttee*.

As far as the British community was concerned, there is a wonderful description of it in the pages of *Harrow on the Hooghly*. One boy fifty years on wrote: 'There was a hierarchy ... My impression is that nobody spoke to people in jute, that Hooghly pilots were similarly a race apart, that tea spoke to oil but not to railways and coal, and that the Raj on the whole did not speak to any of them, unless they had an introduction from "home" – i.e. they came from the same circle in Britain – or unless they had become so rich and so grand that they could no longer be ignored.'

There was probably considerable truth in that summary. Certainly jute was the fiefdom of Dundee Scots, and the Hooghly river pilots were a hard-drinking group of Scots. People in the railways often 'lived the job' in railway cantonments, as did of course the people in the military. Colonial life is somewhat like living in a goldfish bowl. They are all thrown into the same glass jar, and cannot avoid seeing one another, even if under different circumstances they would have little in common. People in the business community were labelled 'box *wallahs*' or desk men. They led a triangular sort of life, based on the bungalow or flat, the office and the club. Aliens in an alien land. It was not always so, of course, particularly before the opening of the Suez Canal, which facilitated the arrival of British wives, and ended (more or less) marital relationships with local Indian women. Across the road from us lived the Rankins, Americans in the Standard Oil Co. of whom more several chapters on. They were a childless couple, but Louise, the wife, was into learning yoga and studying Indian culture. This was regarded as rather odd by the other mems, who at the same time distanced themselves from the authoress Rumer Godden who, to break the monotony of her life, started a school for dancing classes for Anglo-Indian girls, who had to live on the fringe of colonial life. It is, however, a fact that

Americans would be more liberal towards Indians in India than towards so-called American Indians in their own country. As A P Herbert, the writer and MP for Oxford University (until the seat was closed down by the Atlee government in the late 1940s), once replied to an American, who was criticising British imperial policy in India: 'Well, at least most of the British Indians are still alive!'

There were plenty of clubs graded according to rank or preference as in the world over, from the Bengal Club on Chowringee for the members of the ICS and the heads of the large trading companies, to the many sporting clubs like the Saturday Club, which was mainly for swimming, tennis and socialising, to the Tollygunge Club on the outskirts of the city, built on an old indigo plantation, which boasted a racecourse as well as golf, tennis and swimming facilities. All of these were clubs for Europeans only. The only exception that I ever visited some years later was the Willingdon Club in Bombay.

But to return to us children. There were literally scores of hill schools in India teaching a British syllabus, like St Paul's in Darjeeling, or Bishop Cotton's in Simla, as well as schools in the plains like La Martiniere in Calcutta and Lucknow, founded by a French adventurer and friend of Warren Hastings, le Martin, who made his fortune in indigo. However, as another person writes in *Harrow on the Hooghly*: 'By the end of July 1940 it was clear that over 200 British children would soon be arriving in and around Bengal, and there were somewhere around another sixty, who were too young to have been sent home. All would need to be educated. The existing English-speaking schools, several of which like St Paul's in Darjeeling, were of a high standard but could not absorb so many. A new school would have to be founded.' So a committee was formed and in four months flat the New School, Calcutta was created in a large rented house, later to be dubbed by its pupils, since it catered mainly for European children, 'Harrow on the Hooghly'. The name stuck, even though the school only lasted four years (1940–44).

From the outset, Tishy had two significant objections to it. First, the man selected as the headmaster was a young (twenty-eight) graduate in English from Oxford, who was already teaching at a college in Delhi. However, he was a Quaker, and therefore a pacifist and a conscientious objector, which roused my father's Kiplingesque prejudices. Secondly, it was going to cost either £105 or £115 per annum, which was as much as Eton, without the social or educational cachet. So even before the school opened that October, I was told that I could stay there until I had sat the Cambridge School Certificate in December 1941, when I was to be sent on to Geelong Grammar School, outside Melbourne in Australia. Why there? God only knows, except my father's immediate superior in Shell was a Scot married to an Australian (second marriage as for all Burmah Shell Brits in those days, except for my parents) and the British public school ethic was so strong in India that the older friend, who kept an avuncular eye on my mother during her 'home leave' in the summer of 1938, listed his education as 'private' in *Who's Who*, when he had actually been to Manchester Grammar School, virtually the top UK school academically.

So that was how it was to be, and no arguments and no indication of who would be *in loco parentis* while I was down there or where school holidays would be spent. In the meantime, Calcutta was a wonderful place to explore on a bicycle, and to be spoiled for choice. The real Aladdin's cave was the Hogg or New Market, acres of small stalls under cover, selling everything from food to textiles with the whole community, British and Indian, Anglo-Indian and Chinese, all jostling down its narrow alleys. The Chinese were the shoemakers in Free School Street. You would go in, choose your material (leather or skin), and put your bare foot on a piece of A4 paper while the shoemaker drew a pencil around the edge. Then in a week or so appeared a pair of shoes made exactly to measure. The taxis seemed to be under the control of a Sikh mafia, large men with beards and bellies, who lolled in open-topped American Chevrolets, with their left hands on the steering wheel, and right hands on the large horns, honking a path through the traffic and the rickshaws drawn by coolies on foot. Both have since disappeared, the Sikhs probably driven out by the Bengalis, and the man-operated rickshaws banned by law. They are now cycle rickshaws or scooter versions with the two-seater carriage at the rear – not to be recommended to anyone who does not like inhaling exhaust fumes. Another major change in the Calcutta scene since those days sixty years ago is the absence of cows and Brahmini bulls, sacred or otherwise, cluttering up the pavements and slowing down the traffic. When I put this to our guide he explained that once the Metro went on line down below Chowringee and out to the suburbs in the 1990s, there was no way that they could allow cattle to blunder down the steps in their time-honoured way, only to be electrocuted on the live rail. So common sense for once prevailed over caste, and owners of such cattle – for they all do in fact have an owner – were given notice to get them out of the city.

My parents had some friends called the Robsons, who had no children but some polo ponies that they used to exercise on the Maidan each morning. They offered to take me out for a ride, and I turned up on my bike at about 7 a.m. one morning, full of eager anticipation. I had never been on anything larger than a sluggish donkey on Hoylake beach in my life, and this pony of about twelve hands at once recognised that the bundle on its back was a complete and utter tyro or novice After a few steps when I was shown how to post in the saddle to trot, the pony just took off and bolted. Clutching the reins gave no support so I dropped them and just hung on to the pommel of the saddle as I bounced along like a sack of potatoes. Every so often there are narrow asphalt roads that cross the Maidan, and eventually one of these appeared ahead of us. Its surface was wet with the morning dew, which to the pony must have appeared like a strip of water, since it simply launched itself into space. Polo ponies are not jumpers, so its flight did not carry it to the far side, and as it landed on the road surface it slid, and its legs simply did the longitudinal splits with me surfing on its back. The Robsons cantered up in great concern, the pony was retrieved and I walked back to my bike, shaking. Two wheels good, four hooves bad. I did, however, go on to ride hill ponies in Darjeeling and Basutos on the farm in South Africa, but rode nothing trained to gallop. Absolutely not.

When the Christmas holidays came at the end of the first term, the parents of their new-found children went into overdrive to entertain us. The poor dogs that had previously been kept as child substitutes must have wondered what had hit their ordered lives. Any account that one reads of life in colonial India in the 1930s onwards is always replete with descriptions of informal parties where they danced to a wind-up gramophone, including one at our flat, since my mother had a stack of Charlie Kunz records. But some of the more ambitious parents threw these parties at the Tollygunge or other clubs, with live bands and cards where one had to go around and book partners against the list of dances. With a war on in Europe and the Blitz of British cities in full swing at the time, it was all a bit OTT, particularly as most of us could not even dance and had not been exposed to the strict tempo of Victor Sylvester. But then the parents must have been pleased that the accident of war had forced them to live family life for the first time against the previously accepted convention.

One final story before we leave Calcutta. In 1940, there was a lady called Betty Pardy, who was married to someone also employed by Burmah Shell, and who painted portraits in pastel. She did mine, head and shoulders, which eventually hung in my mother's flat in London, and which was so similar to my elder son Peter at that age, that he once asked when he had sat for it. In the late 1980s *The Sunday Times* colour supplement ran an article about the well-known author on Indian Raj subjects, M M Kaye, and there on the front cover was a picture of her sitting next to her sister, Betty Pardy, who by this time had become Mrs Paget-Hoblyn, who had had a third unnamed husband in between by all accounts. My mother wrote to her via the editor of the news-paper, to renew contact. Plenty of mems had two husbands as explained above, but three... well, that was something to be investigated. In due course, we had a reply with an invitation to visit them at their home in Surrey. When Betty saw Lene she asked if she could paint her portrait too, so we paid several visits and had plenty of opportunity for talk. M M Kaye was Molly Hamilton, as anyone who has read any volumes of her auto-biography will know, the widow of General Hamilton. When the film was being made of her book *The Far Pavilions*, she was asked to go out to India for three months to advise on settings, dress, behaviour and so on. She agreed providing they would pay for her sister Betty to go too, since she was by now financially dependent on Molly. At the end of the filming the film producers threw a farewell party in Delhi or wherever it was, during which an Indian gentleman approached Molly and asked her why she was wearing a brooch in a particular motif. She explained that this was the badge of such-and-such Guides (I cannot remember the exact name) and that during his service in India her husband had been the regiment's colonel. The Indian replied that he had recognised it, and that his regiment would be 'beating retreat' the next evening at 6 p.m. and invited the two ladies to attend as honoured guests on the dais where the salute was taken. Sadly she had to demur since their plane to London was also that evening, and they were in the hands of the film people.

When they were woken up the next morning with the usual *chota hazri* or little breakfast, there was a note from the Indian officer to say that the ceremony had been brought forward by some hours, that a car would come to take them to the parade ground, another would collect their luggage, and when it was all over they would be delivered to the airport in good time. That does not happen unless what we read about the relationship between the British officers and the Indian Army is true. For further reading on that subject I can recommend *A Matter of Honour* by Philip Mason, an account of the Indian Army officers and men that reads more like a labour of love than a historical record.

Incidentally my mother, uncharacteristically, did not on that occasion summon up the necessary nerve to enquire about the three husbands.

At the end of the second term – that is, around the end of April 1941 – it was decided that the school would transfer to the cool of Darjeeling, the hill station for Calcutta, for those children whose parents did not want them to sweat in the city through the monsoon months. It was a massive job really, since boarding accommodation had to be found and rented. There were five of these houses, the senior boys from about eleven to seventeen years of age being housed in a mock Moghul summerhouse owned by a wealthy Indian from the plains. We all set off one evening on the night train from Sealdah station in Calcutta northwards to the terminus at Siliguri, located at the base of the

Himalayan foothills. From there we went by the Darjeeling Himalayan Railway, the so-called Toy Train on its narrow two-foot gauge, one of the engineering wonders of the world that had been built back in 1881. The journey up to Darjeeling at about 7,500 feet takes about six to seven hours, providing none of the track has been washed away overnight, and climbs, loops and zigzags through forests of cedar, teak and pine. In places it went slow enough for us children to jump off and pick it up again on its next leg. Since the 1940s a new road has been built for cars and the inevitable diesel trucks that shorten the journey to about four hours. But to its credit the Indian government has declared the train a World Heritage phenomenon (one cannot describe it as a site) and continues to subsidise it for any tourists not in a hurry.

I can only liken one's arrival in Darjeeling, providing that the clouds are clear, to the excitement of arriving by train at Zermatt, Switzerland, which I have done about fourteen times. They both have spectacular mountains that hove into sight as one rounds the last bend – Kanchenjunga, in the case of Darjeeling, at over 28,000 feet high, the third highest mountain in the world, with a row of five peaks. The highest point of the railway is at Ghoom, where there is a famous Buddhist monastery. Above that is Tiger Hill, about eight kilometres out of the town, where one can go up for sunrise at about 6.30 a.m. to try to spot the small triangle of Mount Everest's peak in the far, far distance. In the colonial days one would ride up on ponies, well wrapped up against the morning frost, to sit as a small group of Westerners. Now it is quite different. As one approaches Tiger Hill there is often a long line of four-wheel drive vehicles parked down the hill, and a large crowd of Indians in their sarees and city clothes collected on the viewing platform. Our guide warned us that we would be among the few looking north-west to try to spot Everest, while the rest would be facing east, looking into the rising sun. And so it was when Lene and I went up there. The real sight is as the sun steals up on to Kanchenjunga's peaks, turning them from peach, to pink and finally the blue of the early morning sky in a matter of minutes. Homer I am sure never visited there, but the sight matched exactly his description of 'rosy-fingered dawn'. So the occasion now is really for the Bengali plains people and is no longer exclusive. The Indians have recaptured some of the natural wonders of their own country, having been led there by the expatriates in the first place.

There were no cars in the 1940s, with the exception of the Governor of Bengal's Rolls Royce. For the first couple of weeks we were virtually banned from taking any strenuous exercise due to the altitude, and still had to wear topees against the sun. The rickshaws were like the cab of a hansom cab on two wheels, pulled by two sturdy hill men in the front and pushed by two from the rear. Our cases or trunks were carried up to our houses on their backs with a rope slung under the base and held to their foreheads with a leather strip, as one sees the sherpa porters carrying loads to Mount Everest.

The greatest thing about Darjeeling was its people, short, sturdy, slant-eyed, cheerful Lepchen folk, related to the Nepalese. The young women wore brightly coloured clothes, gold ornaments over their faces and wrists, and almost permanent smiles. The second-best thing that we were given was freedom to roam the district. It was like being back at West Kirby with its Grange Hill, multiplied to the nth degree. The centre of the town was the round 'square' called Chowrasta, where one could rent hill ponies that had mouths like iron, to ride along the Old Calcutta Road. The famous tea gardens fall away down the steep slopes or *khuds* around every side, and in half an hour one could easily plunge down 1,000 feet to see what was around the next corner. Darjeeling received huge amounts of rain during the monsoon months, probably around eighty inches, and the hillsides were laced with deep and fairly wide drainage channels that had to be avoided since a slip into one of those would transfer one to Kurseong far below in fairly short order. There was a Gymkhana Club in the town, a wooden roller-skating rink, and one-armed 'fruit machines'. Each month I received two rupees and eight annas pocket money, of which the eight annas were invested on those machines. I say invested rather than gambled, since it never required more than eight pulls of the lever to win.

Our teachers were a varied lot, as one would expect of a school that had been assembled in four months flat. I had learned ancient Greek at Bickley Hall, so needed it as another subject for School

Certificate. None of the teachers in Calcutta knew it, so a request was put out to the parents, which turned up Mr Cyril Gurner, an ICS man who was in charge of what was essentially the Public Works Department for Bengal. All ICS men were classicists, even if they were in charge of water supply and the removal of ordure. At any rate another boy, Martin Pinnell, and I used to go to his house twice a week to plough through the syllabus of Xenophon and Homer's *Odyssey*. When I remarked to Mr Gurner's daughter fifty years later when we had a reunion, how clever I thought her father was to be able to teach Greek more than twenty years after leaving university, she replied, 'Oh, that was nothing really, the other five nights of the week he translated ancient Greek into Sanskrit!' In that first term in Darjeeling Martin stayed down in Calcutta, so again a request went out just to teach me; this produced John Blandy's father, the Secretary to the Governor of Bengal. His bungalow was on the side of the mountain some distance from the school, so twice a week I would go to Chowrasta, rent a pony and trot out to where he lived, with my textbooks. We sat on the balcony looking directly on to Kanchenjunga if the monsoon clouds had not rolled up the valleys, and I used to think how incredibly lucky I was to be there and not cooped up at Aldenham.

The sports master for the senior boys at Eden Falls was a most unusual character, one Tony Lamarro, ex-All-in Wrestling Champion of Australia on several occasions. Of Italian origin, he was about 5'9" tall, weighed in excess of fourteen stone, was as light as a feather on his feet, and inevitably went under the nom de guerre of Two-ton Tony Lamarro. The main house had a glass conservatory attached to one side, where he caused an eighteen-foot-square boxing or wrestling ring to be rigged up. Above the house there was that rare thing for Darjeeling, a flat area about the size of a tennis court with surrounds. Every morning he would take us up there at 7 a.m. in our PT gear to go through twenty-five press-ups, fifty knee dips and however many circuits he felt like on that day. So after acclimatisation at 7,500 feet, with that training and cross-country runs around the Old Calcutta Road, we were pretty fit. In the conservatory he had added wrestling mats, and he taught us head locks, how to fall when thrown, half-

Nelsons, full Nelsons and the fearsome Boston Crab, where you got your opponent on his back, grabbed his thighs under one's armpits, turned him over on to his front and then sat on his back until he surrendered. Pretty nasty stuff really!

We then came to the point when we were going to have a boxing match versus St Paul's School, the Eton of east India, with vastly more boys to choose from. Tony Lamarro told the team, of which I was a member, that he was going to have two minutes in the ring with each of us to toughen us up and get us used to being thumped a bit, but not too hard – or so he said. The first boy was called into the ring, one of the smaller ones, and they sparred around, quite gently it has to be said. However, when Tony looked around for the next one, there was just a row of empty windows and no other boys to be seen! The match in fact never took place that term, since the school went down with chicken pox. It happened the next year, but by that time I was in sports-mad South Africa, and had put Tony's training to good use by winning my weight in my first term, where all boys had to enter the inter-house boxing competitions.

In 1998 Lene and I visited Eden Falls, which by then had been taken over by St Paul's as their san. There was no point going in, but our guide took us behind, where the servants' quarters stood just as they had fifty-plus years before. There was a lady, who had been a girl there in the 1940s, and now lived with her fifteen-year-old granddaughter in a two-roomed house. They invited us in for a cup of 'char'. The young girl was studying for the equivalent of O levels, and of course wanted to make a career in computing. In the upper corner of their living room was a TV set mounted on a bracket. When we enquired what programmes they could tune into at that altitude, the daughter replied that they had a choice of nine channels at an altitude of 7,000 feet. Times change!

But fortunately, the entertainment value of Indian Railways does not. We drove down to pick up the Calcutta–Delhi express train for Varanasi or Benares, as it used to be called – at New Jalpaguri station, which has replaced Siliguri as the junction. We arrived at about noon for a 12.30 p.m. departure, only to be told that the train was delayed by two hours. This must have been general knowledge since apart from us two there was only a group of seven soldiers in blue turbans, standing around. So we went to the snack stall on the platform and bought some samosas and a couple of Fantas. A young girl of about eight in a yellow dress wandered up to Lene sitting on her case, and started a game of marbles with a broad-edged button that they rolled between themselves. Since there were no other customers and the train was late, the stallholder stripped down to his boxer shorts, jumped over the counter and crossed the first rail to a low wall. Above this there was a large water tank with a wide pipe for filling the tanks on the train for the toilets, restaurant car, and so on. Mounting the half wall, he pulled down on a chain that released the water, anointed himself from a shampoo bottle, and quickly became a pillar of soapsuds from head to foot. Naturally both of us took photos of this activity, which apparently is an old established perk on the railways, and Lene went back to her game of marbles. The next thing I knew was that I was surrounded by the seven soldiers. One accused me of taking the photo because I found it funny, and because India was a poor country. I responded that I had taken it because I found it interesting, and that I knew India was a poor country, but was better off than when I lived there. When was that? Before independence in the 1940s. Really? Nevertheless India was still a poor country; not everyone could shower at home, and this was one alternative. I realised that I had hurt their feelings, not to mention that the odds were 7:1, so I said, 'Look, the reason why we took those photos was because here was a man showing initiative, and you as soldiers should be the first to recognise that. '*Teek hai?*' (Is that all right then?) 'Ah, right, *teek hai*.' Smiles, handshakes all round, not to mention relief on my part both for their assuaged feelings and my physical safety!

Over the next two hours the station gradually filled up with all those who knew that it was going to be late. The would-be passengers squatted on their haunches gazing into the middle distance, contemplating their karma. The young girl had exhausted our amusement value and trotted off. A couple of cows came down the steps and grazed on anything that was available, including some of the vegetables carried by the passengers. Eventually the train came in, and we boarded it.

Delays like this can and do happen on British trains, but one certainly does not have the same entertainment as in India while waiting, and the quiet contemplation of karma is replaced by babbling frustration into mobile phones.

The autumn term of 1941 was supposed to be my last one at the New School before being sent on to Geelong Grammar School in Australia. Unfortunately for this plan, the Japanese made their infamous attack on Pearl Harbour on 7 December 1941, and Hitler compounded the error by declaring war on the USA. Even if passages had been available from India to Australia, the sinking of the *Prince of Wales* and the *Repulse* effectively closed off that avenue. However, when Tishy's mind was made up that a certain course was to be followed, that was it, and he sent three cables to schools in South Africa, St Andrew's, Grahamstown, Michaelhouse and Hilton in Natal, asking if they would take a fifteen-and-a-half-year-old boy, whose headmaster said that he should get such and such grades in School Certificate. Only the head of Hilton accepted, and so on 19 December I sailed down the River Hooghly for Durban on the MV *Inchanga*, one of the Bank Line trio of passenger ships, the others being the *Isipingo* and the *Incomati*. The headmaster, whoever he was, would be *in loco parentis* and would tell me where I was to spend the holidays after arrival.

I have to say that as far as I was concerned it was simply the continuation of the great adventure that had begun eighteen months before, and I felt a bit like a pioneer, since I was the first to go. One or two others followed with their mothers a year or two later, and several of the other boys went on to other hill schools with high academic standards, such as the Royal Indian Military College at Dehra Dun, to study for Highers. My mother was pretty upset at another parting since we had got on well, but as the saying goes, 'When father says turn, everyone turns'. In retrospect, however, it was a parting of the ways, both physically and emotionally. Life in colonial India (or 'imperial' would be a better adjective to describe it, since the expatriates did not settle there as in Kenya or southern Rhodesia) was very circumscribed for folk in the business community. Each major city centre had its own hill station – Simla for Delhi, Ootacamund for Madras and so on – usually built in the imitation of the Scottish Highlands or Surrey foothills. Journeys by train were long and slow, so people lived on well-recognised tramlines working towards their retirement at 'home' by the fairly young age of fifty or so. In those pre-penicillin days of limited medication their health would have taken some knocks over the previous twenty-five years or so, as a result of which it was estimated that most of the men would be dead by sixty. And so they were. Their wives seemed to survive for longer, either because they were innately tougher, drank less, smoked less, or a bit of all three.

Having sampled it I resolved never ever to get sucked into expatriate life anywhere, with its social round of parties, bridge and transient relationships. It came close in my career with Brussels a couple of times, but I managed to hold out.

6.

The Second Leg to South Africa (Years 15–18)

19 December 1941 saw me boarding MV *Inchanga* of the Bank Line to sail at fairly short notice for Durban instead of Australia. As I said at the end of the previous chapter, it was all part of the adventure that had started eighteen months earlier on departure from Liverpool. Christmas, the northern European construct as we know it, has always seemed to me to be a bit of a damp squib when celebrated either in the tropics or the southern hemisphere, as I did on several occasions thereafter. The ship's crew came up with the usual British festivities for its passengers, who numbered no more than eight to ten for the first phase.

Those three passenger ships of the Bank Line had berths for forty-eight passengers only, and therefore must have paid their way through freight. They had beautiful lines with a single funnel, slightly raked, wooden decks, and even in her wartime shades of grey the *Inchanga* still looked like a royal yacht or a tycoon's floating statement of supreme affluence. Mounted on her stern was a four-inch naval gun to deter any surfaced submarine, but certainly not any surface raider. The gunner in charge was the dissolute wreck of a three-badge A/B otherwise known as a 'stripey', whose service had been extended by the war. I was taken aboard by my parents and introduced to the captain, a bluff, bearded merchant marine skipper in his forties, who assured them that he would keep an eye on me during the voyage. Fat chance. The passengers consisted of a South African doctor from Johannesburg (who was to come to my help later), a blonde lady of ample proportions, another lady recently widowed and dressed in black, a pair of married couples and a Mrs Mallinson, with her seven-year-old son. The last two had just escaped from Burma, leaving the husband behind to blow up the oil fields belonging to the Burma Oil Company, and were being sent to

South Africa for their safety. She was clearly extremely worried for her husband's safety, had no idea if or when they would see him again, was short of money and therefore did not join in the general shipboard social round. It was hard for her.

We set off down the Hooghly early the next morning on our way to join the main Ganges River and the sea. The Hooghly is well known for being one of the most difficult rivers to navigate, because of its strong currents and shifting sand banks, from which every so often the remains of a previous wreck showed up in the form of a mast or superstructure. The pilots, mainly Scots who lived across the river from Calcutta itself, rightly prided themselves on their skills and to an extent operated a 'closed shop'. However, shortly after Indian Independence they were told to pack up their bags and go. Their reaction was disbelief, consternation, contempt for the Indians. Did they not realise how irreplaceable those pilots were, how in a matter of weeks the Hooghly would become a graveyard of sunken ships, Calcutta would be cut off from international trade, and so on? Well, the Indian government replaced them with Romanian and Ukrainian pilots, familiar with the shifting sands and shoals of the lower Danube and Volga rivers, at a fraction of the wage cost, and so an early post-imperial lesson was learned. It had to be repeated in 1956 after the nationalisation of the Suez Canal, when we assumed that it would soon silt up and we would all be back to the pre-1868 situation with Nasser pleading for us to return. Fifty years on when visiting India, one cannot help but be impressed by the sheer efficiency and attention to their charges' welfare that Indian travel agencies exhibit towards tourists. Any nation that can raise a volunteer army of 2.6 million to fight for a ruling power must have reserves of loyalty and responsibility. They finally had their war memorial unveiled at the top of Constitution Hill.

It only took a few days for us to go down the east coast of India to Madras, where we put in to take on more cargo and perhaps the odd passenger. I was surprised when friends of my parents Marie Priestly and her husband came on board and asked if they could join me for dinner. It must have been Christmas Eve by then, but I had already had my presents. During the course of the meal it became clear that they had a mission. When I was at school in Darjeeling, like many of the other boys I had bought a Ghurkha kukri (a curved knife) from a trader at the school gates. It was not full-sized, but about eighteen inches long and sufficient to do some damage if wielded carelessly or with intent. My parents had noted that it was no longer in my bedroom; had I packed it by any chance, since there was no way that they could allow me to arrive in a new school with a weapon like that? Of course I had it, so it went ashore with the Priestlys to be recovered when I next saw my father in Calcutta in March 1946 on compassionate leave from the RN.

After sailing round the southern tip of India we put into Colombo in Sri Lanka and then headed west across the Indian Ocean for Mombasa. I don't know at what speed the *Inchanga* could sail – probably slower than the *Strathmore* at ten to twelve knots, and the voyage was extended by the need to zigzag to avoid any German submarines that may have been operating in the Indian Ocean. So we were back to those lazy, tropical days of deck games and refreshments that I had experienced on the way out from England. I was the only unaccompanied youth on board and after a while listening to adult conversation all the time had its limitations, so I found myself drawn into the circle of the three apprentices, aged between seventeen and nineteen years for company. Just as estate agents say that property values depend on location, location and location, so apparently were the lives of those three motivated by sex, sex and sex – or the lack of it at sea.

Somewhere after Colombo I began to wonder why I had not seen the captain since my parents had entrusted me to him on that first evening. They looked at me pityingly. 'Didn't you notice the blonde lady with the large bust?' (or words to that effect) one of them asked me. I agreed that I had, but not since the early part of the voyage. 'Well exactly,' came the withering comment. 'You don't think the skipper is thinking of you when he's got her in his cabin up on the bridge, do you?' By Mombasa they were running a sweep on how long it would take the Electrical Officer to secure his 'wife for the voyage'. As we left that port we noticed among the new passengers a lady clinging to the neck of her husband, who looked like a colonial servant, before coming up the gangway with tears streaming down her face. By all accounts the Electrical Officer had secured his prey within a couple of days. I was amazed; she looked just like any one of my mother's friends. Was that what went on? Well, well, travel certainly does broaden the mind! My father, who was dead straight in that and other ways, and somewhat prudish, never did ask me how I got on during the trip, and I never told him. He would not have approved of my shipboard company.

As we left, Mombasa security was tight to the extent that we were not informed of the next port of call until after several hours, and then we were disappointed that it was not to be Zanzibar, with its reputation of being an exotic location in many ways – an Omani sultanate, the centre of the clove spice trade to the Persian Gulf and Indonesia, as well as its dark connections with the slave trade. However, the next few days did enable me to observe that humans do not behave all that differently from pack animals. Our days sailing across the Indian Ocean had fallen into an easy, relaxed routine. After breakfast we passengers would take up our daily activities, walking countless circuits around the cabin deck, reading in the saloon or playing deck games under an awning on the boat deck. By 11 a.m. they were all ready for a change and an exchange of gossip so we would repair to the port side of the boat deck, which was not occupied by the shuffleboard markings, pull our deckchairs into a semicircle to be able to watch what was going on, and order drinks. Tonic water had not been invented then, so those who wanted the hard stuff called for pink gins, while most stuck to that refreshing and cheap tropical beverage of fresh lime and soda with a bit of sugar. In short, we had bonded. After a couple of days one or two of the new passengers from Mombasa tried to break into this cosy little circle. It was like a wildlife programme that one sees on TV where a lone male lion tries to ingratiate itself into an established pride. At first they would circle round watching the deck games in progress, before sidling up to our *laager* or encampment and making a few diffident attempts at conversation. No deckchairs were moved; no spaces were opened for them. After all, as one lady pointed out, we were from Ind-jah and they were only from Keen-yah, lower in the colonial pecking order. It took a few days of mingling during meals in the dining saloon before true fraternisation was accomplished.

Before leaving Calcutta I had been told that my uncle 'Mac' (I never knew him by any other name, nor knew what his true first name was) lived and worked in Dar-es-Salaam. At the time of my parents' wedding in 1925 in Mombasa he was either managing a cattle ranch on an island in the middle of Lake Victoria or was putting himself through Cedara agricultural college in Natal, and by 1942 he was in the sisal business in Tanganyika. I had barely heard of him, and had never met him nor seen a photo of him, but he was simply advised by cable that I was on my way to Durban, and might put in some time, without any dates or the name of the ship, for the usual security reasons. We entered Dar-es-Salaam harbour on a Saturday evening early in January, passing the wreck of the German warship that had been sunk there in the Great War, and dropped anchor with our lights doused by the blackout.

On the next morning passengers were more interested in looking across the harbour at what activity there was ashore, and wondering how to get there, so we had assembled on the boat deck. At about 10 a.m. we noticed a dinghy pull out from the landing point, heading more or less in our direction, with a European sitting in the stern dressed in the regulation khaki shorts, long stockings and bush jacket, a squashed hat on his head, being rowed by a local African. As they drew closer my fellow passengers speculated on who they could be.

'That's my uncle,' I piped up.

They swung round as if I was Oliver Twist asking for more and chorused, 'Who?'

'That's my uncle,' I repeated.

'How do you know?'

I stuck to my guns. 'I just do.'

So the dinghy came alongside, Mac stepped on to the bottom of the gangway and bounded up the steps to greet me with outstretched hand. Almost a 'Dr Livingstone I presume?' meeting. So began a long avuncular relationship that went well from the start. As a Hilton boy might have said about his latest girlfriend at the start of a new term, 'Ja man, as soon as we met, we just clicked!' I went ashore to spend the day with the son and daughter of one of Mac's friends, sailing in a dugout canoe with an outrigger and lateen sail, the most exhilarating experience since sitting on the back of a polo pony, and a lot less frightening. Although I did not know it at the time, Mac immediately wrote off about my visit to his father, 'the old pirate' in New Zealand, whom he had visited on one of his leaves, and that set off a very long-distance correspondence from school over the next few years.

The *Inchanga* must have been taking on cargo as the mainstay of the voyage, since we put into both Beira and Lourenco Marques in Portuguese East Africa without adding to the passengers. The entrance to the port of Beira was up a wide, flat, muddy estuary, in colour like 'the great, grey, green, greasy Limpopo'. Short, swarthy Portuguese officials in uniforms replete with gold decorations bustled about the quayside. In our superior British way we regarded them as slightly comical, with never a thought towards the feathered headdresses and other trappings of our colonial governors. I bought myself a beautiful model of a retriever dog, carved out of vegetable ivory. It cost the equivalent of 8s, which virtually cleaned out what balance I had left after buying the odd round of lime juice and soda for our group. I was fretting over this when the doctor said that he would take me back to the shop and get the money back if that was what I really wanted. Needless to say, it still stands here on a book shelf in pride of place some seventy years on. But it was not until 1987 when Lene and I went on a camel safari along part of the Uaso Nyiro River in the Laikipia district of Kenya that I saw the Doum palms from whose fruit the vegetable ivory comes.

We finally reached our destination of Durban towards the middle of January 1942, and sailed inside the Bluff to tie up at the quayside. Those were the days of *civis Britannicus sum* when anyone with a British passport could wander over the bits of the world covered pink without restraint, and if one got into trouble anywhere else, the Foreign Office still had enough clout to come to one's rescue. It bred a certain arrogance, I have to say. The immigration officers came aboard, checked our passports, asked what my father did for a living in India, as they did in those days, and who was going to look after me. The headmaster of Hilton knew neither the name of the ship nor its date of arrival, and a phone call elicited the information that he had gone off with his wife for a few days' holiday by car to the Transkei, and had not left an address. So the immigration officer, who probably thought I was a bit stroppy by this time, dropped his bombshell. Anyone entering the country to reside had to have £30 so as not to be a burden on the state. Did I have it? Of course I didn't, I hardly had 30d by this stage. At last the captain put in an appearance, and when asked what would happen if they could not find the headmaster in time, he jovially told me that he would take me back to England. Not very helpful really. So after everyone had disembarked, I stayed on board. One is fairly resilient at that age, but on the second morning as I was leaning over the side, who should come up the gangway but my friend the doctor, observing, 'I see you are still here.' He had traced the head and his wife, who were now on their way to Durban, and he would put up the money and take me ashore until they arrived. A kind man to all who needed his help on that voyage!

The headmaster was Terence Mansergh, unofficially referred to as 'the Duke' by the boys at Hilton. In those days of deference to the mother country by the white Dominions, most heads of such private schools in those countries came from the UK, as did many of the masters. It was thought that South African or Australian universities did not produce men of the necessary academic calibre. This was what the former Australian Prime Minister Roy Keating referred to as 'cultural cringe'. In return they got their own back by consistently beating the home country at Rugby Union. Sixty years, on the situation has reversed and come more or less into equilibrium. Mr Mansergh was about 5'10" in height, athletic since he had played hockey for England, had deep-sunk eyes and a mathematical rather than the usual classical background. His wife was broadly built with an imperious voice, tended to carry all before her in physique, and was therefore known by the boys as 'the Battleship'. They loaded my trunk into their car and we set off up the old road through 'the Valley of 1,000 Hills' to Maritzburg, the 'Sleepy Hollow' capital of Natal Province. A great introduction to a new country.

From there the road wound up to the small village of Hilton Road at about 1,000 feet or maybe more, passing an extravagant Austrian castle-like house built by an Italian on the right-hand side. From Hilton Road a dirt road led north for about five miles through wattle plantations to the school.

I cannot imagine that any other school in the world has such a location. Many schools have spacious grounds, but this consisted of what can only be described as a campus perched on the rim of the wide Umgeni River valley, hundreds of feet below The actual grounds are entered through a pair of sandstone pillars from where one sweeps up a long drive, past the cricket oval circled with eucalyptus trees, to the collection of white, neo-Cape Dutch buildings of the various houses into which the boys were divided, with the main two-storied edifice of the dining hall and offices. Only the head's family house and the san were single-storied, but still in the same style of architecture. To the left of the main classroom blocks was the school chapel built in a mellow, brownish stone, which acted as a visual resting point. It has recently been expanded with the increase in the numbers of pupils. The whole layout is homogenous and unforgettable in that location with clear blue skies. To the north across the width of the Umgeni valley one could just detect the white strip made by the Karkloof Falls, which are in fact a series of low drops, as I discovered when I visited them for the first time in 1995. To the west in winter we could see the snow-capped tops of the Drakensberg plateau of mountains, which were not visited during the war due to petrol rationing, but I got there in 1990.

When we arrived there were no boys since it was the Christmas holidays, and after assigning me to a dormitory, the Manserghs just told me to look around the grounds on my own, and watch out for the sunlight at that altitude if I chose to go for a swim. I set off along the perimeter road past the main building until I reached a small car parked at the side, with someone who turned out to be one of the masters standing next to it. This was the maths master Frank Morris, universally referred to as 'Fronk', since he pronounced his 'a's as 'o's, just as the Dutch refer to 'Omsterdom'. He was in fact English, in his early sixties. 'Hello, boy, and who are you?' he greeted me. I told him my name adding 'sir'.

'Do you know anything about cars?' he inquired.

'No, sir.'

'Well then, get down and look under the bonnet and see if you can see what is wrong.' I crouched down on the burning tarmac just long enough to see a widening circle of oil draining from the sump. Fronk went off to make a phone call, and I disappeared to the pool. Tarmac in midsummer is hot when applied to bare flesh.

The following day, after a phone call, I was put on to the train back to Maritzburg station, where I was collected by a pickup truck to join a group of six or seven boys from Kenya, who spent their holidays on the farm near Wartburg, about fifteen miles or so north of Maritzburg across the Umgeni river. Wartburg was just a *dorp* (a rural village) in those days, made up of mainly German families that were assumed to be members of the anti-British 'Ossewa Branweig'. By now, German dedication to the Protestant ethic has turned it into a prosperous small town. The Hollys' farm consisted of 5,000 rolling acres of mainly wattle plantations for the pit props of the Rand mines, with some stands of eucalyptus for telegraph poles and so on. The Hollys by then must have been in their late fifties to early sixties, with two grown-up sons, Jimmy and Geoffrey, one of whom had got a rowing Blue at Oxford. During the 1930s they had been hit hard by the Depression and when business was bad they had taken in paying guests to swell their income. Both their sons had gone to school at Michaelhouse, the rival to Hilton in the same way that Toronto rivals Montreal, or Sydney rivals Melbourne. Michaelhouse was always considered to be the more cerebral school and Hilton the more physical, as demonstrated in the oft-told tale that when in a rugby scrum the Hilton pack leader would bellow, 'Shove, you buggers, shove!' while his equivalent at Michaelhouse would exhort, 'More pressure in the rear, Michaelhouse!' I am sure that there was some truth in that assessment, since I have noticed that ex-Michaelhouse boys have made a greater mark on the world stage than our lot. Holmes à Court, born in what was then Rhodesia, comes to mind, as does the man who took charge of the Channel tunnel enterprise, and before him Michael Edwards, who was brought in to run British Leyland – though not with much success it has to be said. At any rate the Hollys, when approached by Hilton as a potential holiday home for this group of boys, said they would take them on approval at first, and then, finding them to be tolerably civilised, made it a regular arrangement. What a bit of luck! Goodness knows where I would have ended up if Michaelhouse had accepted me. On that first trip I just remember standing up in the back of the truck, hanging on as we bounced along the dirt roads, and thinking that this was the life.

I was probably there for less than a week on that first occasion, and will come back to the farm in more detail later. But I recall the usual new boy situation of being looked at blankly by a group which had already bonded and was sizing up this interloper, and having the 'native' store pointed out on the side of a hill, where the roof was unaccountably red in colour among all that green. This apparently was how red chillies were dried in the sun, and it was the first time that I had seen them.

When the time came to return to Hilton we were taken back by truck to Maritzburg to join the school train that came up from Durban to Mooi River, or somewhere like that. Michaelhouse boys were at one end, Hilton boys at the other, and the girls from St Anne's at Hilton Road occupied the middle carriage. The tradition for those joining at Maritzburg was to have tea at a café, the name of which I have forgotten, before the train arrived. Within the café the same segregation between the groups of children was maintained. Boys on the whole, in those days, did not chat up girls when surrounded by their peers. Nevertheless, after a few minutes I noticed that one of the St Anne's girls on the other side of the room was giving me the once-over, and there was something familiar about her. After giving it some thought I decided that she could have been my cousin Ann, whom I had met just the once when she came to stay with us at the West Kent Hotel in 1938, four years previously. So I got to my feet and walked the length of the room to the girls' table. Shades of Gary Cooper walking down the centre of the street in *High Noon*. Conversation dropped and everyone looked up. From my lot, 'Who does this bloke from India think he is, just going across to talk to the St Anne's girls, when he has hardly arrived?' and a similar query from the Michaelhouse representatives. 'Are you my cousin Ann Hillcoat?' I asked, and had it confirmed. Neither set of our parents had communicated to the other that we would be at schools only five miles apart from one another, and that was the only time we met.

Hilton College, like many of those schools overseas, was based on the British public school system, but mercifully without those aspects that gave them a somewhat warped reputation – namely fagging, flogging, and fatuous customs dressed up as traditions. It has to be said that as with all schools during the war years, some of the best teachers were in the services 'up north' and prowess in sport, if not the be-all and end-all in the pecking order, was pretty close to it. I was grateful to Tony Lamarro and all his early morning press-ups and knee dips in Darjeeling, which enabled me to win my weight in the school boxing that first term, and so to be accepted straight into the Matric form with something to offer.

The boys really had a wonderful free and easy life in the immediate spacious school grounds, with access to the hundreds of acres of land running down to the Umgeni River. One could stand on the perimeter and look down on to the rondavels of the Zulu kraals that were dotted around the landscape with their patches of mealies or maize plants beside them. On Sundays we had to get out of the immediate school grounds after chapel and were not allowed to return until 4.30 p.m., so we all went off in groups, in winter to camp in the wattle plantations and cook up whatever tinned food was available from the tuck shop over a fire, and in summer to walk either to Gwen's Falls, where there was a pool, or to hike right down to the bottom to swim in the Umgeni. In summer when the river was in flood, this was more like surfing, entering the fast-flowing water at one point to be carried down feet forwards liable to bounce off any rocks before catching an overhead branch and pulling oneself out. The negative to such days was having to climb back up the 500 feet of the rocky path in the summer heat in the late afternoon. No one was ever drowned so far as I know, although the same could not be said of the Howick Falls, 360 feet or so in height and a couple of hours of good walking away. These were out of bounds since a boy had chosen to dive off a ledge at the top the previous year. I don't think that any trace of him was ever found in the fast-flowing water.

I was there for nine terms altogether until March 1944, South African schools having four terms per year. It was long enough to meet some interesting characters and to make some lasting friendships. There was a boy called Dalglish in my schoolhouse (Pearce's), who had an incredible rapport with wild animals. He kept a genet as a pet, a small animal with a bushy tail, a bit like a grey squirrel but with big, brown eyes like those of a bush baby. This he carried around with him next to his skin under his shirt. When it was time for us to go to chapel the boys would line up outside by houses waiting to enter, whereupon Dalglish would take the animal out of his shirt and put it on the grass for it to scamper back to his dormitory, where it would go to the locker beside his bed. It really had a homing instinct.

His other 'friends' were not quite so acceptable. They were adders. Just below the chapel was the school farm with the herd of dairy cows and the milking parlour, as well as a dam for the water supply. Dalglish caught frogs there, which he then asphyxiated in one of the labs. One day I came across him training a snake to eat what he had recently caught. He had chopped the frog up and, holding the snake behind the head to force its jaws open, he fed a leg into its mouth and then gently teased it down the length of its body, tying a piece of string or straw above it to stop the snake regurgitating the meal. Of course it thrashed around, but finally digested it. He kept these snakes in his pocket, one at a time. I once asked him what he would do if they ever bit him. 'They wouldn't dare,' he replied. 'They would know that as soon as they hit the ground my heel would be on their head.' Since we all went around with bare feet out of class hours, that did not seem to be much of a disincentive, although the soles of our feet could get pretty tough. In fact on the Hollys farm we used to compete who could walk furthest over the newly burned grass in the spring. At meals in hall, Dalglish would often have one of his little friends in his blazer pocket so that he could put down a saucer of milk on the bench and let it have a drink. Understandably there was often a vacant place to either side of where he sat!

While on the subject of food, I should say that the quality was far ahead of what used to be served up to us in peacetime England. I can't say that I liked mealie meal porridge, but there was a dark purple sort of porridge called *mabela* or something like that, which I really liked, although I was in the minority who did.

I was also fortunate in having Hugh Bryan as my housemaster in the last year. He also taught me French, and once again ancient Greek on a one-to-one basis. The latter was a very useful subject since I met some interesting men through studying it, albeit to a modest level. But Matric included Plato's *Phaedo* for the first time (in addition to the usual Xenophon and Homer), the account of how Socrates stoically met his death surrounded by his friends as the effects of hemlock slowly passed from his feet up his body. I recall being quite affected by that. Hugh Bryan was seventy years of age and had returned to take the place of one of the younger masters away at the war. He was a stocky figure with flowing white hair, and when I left he gave me two books, *No Outspan*, the autobiography of Deneys Reitz, and *Commando – a Boer Journal of the Boer War*, by the same author. In one, Hugh Bryan wrote a small motto in French, and in the other one, in Greek. I can still translate the former, but not the latter. They were both bought from Shuter and Shooter, Booksellers, Pietermaritzburg, and since Maritzburg (until recently at least), claimed to be the last outpost of the British Empire (along with Victoria, BC, Canada, where they really do still serve cucumber sandwiches at tea!) it probably still exists.

It was back to normal so far as my parents were concerned, 3,000 miles or so apart and the usual weekly letter. Those from my father usually ended, 'Work hard, my lad.' After thirteen years that phrase began to lose something of its originality. There were times – not many – when there would be a gap of a couple of weeks or so between the incoming letters, and one had to assume that the mail ship from India had been sunk, since by 1942 there were German submarines operating in the Indian Ocean. The Japanese, I think, were fully involved with fighting the Americans further east. However, what was more remarkable was that I began to get correspondence from Grandpa Sam Watkins in New Zealand, where he was living at Whangerei in the north island.

He even sent me two books on sailing, since he had started his career 'before the mast' and worked his way up. One was by John Masefield and the other on all types of sailing vessels. These I have passed on to my cousin Colin, but how they ever got to me in South Africa with a war going on against the Japanese in the South Pacific, I will never know. I can only assume that the ships went south below Australia and then west across the Southern Ocean to the Cape to keep out of the way of hostile warships or submarines. No doubt convoys of Anzac troops going to the war theatre in Egypt went by the same route. Little was I to know that I would come very close to joining Sam in New Zealand in 1945–46.

The Hollys' farm, where I spent all the holidays in 1942, was about three miles from Wartburg at the end of a dirt road. Just before the farm entrance this crossed via a drift a small river that ran through their land from another adjacent farm. This flowed over some flat sandstone rocks for a few metres and then fell probably a couple of metres into a wide, deepish rock pool surrounded by high krantzes. At least, it was deepish until just before the end of my stay, of which more later. This was our main and nearest swimming hole, reminiscent of those old *Saturday Evening Post* pictures of skinny young boys larking around in American scenes with the nostalgic caption 'the old swimmin' hole'. They represented an era of unsophisticated and innocent enjoyment. Through the farm gates the ground opened up on to a wide grassy area of Kikuyu grass, almost a lawn which led to the single-storied farmhouse on top of a rise. This was built in the traditional South African style with cellars below and steps running up to the *stoep* that ran around two sides of the building. Behind the main house was another smaller one for Mr Norman, the farm manager, and his family, which included a son and his daughter, Jill. Ma and Pa Holly, as we referred to them informally but not to their faces, lived in the main house with Mrs Holly's mother, a quite old but fierce lady. There was also another lady who stayed there with her small baby, a Mrs Packard, the wife of a British Army Brigadier 'up north'. Our quarters were to the right of the house in a couple or three rondavels, where we slept three or four to a room. We had the usual bowls and jugs of water to wash in, although that was not all that necessary for boys of that age, who swam in the river or the rock pool most days. There was no electricity so we had paraffin lamps in the house and candles for our bedrooms. The domestic water supply was pumped up from the dam by the swimming hole through a long pipe by the aid of what I believe engineers refer to as a 'ram pump'. Whenever I mention this to any of my engineer friends, they get a dreamy look in their eyes. Apparently it worked on the principle that once the whole pipe and pump were primed with a head of water, then it would start off and keep going until it lost the head of water for any reason. So we could hear the regular 'thump, thump, thump' of it going about every second, day and night.

Although South Africa was relatively unaffected by wartime shortages, there was still petrol rationing, which was one of the reasons why I never got up to the Berg. There was one big truck on the farm as well as the pickup truck, and the Hollys had a Chevrolet for driving into Maritzburg in more comfort. There-fore, for hauling the timber from the plantations to the saw mill, they relied on the traditional wagons with their spans of fourteen oxen, controlled by the Zulu drivers with their long whips that had a thin strip called the *vorslag* attached to the end, which they cracked over and on the backs of the animals. We boys also had our whips attached to a two-foot wooden stick for cracking around and making a noise, or using the thick end of the stick to kill iguanas, between four and five feet long, as they basked in the pastures after clearing out another nest of duck eggs on the banks of the river. All this is probably very politically incorrect now, but that is what we did. Sometimes we ate the lizards at a *braai* (where one grills meat over an open fire) and they tasted rather like chicken. The skins we would give to the Indian supervisors to tan and make into fancy belts for us, and apparently they liked the fat to rub on their joints as a cure for rheumatism – or that is what we understood. The river was wide and deep enough for Geoffrey Holly to keep his skiff there before he went on to win his rowing Blue at Oxford, and it was still around for us to use when we swam there.

About ten minutes' walk below the farmhouse was the saw

mill, for cutting the main part of the wattle trees into pit props, and the tall eucalyptus trees into telegraph poles. The strippings were stacked into tall, conical kilns sealed with mud, to be converted into charcoal. There was not much health and safety in those days. The timber was sawn up on open circular saws making that high-pitched scream. Occasionally one would jam and one of the operators, being too careless in how he cleared the obstruction, would lose some fingers or worse in the process. In the spring the wattles would all bloom into a yellow haze of mimosa across the hillsides. The side branches were stripped off before loading on to the wagons and this material would be laid in rows around the contours of the hills to break down over time, thus preventing the rain run-off and soil erosion that was endemic in Natal. In the last summer there, the neighbouring farmer, who did not do this and had also burned his grass to the roots, suffered enormous erosion when the river that came across his land swept tons of soil into our swimming hole reducing it to only a few feet in depth. The Hollys planted about 600 wattle trees to the acre as a conservation measure, where, as Pa Holly constantly told us, on other farms they would pile in up to 1,200 trees in the same space. All this was only a few years after the two American agricultural scientists, Jacks and White, had written their book on the subject of soil conservation entitled *The Rape of the Earth*. This was their description of how the dust bowl had been created during the 1930s on the American prairies, by ploughing up the grasslands and replacing them with the monoculture of wheat. The newspapers had been full of pictures of whole fields just being blown away across the darkened skies. In terms of soil conservation, Pa Holly was forty years ahead of his time.

By any description, Pa Holly was a character. A strong, thick set man with a face burned red brown by the sun, crinkly grey hair and blue eyes, he used to claim that in a country where many people were bilingual, English and Afrikaans or English and Zulu, he was tri-lingual: English, Zulu and bad language! The latter would be considered pretty mild in today's verbal environment of barrack room obscenities, but his remarks were peppered with 'damns' and 'bloodies'. It was also said that he was so fluent in

Zulu with its verbal clicks that he could join a bunch of workers on the road after dark and enter into conversation with them without being identified. In that he was probably a match for Charles Chatterton.

Pa Holly also invented a grader for smoothing out the roads, which was his pride and joy. Compared with the large yellow Caterpillar machines with their slanted metal blade attached to the front, this was simplicity itself. It was made of railway sleepers bolted together and with the forward timber set at an angle to scrape and deflect the bumps on the road to the side. It probably had some extra weights on top and a couple of oxen pulled it with chains attached. Pa Holly used to boast ironically to us that there were three things wrong with this machine: 'It was too simple, too cheap and no bloody good!' He used to take a wicked delight in this subject when we were having meals in the large dining room of the farmhouse. There was a long, wide rectangular table around which we all sat, with a round table in the window for any overflow in numbers. Pa and Ma Holly sat together at the head of the main table, with Mrs Holly's mother, an elderly lady who disapproved of some aspects of her son-in-law, sitting immediately to his right. Every so often a spirit of mischief would take him and he would ask, 'Well, boys, tell me what's wrong with the grader I invented.' So we would start off, 'It's too simple, it's too cheap, and—' words would then tail off because we knew what was coming. 'And it's no bloody good!' Pa would end the sentence with a roar and a wicked twinkle in his eye. Whack! Down would come any available knife, fork or spoon across his knuckles, unless he moved them in time, wielded by Mrs Holly's mother, with a disapproving remark to back it up. Pa also had a low opinion of black and white Friesian bulls. Whenever we were walking across the pasture with him and he saw one, he would grunt, 'Those Friesian bulls are no bloody good, all bellow and no poke!' We never did find out why he continued to keep them.

There really was no discipline enforced on us; we were just expected to behave reasonably, and knew that the penalty of the opposite was to be chucked out. I can only think of two occasions when we were taken to task. One afternoon we were larking around on the front lawn unconsciously indulging in the casual swearing affected by schoolboys (mild as mother's milk by today's standards) when Mrs Packard stormed on to the *stoep* from the sitting room and said that she was fed up with listening to us, and it had to stop forthwith. Which it did – at least in her hearing.

The second incident was more serious. As written above, it was assumed that Wartburg was a nest of Ossewa Branweig, so one of our number, who went on to become an architect in Nairobi, made some stencils with appropriate derogatory messages. We set off at around midnight with pots of paint to daub the sides of the store and other buildings. It took about two hours to walk the three miles there and back again under a beautiful clear moon, and not a dog was disturbed, so we were back by about 2.30 a.m. Nothing happened for two days, until late in the afternoon the local sergeant of the Natal police rode up the drive on his palomino pony to the main house, greeting us as he went by with a cynical look. We had enough savvy to stay put and act innocent. He told the Hollys what had happened and asked them if they had any idea who might have done it. They genuinely pleaded ignorance, and after about half an hour he rode off. But Mrs Packard was made of sterner stuff. Before supper we each always changed into a shirt, tie and school blazer, with shoes of course, and assembled in the large sitting room. That evening we were confronted by massed adults, asked if we were responsible for it, and told that if we did not 'own up' as the phrase went, and were later found to have been responsible, we would be thrown off the farm for all time. So that was that, and we got the message. A nice chap, that police sergeant. We saw him again once or twice as he rode that pony in the gait known as tripling, a trot with the fore legs and cantering with the hindquarters.

At one end of the large sitting room there was a baby grand piano. Apart from us and Mrs P, other visitors used to come and stay from time to time, girls from St Anne's or, in the second year, a Czech mother with her two daughters called Redgrave, nieces of Sir Michael Redgrave, the actor. The mother was a fine classical pianist and used to play sometimes in the evening before we went into supper. After I returned to England I read in the papers that the elder daughter, Mary Maude, was killed in a car accident in this country around 1948.

A farm of that size would not be complete without dogs and horses or Basuto ponies. The dogs were Himmler, a liver and white pointer and Sambo, a black curly-haired retriever. No doubt that name would not be acceptable now. They were great friends and would spend hours sitting on the front lawn socially grooming like a couple of monkeys, which was mainly Himmler biting the big, fat, grey ticks out of the fur of the other. No doubt he liked the taste of the blood.

There were also three or four horses; a large Waler, a smaller female called Zonde and a pony called Tigger. Zonde had a foul temper and I was scared stiff of her. As soon as one went into the stables to saddle them up, she would start stamping around and throwing her head. But one of the Kenyan boys, 'Skinny' Richardson, took absolutely no notice. He would simply walk behind her in the stall, throw on the saddle and start pulling on the girth, at which Zonde would stamp some more and throw her head around, baring a set of teeth like tombstones. Skinny took no notice, slapped her around her chops and told her to shut up. And she did. If possible I stuck with Tigger, who was about the size of the Darjeeling ponies.

To the south the main part of the farm ran up to higher ground, where all the plantations were laid out, through which another river ran into an area that at that time was known as a Native Reserve complete with a small mission chapel. All sorts of earth roads crisscrossed that area and when a plantation was felled the whole appearance would be changed, so one had to develop a bump of locality. If one did not, it was no great problem, since after riding as far as one wanted to go by the sun, one would just turn around, relax the reins and sit back as the pony went home.

On a couple of occasions that bump of locality came in useful as we decided as a group to walk from Hilton to the farm at the start of the holidays, thus saving several shillings of the rail fare, which we could pocket. The distance was about twenty-five miles – quite a way with bare feet. We left the inner school grounds at about 7 a.m. and headed for the end of a peninsular of land jutting into the Umgeni valley, known as Otto's Bluff, named after a farmer who farmed the land. From there we would drop down and head north-east into the morning sun to swim across the river, holding up our few clothes and tuck shop grub in one hand. That was before the river was dammed higher up for power supplies, so it was reasonably full and fast flowing, but one just angled across the stream. We all carried so-called snakebite outfits in the pocket in our belts made out of Duiker skins, but fortunately never had to use them. I now understand that slicing open the bite and rubbing in permanganate of potash would have been totally useless. After clearing the river, it was a long haul on the other side of a long valley with a depressed saddle on the horizon. Such images stick in one's mind. In 1990, when we were visiting the Chattertons and were driving to Hluhluwe, I asked if we could go cross-country via the Hollys' farm. After leaving Maritzburg and crossing the now shallow river, I knew exactly where to head for when we came in sight of that saddle. At the top of it was a neighbouring farm, which back then we reached at about teatime, and the lady had been warned that we would be coming through. So that was a nice break before we eventually made the Hollys at about 7 p.m., more than somewhat footsore. But it was good training for independence in life.

I failed Matric on the first attempt due to maths, which was of a higher standard than I had been taught. In fact, I was talking to my neighbour across the road a couple of years ago, who also had spent some time in South Africa and took Cape Town Matric. Without prompting he said that he had found the maths very tough, and since he became a civil engineer, that put things in perspective. At any rate, the net effect was that I joined the class coming up from the first year Matric form and thus found myself among my own age group, instead of seventeen year olds. So I got to know Michael Noyce, who was in the same school house as I was, and early in 1943 he invited me to his home for part of the holidays. It worked out well, and although they were almost overwhelming in their hospitality, they appreciated my attachment to the Hollys' farm so that for the next year and a bit my holidays were divided between the two locations. Durban in those days was the largest port on the east coast of Africa, with a subtropical climate and a social structure that was almost neocolonial, the whites at the top of the pyramid, the blacks at the base, and the Tamil Indians sandwiched in the middle. Gordon Noyce was a partner in a local firm of chartered accountants called Murray, Smith Berend and Noyce, and the family lived up on the Berea from where we could cycle down Burman Drive to the country club at the north end of the beach. I could not have landed with a better family; they were kind, generous and quite musical. Gordon had a baritone voice and would sing while Dorothy accompanied him at the piano, mostly light opera or Gilbert and Sullivan. Their daughter Megan, six years younger than her brother, reached higher musical accomplishments, before dying young in a tragic accident. Most of our holiday friends were from Durban High School with the advantage of having sisters who attended the local Girls' High, and we led a very carefree social life. The parents were extremely generous, and Christmas holidays were a round of parties and dances in their homes. I could not help but contrast this with the food rationing and blackout that would have been my lot had Dunkirk never happened.

Cape Town and Durban were renowned for their hospitality to the Allied troops going in convoys up to the Western Desert, whether they be British, Poles coming down from Russia through Persia for retraining, or Australians. The latter, however, soon eroded their welcome by insisting that they still had to maintain their rough, tough, 'digger' image, about as welcome as today's English football hooligans. When they had come through Bombay before I left India they had taken over the 'garries', horse-drawn carriages usually plying for hire, unhitched the horses and held impromptu horse races around the Gateway of India, all of which went down like a lead balloon with the Brits and of course the 'garry *wallahs*', whose horses, already pretty broken down, were wrecked as a result. However, in the case of Cape Town, their humour was more creative. A story went the rounds that a lady in an Austin 7 car stalled at a set of traffic lights outside the General Post Office. She was unable to start it, whereupon four Australian soldiers picked up the car and driver together, deposited them on the pavement, put money in the slot machine and stuck the stamps to her windscreen! Whether true or false, a good story.

Nevertheless, they outlived their welcome, and after the first or second Australian convoy their ships were not allowed to tie up at the quay, but had to anchor offshore, with the sharks to contend with should they decide to try to swim. For the British soldiers, those from the so-called working classes, who had never been out to a restaurant let alone lived in a decent house, Durban was simply paradise. They came down the gangways to be met by the waiting citizens who took them off in pairs to their homes, regardless of rank. The only group I can recall that had a bad name were the Liverpool Irish in the RAF ground staff up in the Transvaal, who were known locally as the 'Blue Plague'. A couple of years later when I found myself on the lower deck in the RN, some of the sailors who had been in for a few years started to reminisce on where they had the best run ashore, Durban and Cape Town usually came at the top of the list. As a last sentimental farewell, a large lady called Pearla Siedle, with a strong voice, would stand on the Bluff singing the Maori song 'Now is the Hour' as the troopships steamed past, going north to an uncertain future. The party was not over until the fat lady sang, and not a dry eye in the house, as they say!

When Christmas 1943 came, I had to decide on the next move. The Noyces must have thought that returning to England with all its problems was a downward move, so they offered to look after me until I had done my military service there, and would then start me off in a career in Natal. However, despite having had a wonderful two years, I still felt a bit like a bird of passage and hankered for the England that I thought I remembered from my days with Mr Cove. There was also a fair bit of friction between the Afrikaans and English speakers that did not bode well for the future, and last but not least the Duke encouraged me to get to a British university by some means, and that could not be done if I went into the South African armed services. So I had one last family holiday with the Noyces and several others that we knew at Umkomaas, then a holiday resort south of Durban, with a long beach, rock pools and everything else that goes with such a place. It was the nearest thing to Cornwall in Natal, I should think. Now I am sure it is subsumed into Greater Durban, the third fastest-growing metropolis in the world, or so I have read.

By January 1944, travelling by sea was much safer so it was decided that my mother would return to the UK with Tim via the Suez Canal in order to return him to Bickley Hall. I was to join them there until I got into the services, and therefore spent the last Easter term at Hilton, marking time in post-Matric. I was sorry to leave it all, but the homing instinct was just too strong. Furthermore, one cannot go on living on the generosity of others with no means of returning it. But my mother visited Dorothy Noyce in Durban in about 1962 and saw her in London on several occasions after that, while I was in touch with Mike until his relatively early death a few years ago. Somehow longevity did not go with that family.

So it was to be the SS *Chinese Prince*, one of the Prince Line ships from Liverpool for the three-week voyage home, calling in at East London, which did not seem to have many attractions, Cape Town and the long zigzag up the Atlantic. She was smaller than the *Inchanga* but went at about the same speed, and had about a dozen passengers aboard. I recall the stay in Cape Town for two reasons. First the obvious one, going with two or three of the officers to the top of Table Mountain by cable car and walking around admiring the local flora, which is quite distinctive. The second came into the category of 'where were you when...' as in the case of Kennedy being shot. In this instance it was a case of where and when did you first see *Casablanca*? Well, in my case it was Cape Town in early April 1944. It must have put more phrases into the English language than most other films from 'Play it, Sam, play "As Time Goes By" ' to 'Round up the usual suspects!' Crikey, what an impact it had!

The long leg up the Atlantic was pretty boring, the rest of the passengers mainly senior British officers and their wives. There was a Rear Admiral RN, who regaled me with patronising stories of how stupid his South African fellow officers had been in Simonstown. No wonder the colonials found some Brits to be a pain in the neck. But the skipper had by all accounts secured his 'wife for the voyage' although she never came off the bridge until the end. And then there was the Atlantic, all that water with no dolphins or flying fish. After a few days of being on anti-submarine watch in the wings of the bridge, I got a bit restless, so went to the bo'sun and asked for a proper job and spent as much time as I wanted painting the ship – grey, of course. I determined that a life on the ocean wave was not for me, and that when we arrived I would volunteer for the Army or RAF, from either of which one had the chance to escape from the constipating confines of a piece of metal.

On arrival at Liverpool I took the train up to Claud Stephenson at their vicarage in Yorkshire, and joined Tim and Dorothy. Claud and Aunt Tommy were their usual kind, hospitable selves, while we stayed for a few weeks and sorted out the nitty gritty of returning to wartime Britain, ration books and mundane things like that. Since I would be eighteen in two months' time I took a bus to the local recruiting office at Morley, near Leeds. There were two men in an office behind trestle tables.

'I want to join the RAF,' I told them.

'Sorry, lad,' one of them replied, 'RAF's full up.'

'Then how about the Army?'

'Sorry, lad, Army's full up too, it's coal mines this week.'

'Bloody hell, I haven't come all the way back from sunny South Africa to end up down a mine.'

'Well, coom back in two weeks' time, we're recruiting for Naaavy then.'

'I don't want to go into the Navy, just looking at all that water day after day.'

'Sorry, lad, taaake yer pick: it's coal mines or Naaavy.'

Too late I realised that I had gone to a recruiting office in the middle of the Yorkshire coalfields, and that there was no way out. Given the alternative, Navy it was, and the start of a new social learning curve where at long last I was to learn how the other half lived.

7.

Naval Service: Around the World in 365 Days (Years 18–21)

After a couple of weeks or so with Claud and Tommy in their new vicarage at Woodkirk near Morley, Dorothy, Tim and I were ready and fully equipped with the necessary wartime rations and other documents to make our way south once again to the West Kent Hotel at Bickley. We must have made an unusual trio with all the large luggage associated with colonial life: green trunks bound with wooden bands, stand-up dark-blue suitcases for hanging dresses or suits in without folding, and the inevitable tea boxes for storing all the miscellaneous odds and ends. I assume that we arrived at King's Cross or Euston Station, where lines of people patiently queued for the available taxis. Since our journey out in 1940, the place got shabbier and shabbier.

The one thing that struck me was the apparent lack of security regarding the units to which the soldiers belonged. There were groups of them constantly on the move, and they all wore their regimental shoulder flashes to denote to which one they belonged. Many of them, such as the Royal West Kents, the Dorset Regiment or the Durham Light Infantry, have been eliminated or amalgamated with other regiments over the years, but I had imagined that security would have overridden pride in regiment. There was further general identification brought in after the beginning of the war with the new units, red berets for the Airborne, green for the Commandos and black for the Artillery, while most of the rest wore so-called forage caps. I never did work out how the squaddies got to make them stick to the sides of their heads, but then I don't suppose they could understand how sailors could wear their caps flat a'back – until a Regulating petty officer hove into sight that is.

The West Kent Hotel was no longer the busy place with the

various associated sporting activities pre-1939, but was full of long-term residents paying five guineas a week all in for full board. The adjacent golf club was closed and was a massive site for anti-aircraft guns, which would soon be needed again versus the V1s or doodlebugs, since that part of Kent was on the route to London. The residents were like something out of an Emlyn Williams play. There was the colonel, who worked in the War Office, with his wife. At the other end of the military ranks there was another man and his wife, who owned a glove factory and were pretty wealthy, but the husband was a corporal in the Army, based somewhere locally. He claimed to be the only corporal who paid for his own batman out of his income to avoid the boring tasks of keeping uniforms clean, and boots, belts and so on polished to the exacting standards of the sergeant major. He used to come back for weekend leave, which seemed to be pretty well every weekend. Joan and Jack Rosselli seemed to have made their home there too. Jack was a major in the Army, while Joan was a VAD (Voluntary Aid Detachment) nurse, who used to walk down to the Chislehurst Caves every morning in her smart white uniform with a head tie that blew in the wind, to look after the East Enders who had gone down there with their families for safety during the Blitz; some had just stayed on. Probably their houses had been destroyed. The caves were very old, tunnelled into the chalk hills around Chislehurst, and were and are a tourist attraction. At that time they were filled with bunks in long lines, where the occupants hung sacking from the sides for some privacy. According to Joan, everything went on there from conception to resurrection. She must have had a very tough constitution, since the restricted air was rife with family germs and ailments. She was a delightful lady and became my mother's closest friend.

There was also a theatrical agent, a charming man in his forties. Why he was not called up I don't know – must have had flat feet. But that did not stop him entertaining his extremely pretty WAAF girlfriend whenever she could get leave, which was quite often. It was generally considered that Wrens were mainly recruited from the upper social groups and that their dark blue uniforms were the smartest. WAAFs however, looked the sexiest in their light-blue uniforms, while those of the ATS were at the bottom of the social scale. I always thought that their uniforms were made from more utilitarian material than the other two, maybe because they had harder work to do on gun batteries, driving and maintaining lorries, and so on. The last person that I recall there was a Swede called Dougal Halstrom, or Dougie for short, who worked in a bank in London. He was a very good skater, and when the swimming pool was frozen over in the winter of 1945 he used to entertain us with his swirls and twirls.

If the cast was from Emlyn Williams, the mealtimes were from *Separate Tables*. There was a large dining room with a crescent of windows facing west over the extensive lawns and tennis courts. The food was basic wartime fare, but we should be so lucky that we did not have to live as a unit on the ration books. These were handed into the hotel management and pooled. Spam was a staple part of the menu – boiled, fried, in fritters, any way they could think up to disguise it. There was a large, walled kitchen garden that produced fresh fruit and vegetables in the summer, so we were relatively well off. Most of the tables were positioned around the walls and across the window area of the dining room, with Dorothy and me occupying the table in the centre – that is, well within the earshot of everyone else in the room if they cared to listen in, which they did, judging by the deafening silences that used to descend when Dorothy's stream of consciousness (*Chambers Dictionary*, 'the continuous succession of thoughts, emotions and feelings, both vague and well defined, that forms an individual's continuous experience') hit an 'interesting' subject. The problem was one never knew what was going to come out next, which made one somewhat uneasy. I believe that she shared this characteristic with her sister. Nevertheless, it was enjoyable for both of us to catch up on some family life together after a two-and-a-half-year interval, and that part of Kent then was unspoiled and more or less traffic free, so it was good for extensive walks.

Apart from the Farnfields of Bickley Hall School, the only people that we really knew in the south of England were the Bigg-Withers, Tishy's boss when they were on the three year tour in Kenya from 1923–26 to start up the local Shell Company. Betty was my godmother; they had two daughters, Carol, my age within a month or two, and Anne, two years younger. I don't know what the other services were like, but the RN seemed to be in no hurry to have us, who were registered with them, to join their ranks. Tim by this time had re-entered Bickley Hall after leaving it in August 1940, so in June Dorothy and I went over to spend a few days with the Bigg-Withers at Crowborough in Sussex. That area was an armed camp, mainly of Canadian and American soldiers, both infantry and armoured. As the girls and I cycled around the local roads one had to keep a weather eye for their tanks, which could spin off the crown of the road. It was said that some of the fights between the Canadians and Americans after the pubs closed were monumental, and that it was all part of the training for the coming battle against the Germans.

It was a lovely summer, approaching the longest day, and at about 10 p.m. on 12 June (happens to be the day before my birthday), I was leaning out of my bedroom window soaking up the warm, balmy air when, from across to the right, a strange plane approached on a fixed flight path. It had an odd, sputtering note to its engine noise, rather like a Heinkel as I thought, but there only appeared to be one engine in the nose and as it passed on to the east there was a faint glow from its tail. Very odd. It must have been about three days later, when they began to come over in increasing numbers and exploded on landing, that the day of the doodlebugs was officially announced, and Londoners could look forward to another, but different, bombardment from the air. So we decided to return to Bickley.

It was easy to get up to London by train, only about twenty-five minutes to Charing Cross or Victoria depending from where one started. London, although shabby and knocked about, was still full of people, particularly Oxford Street where the pavements were packed, probably because of the curtailed bus services. The 'clippies' or conductresses on the buses were among the most cheerful members of the population, women for whom the war had offered a way out of the home to earn some money in the open air, meeting thousands of people and enjoying the banter, which was reciprocated. No doubt the women in the factories felt the same. Fifty years later when I was taking my OU degree I met many female schoolteachers, who were upgrading their diplomas into degrees, and almost all used to complain about their ghastly experiences of working in industry. By chance I was in London on D-Day and the atmosphere was electric, with flight after flight of bombers and fighters going overhead, flying east to support the landings. So the *Evening Standard* got the news out first before the daily papers, since there was no way of suppressing that event, which had been anticipated for some time.

The doodlebugs did an enormous amount of lateral damage, particularly if they landed in dense streets of council houses, which would simply be flattened. The nearest that we had one was about 300 yards down the lane; it took out the clubhouse of the West Kent golf course. Once again it was clear that Bickley Hall should never have kept the boys there, even in the cellars, since the windows and wall plaster were regularly blown out or shaken down. Still, it provided me with a job while kicking my heels, to cycle over and help with the clean-up. I was going up St George's Road one day when a V1 cut out overhead, so I nipped over a wall and landed between a couple of gravestones in the churchyard. I felt pretty stupid, and with the rest of the population soon learned that when they cut out, they then had some distance to glide before landing.

In July the school had its annual open day with a cricket match between the two houses, and many old boys turned up, several from my year. Four years is a long time at that age, particularly when one has had such varied experiences compared to the others that had stayed put. I was talking to another boy about it, whose parents were tea planters in Assam, and he explained, 'Well, of course, you're on a different wavelength to them by now,' and it has never really gone away. I believe that the French have a term for it: 'an escaped Englishman'.

By August, the Navy decided it needed me and the rest of a motley crew, who turned up at a London station for the north, complete with our rail warrants and minimum bundles of clothes, which were soon to be replaced with uniforms, which because the jumpers were tight more or less fitted, whereas Army uniforms tended to fit where they touched. Our destination was Butlin's holiday camp, on the east coast of Lincolnshire at Skegness overlooking the Wash. If this was a holiday resort, I thought, then

I'm a Zulu. The camp of chalets and the central blocks for feeding and entertainment looked out on to a grey, cold North Sea even in summer. The beach was deserted apart from anti-tank obstacles and rolls and rolls of barbed wire. The nearest town, Skegness, a bus ride away, was a dump. Reality did not so much set in as land with a thud. The master-at-arms, one Dusty Miller (all Millers were called Dusty for some reason) told us on every occasion possible, which was at least daily, that he was a bastard and that he was the only sane man in the RN, since he had had a spell in the loony bin, and now had a certificate of sanity. We believed the first part of his claim, but not the latter.

Each chalet had three bunks, and I shared one with a chap called Jim Wall, who came from near Canterbury, and another fellow. In the next chalet there was a young Welsh lad of barely eighteen, who came from a mining family, sharing a bed with his brothers top to toe, and who was away from home for the first time in his life. Poor little sod, the first night he howled, 'I want my mam, I want my mam,' while the occupants of the neighbouring chalets yelled to him to shut up. This went on for two more nights, until a group of us sleepless ones went to the petty officer and told him he would never make it, and should be returned as a Bevin boy in the mines. So the RN did the right thing. There was another chap called John Inch, who was 6'4" and wore size-fourteen footwear. There were no boots of that size in stock, so since the first few weeks were more or less perpetual square bashing; he used to go through a pair of shoes every ten days or so. At the end of our basic training when we were allocated to various branches of the service, he was assigned to submarines. Clearly the drafters of such orders took more notice of his name than his height.

Although we were tested for sight and fitness before being called up, I had not faced the system of Japanese dots of various colours and numbers that were used to test colour vision. To my surprise I was graded down for colour vision, since I could not tell the difference between purple and navigational green, or something like that, and there was absolutely no way of flannelling one's way through those dots with inspired guesses. You either recognised the concealed numbers, or you did not. So I was given

Chatham barracks as my home base, from where I was sent off to various places to be trained as a gunner, destined never to hear a shot fired in anger. The barracks had been built in the Napoleonic Wars, when the south-east of Britain faced a direct threat from the French just across the Channel. It is easy to criticise them under wartime conditions, when they were grossly overcrowded, but they must have been well built since within the past ten years since the barracks were closed down, the buildings have been refurbished and taken over by the University of Greenwich.

The first challenge to be mastered after the bunks of Butlin's was how to sling and get into a hammock without falling straight over the other side, as pongoes (soldiers) did to our huge delight when we returned from India by troopship. Then there were the officers' 'rounds' with the petty officer bellowing, 'Stand by yer 'ammicks,' a call that had come down from Nelson's day, now made redundant by bunks. There was also the naval store called 'slops' for some unfathomable reason, where apart from our normal needs of new socks, underwear and so on it was possible to buy items like Bronnleys and Pears soap, which could not be had for love nor money in the retail shops like Boots. Thus I was a welcome visitor to the West Kent Hotel just up the road with my spoils.

Chatham had its own gunnery school for anti-aircraft guns like Oerlikons and Bofors, and medium naval guns up to six inches. But for the big stuff – that is, fifteen inches, as on battleships we were sent to Portsmouth or 'Pompey', where the old HMS *Queen Elizabeth* was laid up. To this was added a spell at Whale Island, which once experienced was never forgotten, since everything was made to go at the double. It was a good way to get ex-schoolboys fit, however. It seemed that we were not really needed for the war at that time since our batch was sent on a Royal Marine Commando course, not something directly applicable to life on board a ship. This took place at Sheerness on the Isle of Sheppey, at the point where the Medway River from Chatham flows into the Thames estuary. Environmentally, that was the low point. Sheerness in the depths of the winter of 1945 made the strand at Skegness appear like the Promenade des Anglais at Nice. It had absolutely nothing to recommend it, and the few people living there looked utterly depressed. However, the course was amusing for fit young men, sliding along steel wires with one leg hanging down and the other foot tucked into one's bottom for balance, slithering under nets or through drainage pipes while petty officers threw whizz-bangs at us and climbing up wooden walls as now shown on TV programmes. The military habits do not change much. The trouble was that we were not all fit young men. One twenty-eight-year-old with a brewer's belly had a hernia about the size of a tangerine, so was excused the heavy stuff. But the daddy of our group was a Yorkshire man of thirty-two, which to us was *old*, called Darrah, inevitably known as 'Pop' Darrah. We had lectures on stripping Bren guns and priming hand grenades after a reasonable lunch. At one such session the instructor imagined that we were in a trench, had taken the pin out of the grenade, thrown it only to see it hit the top of the parapet and bounce back to our feet. Looking in the direction of the somnolent Pop, the instructor asked, 'And what would you do then, Darrah?' Pop's survival instincts took over and, opening his eyes, he replied, 'What would Ah do? Why, the hoondred yards in five seconds!'

In due course we were told that we were going to be drafted to our ships, and were issued with long, greased woollen underwear suitable for Arctic conditions. Because of one's exposure to others who had seen it all before, it did not take long for new hands to become cynical. Clearly the issue of such kit indicated to us that we were not destined for Russian convoys, but rather for sunnier climes such as the Mediterranean. After all, why else would the idiots who ruled our lives issue us with gear that was going to fill up at least the bottom third of our kitbags, making it difficult to fit the D clasp through the holes at the top, when all the correct tropical kit was added to it? It was obvious. So vastly relieved, we clutched our one-week embarkation leave passes and set off to enjoy ourselves.

Tim, Dorothy and I, with the Farnfields, and the Holdsworth parents through whom I had been introduced to the school in the first place, all trooped down by train to Rock on the north Cornish coast opposite Padstow, and near Polzeath. The Holdsworths had tragically lost two sons in the RAF during the

Battle of Britain, and when our parents returned from leave to India, they took over Tim for his holidays, together with the ever-reliable Claud. I visited Rock again in March 2001, and it is one of these places that simply do not change in appearance, since it must be protected from development. In the summer it is now the destination for the Hooray Henrys and the female equivalents. It was always known for the secretive St Enodoc church set in the middle of a quirky golf course, where one has to shoot blind over sand dunes on several holes. Since then it has become even better known as the resting place for the late John Betjeman. Tishy arrived back on the last day of my leave with one thing on his mind, English bitter, which he used to crave for in India. By this time the alcohol content had been reduced to 2% so one had to drink a fair amount to receive any effect. English expatriates have some odd dietary cravings, including Marmite, lamb chops and baked beans.

So it was back to the barracks to prepare for the draft to an even larger and warmer destination than we had thought, namely the width of the Pacific. My parents came to Chatham to take me out for a meal, but we were confined by that time in case anyone decided to go AWOL, and we communicated for five minutes or so through the iron bars of the gate in the stilted manner of such partings. Our troopship, the SS *Argentina*, awaited us at Southampton, bound for New York. There were 250 of us and thousands of American soldiers, all hot-bedding, so there were twice as many on board as the number of bunks. We were accommodated several decks down with only a two-width ladder with a bar down the centre to exit by, but happily by this time the U-boats had been defeated. The American soldiers consisted of men from the 82nd Airborne Division and others, who had been taken prisoner in the Battle of the Bulge in Belgium in 1944, and had then been recaptured by the Allied advance into Germany. The Airborne treated the rest with scorn and would not mix with them at all. Since the *Argentina* had been an American liner, it had all the facilities, and the Airborne lot occupied the first-class dining saloon and lounges, and played poker or craps on the grand stairs all down from the boat deck. It was a Runyonesque scene of that permanently floating craps game. Nor did they shave from one end of the voyage to the other, which must have taken about one week, since we still followed a zigzag course.

This was our introduction to the American forces standard of living via the so-called 'chow line', where plentiful portions were dolloped on to aluminium trays with scalloped sections. One thing the RN taught its men was how to keep clean and tidy in small spaces. We more or less lived on the upper deck since it was early May 1945, and the kitchens had large empty wooden tubs that had stored marmalade. These became prized items for doing our dhobi-ing at the various steam jets. That sort of basic training comes in useful. In 1986, Lene and I went on a week's camel safari on the Laikipia plateau in Kenya, following the Uaso Nyiro river course. When we returned to the base camp, whose rondavels were next to pools in the river free of crocs, we were pretty mucky. So I took my dirty clothes and a bar of soap down to wash them out. As I was crouching on the bank, a Scottish barrister in the party approached Lene to ask what I was doing. 'He's washing his smalls, of course,' she replied.

'I don't believe it!' he said. A precious lot, lawyers.

Our arrival in New York was spectacular, sailing up the Hudson River to Pier 92 at 5.30 a.m., with Manhattan partly lit up since the blackout had more or less been lifted by that time. We were not allowed to disembark at once, but in the meantime an Army band entertained us with 'Rum and Coca-Cola' and 'One Meatball Without the Gravy'. Clearly the Americans took a more relaxed attitude towards martial music.

A couple of days after we arrived, VE Day was declared, with all its celebrations. I went down to have a look at Madison Square Gardens to see where Joe Louis and others had fought, and went up to the bar and asked for a beer. Taking out my fancy Egyptian purse with the usual decorations, I put it on the counter to count out the money and the next second it was gone. Lesson number one: don't ever take your hand off your wallet. Since New York was no place to be skint in, and at any rate we were only paid 7s per day, I called collect Everett Rankin, a friend of my parents working for Standard Oil in Calcutta in 1940, now living in upper New York state. He put me on to some friends called Smith, who took me out and showed me the sights. There was also another way that British sailors found to supplement their pay, and that was to donate blood at one of the centres. I think the going rate was $5 per pint, and a cup of tea afterwards. There were stories of matelots returning and saying, 'Bleed me dry,' but no doubt they were apocryphal.

After about four days in a really plush barracks in Pier 92 we entrained in Pullman carriages with bunks and day seats for the three days and nights' journey across the continent to Vancouver. When the German war ended, Canadian servicemen were given the option of staying in, or being demobbed. Unsurprisingly, most of them elected to take the latter course. A series of repair and maintenance ships were being built in the yards on Victoria Island for the British Pacific Fleet Train, to meet Churchill's wish that we would be in at the end of the Far East war to recover our colonies such as Hong Kong. There were three memorable sights from that journey. The tracks went through the south side of Chicago, where the poor black people lived, and on virtually every modest house porch there was a massive refrigerator or other electrical appliance, due to lack of space, much like some of the English now keep their freezers and God knows what else in the garage, and their cars in the drive. Secondly, as the route swung north, we went through the Badlands of North Dakota, miles of nothing in May, and no doubt fit for nothing in the winter. Then once we entered the Rockies we added an engine and became a so-called 'double header', stopping every so often at a 'halt' to take on water, where the local Canadians came out to greet what was clearly the big event of the day. Thus we arrived in Vancouver, en route for the barracks, HMCS Esquimalt, on Victoria Island, which along with Maritzburg claims to be the last outpost of the British Empire, since many Indian and Malayan colonials retired thereto.

We were not the first draft of British sailors into Esquimalt, but the second. A series of ships were being built, upmarket Liberty ships, with holds fore and aft surrounded by derricks, and engineering and electrical workshops below for servicing small ships such as mine sweepers or sloops. Our ship was the *Flamborough Head*, followed by the *Berry Head*, *Raine Head*, *Mull of Galloway* and some others, each powered by a single screw that enabled them to steam at a maximum of nine knots, which would be far behind the main fleet. Since they only had twelve 20 mm Oerlikon guns for protection against Japanese attacks, that was probably just as well.

Before we were allowed 'ashore' from the barracks for the first time, we were paraded and received a warning on behaviour from the commander. In the past week there had been fights between British and Canadian sailors, and the genteel inhabitants of Victoria had complained. If it happened again we would be stopped from taking shore leave. Such a repeat occurrence seemed very unlikely to us, who were mainly eighteen-year-olds, and Canadians on the whole were bigger, and the main desire seemed to be to tuck into as many banana splits – those confections of ice cream, cream and fruit – as affordable, since most had grown up without access to such goodies. Nevertheless to our surprise we were paraded the next day and read the riot act by the commander, and leave was stopped. In the end the culprits were tracked down, a group of Newfoundlanders, or Newfies. They were primitive fisher folk, and I mean *primitive*, who had made their livings off the fishing banks of Labrador and Greenland. Newfoundland at that time was still a Crown Colony, so its men were on British rather than Canadian rates of pay, and they did not like it one bit, and vented their frustrations in the town. Since then Newfoundland has joined the Canadian Confederation and tied its currency to the Canadian dollar, so it has been priced out of its fishing markets by Icelanders, who resorted to a series of devaluations.

It must have been about the end of May when we set sail for the South Pacific, but within a couple of days had to put into San Francisco with minor engine trouble, enough to keep us there for a couple of days. As it happened, that coincided with the opening of the United Nations at the Opera House, whose steps flew the national flags of all the countries that were joining. Once again we were paraded, issued with white belts and gaiters and as many rifles as could be mustered, and given another inspirational address, this time from a rear admiral, who advised us that as the only crew of a British ship in San Francisco at that moment we represented the Empire and had to put on a show of marching to match, which since we were mostly newly trained, we probably did. I have a black-and-white photo taken with a Brownie camera to record that historic occasion.

The Americans were their usual hospitable selves – not so much the civilians as the US Navy sailors, who showed us the main sights since the naval yards were some way from the city. That evening they took a few of us to a bar near Union Square for a drink. There was nothing special about the bar except there was a huge rough-looking type sitting at one end of it, muttering away. Before I had finished the first glass a studious-looking American sailor with glasses told me to drink up. When I protested that I had not finished and it was my turn to buy a round, he just told me to drink up fast, and we were propelled out by our respective elbows. 'Did you see that big guy along the bar?' asked our host. 'He was beginning to mutter about "goddamn Limeys", and you would not have stood a chance.' He was right. Before dawn several of our crew turned up with cuts, bruises and black eyes, as though the boot had been put in. The general opinion of the older hands was that they had probably asked for it, being either Glaswegians or Liverpudlians, whose idea of a good run ashore was to get absolutely sloshed and then go around looking for a fight to the raucous tune of 'We are the boys of the bulldog breed'. Hence, lesson number two: never go ashore with the young citizens of those two great cities.

Our voyage across the vast Pacific was at a stately pace, without a sign of any other ship or anything remotely connected with the war. It was soon clear that the latter was the best thing that had happened to the whale population for many years, since all hunting was curtailed and they were forever surfacing and blowing their tops. Dolphins too, attached themselves to our ship, and there was a favoured position to watch them, sitting on the flange around the bows protected with a guard rail just below the jack stay, where dolphins could be seen through the hawse pipe surfing on our bow wave, rolling over to look up at us. We were all sure that some of them winked back. After several days we arrived at Hawaii and were taken out to an idyllic R and R camp on a beach several miles outside Honolulu, which was off-limits to us to avoid the usual inter-allied fights! Nevertheless, we were bussed into the US Naval yard to see the damage inflicted by the attack of 8 December 1941, while an aircraft carrier called the *Hornet* had its starboard flight deck folded down like the page of a book, the effect of a massive wave in a Pacific storm.

From Honolulu we set off again for our final destination, Manus or Admiralty Island, an archetypal South Sea island base just north of New Guinea, complete with coral reef protecting the harbour from sharks and other such nasties. Somewhere along that leg I celebrated my nineteenth birthday and learned lesson number three, that is, to sling one's hammock before rather than after accepting the traditional offer of 'sippers' of dark Jamaican rum from all the other members of a mess of twelve, to wake up a couple of hours later with a thick head. For good turns above average, such as standing in for a mate on watch who wanted to go ashore out of his turn, the reward would be 'gulpers', but in that case only from one tot. That tradition of the daily rum ration has of course has now been ended, and it is probably just as well since there were always those who used to accumulate the daily tots in a bottle, and then go on a bender.

Frankly, most of us had not the faintest idea where we were. There were no islanders, just the RN and Australian navy mine sweepers in this huge lagoon. We then got down to do what we were designed for, namely repair and maintenance, and I found myself assigned below decks to the engineering workshops, full of large lumps of metal with wheels on the sides. These turned out to be lathes, which were quite new to my experience, and I was told by the artificer in charge that my job was to keep the trays clean by sweeping out the metal filings that came off whatever was being turned. It would be an exaggeration to say that this occupied me for more than five minutes in every hour and I told the petty officer in charge that I was going to look for another job. He thought I was mad to renounce such a cushy number, but I got the job of fleet postman. This involved setting off in the morning in a motor launch with a helmsman and a stoker to pick up the home mail from all the ships and take it to the large depot ship, HMS *Maidstone*. The ships varied from the fleet carriers such as the *Indefatigable*, to the mine sweepers and small merchant ships. There was one small water tanker, a rust bucket with a very low freeboard, manned by an older English captain and a black crew, presumably Pacific islanders. Whenever we came alongside, which was often, since he must have been a prolific letter writer, the skipper would be sitting in his wheelhouse in a dirty singlet, hunched over a book borrowed from the *Maidstone*. There must have been thousands of those old vessels in our merchant marine, limping around the sea lanes of the world in those days.

In the late afternoon we had to make the run in reverse and delivered letters collected from the *Maidstone*. Since our little crew were all of a similar disposition towards sun and swimming, we used to spend the meantime on a small lump of coral with a wooden glass-bottomed box, which the chippie had made up for us, to look at the wonderful variety of tropical fish. We also discovered that the Australians had beer on board in place of rum, which they would sell to us, and we arranged to play water polo with them between the booms let out from the ships' sides. They always beat us of course, but it was worth the swim across to float back afterwards to our ship with the internal and external liquid content of our bodies more or less in equilibrium. All this was a far cry from the death and destruction that was going on far to the north off the islands such as Okinawa, and we had no doubt that we were favoured members of what was generally referred to in the 'Andrew' as 'Harry Tate's Navy'. Who Harry Tate was I know not, but nowadays folk pay thousands of pounds to experience such a lotus-eating life as we did, courtesy of King George VI, God bless his memory.

In the middle of August came the news of the bomb, which was completely beyond our comprehension. We were all relieved that the fighting was over and the older ones, many married, wondered what sort of a world they would be bringing their children into. There was absolutely no thought of sympathy for the Japanese, and the next item of conversation to occupy the mess decks was talk of the coming general election. Words that I had hardly heard of before were hotly discussed: trade unions, Labour and Tories (the latter usually proceeded by a derogatory adjective). It would not have taken a sophisticated pollster to discover which way it was going to turn out as we sailed for Hong Kong, threading our way through the pattern of islands that make up Indonesia and the Philippines, experiencing a typhoon on the way that shook most of the crockery out of the shelves and anything else that was not lashed down, and sorted the men from the boys when it came to sea sickness, and even courage. There was one fairly tough, bullyboy character down on his knees calling on his mother and praying to 'holy mother of God'. We had no trouble with him after that performance. For some reason, rough seas always stimulated my appetite and I cleaned up on several portions.

As we entered Hong Kong harbour early in September, the skipper, who was a nice old commander brought out of retirement by the war, came on the Tannoy and addressed the crew. We would find the place a mess, the people would be starving, and we had to look after the British and Canadian POWs because of the Japanese occupation, the local girls would be rife with VD, so think of your wives, your sweethearts and your mothers back home, and avoid contact with them. The town certainly was a mess, with all the houses up the Peak stripped bare of wood and anything else that would burn. The majority of Japanese just surrendered because their emperor told them to do so, but there was a group of about a dozen Koreans who took to the Peak and refused. Rather than risking lives to go after them, the decision was taken to leave them until hunger drove them down, or until they held a grenade to their stomachs and removed the pin.

Our stay in Hong Kong for about two months allowed us to observe the differences between our various types of officers, which included old-style RN, wartime RNVR (Royal Navy Volunteer Reserve) and ex-merchant marine RNR (Royal Navy Reserve), the latter due to our ship having holds and derricks to handle. On the way up the First Lieutenant, a regular two and a half ringer had shown signs of stress, screaming at the seamen as if we were still recruited from 'the scum of the earth.' The arrival of the British Pacific Fleet in harbour after sixty days at sea sent him further over the top, and for two consecutive nights he called out the little high-speed motor launch called a 'skimming dish', and toured the fleet, hurling abuse at the rest of the ships and questioning the parentage of their officers. On the third day, two men in white coats came aboard and took him ashore, to be replaced with a prince of a regular RN officer. But on the whole the RNR were the best – better seamen, with a more easy and hands-on control of the crew members by force of example, rather than force of old-fashioned discipline.

The crews of the fleet ships, when they arrived later, went on a monumental bender, mainly on rice wine since beer was lacking, and each evening a fleet of rickshaws brought the prone bodies of matelots back to Queen's Pier where the ferries came in from Kowloon, tipped their bundles out of the back, put their caps under their heads, and headed back for the next. Each night the duty part of the watch had to go ashore in the liberty boats, identify their shipmates and bring these inert bundles back on board. The first time you carried them up the gangway by both their arms and legs; repeat offenders were just dragged up by their arms to feel it in their backs the next day. The Americans were much better organised, sending out men to tack up signs directing their sailors to 'prophylactic stations' on the basis that prevention is better than cure. However, the town soon began to recover.

I had a mate, one Bill 'Ginger' Matthews from Suffolk, whose father was an estate manager near Horsham in Sussex for a Lady Loder. We both felt the need to stretch our legs and get away from the confinement of the crowded mess deck, so used to climb up over the peak, since the cable railway had not been repaired, and drop down to the empty countryside around the reservoirs on the other side. The Chinese are a resilient, commercial race of people, and by their New Year the balconies of their houses were decorated with lanterns and streamers. After nightfall the crackers began exploding in one long staccato burst of noise. They also put on a pantomime in the local theatre with exaggerated characters swaying around the stage on stilts, which reduced the locals to screams of mirth.

But it has to be said that the overriding interest of most of the sailors was when their call-up group number was going to be announced for repatriation to Blighty. For us who had barely joined it was an academic subject, but the rest of the ships started to fly their 'paying-off pennants' as they steamed out of harbour, bound for the UK. Before leaving they would keep a naval tradition of 'ditching their skates' (offloading their hardest cases) on to any unsuspecting ship. Thus at one stage I found myself in No. 11 mess, where all the other sailors had done time in a civil or military prison, better known as a 'glass house'. The next mess was No. 13, also known as 'Rose Cottage', reserved for those suffering from VD, despite all the awful warnings and ghastly pictures we had been shown of diseased members dropping off. One evening my other eleven mates began to discuss the relative merits and demerits of establishments such as 'the Scrubs' or Maidstone and Colchester gaols. They were a bunch of thieves. Whatever they wanted they filched – booze from the wardroom, better food from the petty officers' mess, clothing from the mess decks. During a lull in this fascinating conversation I pointed out to them that my locker was just over there, it contained a nice new tropical No. 1 suit that I had had made up by a tailor in Hong Kong at relatively vast expense, as well as a new pair of shoes and the black silk worn round the neck in mourning for Nelson, that ever-present memory in the RN. To pick my padlock in the middle of the night would be a second's work for most of them, so I asked diffidently where I stood in their scheme of things. A look of genuine alarm that I should harbour such an evil thought spread across their faces, and the bloke next to me put his arm around my shoulders and said, 'Don't you worry, lad, you're one of us!' Compliments don't come any greater than that!

The hardest nut that I ever met was a Glaswegian called Fluker, who had grown up in a violent household where his father beat up his mother, until the son chucked him out of the house. Fluker had made a living totting (salvaging) coal from slag heaps and taking on all comers in boxing booths, and communicated in a series of glottal stops and grunts. One evening when he was cook of the mess on his own, his oppo (opposite number) having gone ashore, Fluker was elbow deep in water full of greasy plates and cutlery and the minimum of soap, so I gave him a hand and got to talk to him about himself. After we set sail I was the helmsman on the bridge, and Fluker would appear in the middle watch with a steaming mug of 'chai' or drinking cocoa that he would plonk down on a ledge grunting, 'That's for you, mate,' and leave. In the end I had to tell him that he needed sleep between 12–4 a.m.; more than I needed a scalding hot drink in that climate.

Some days after we had put to sea I was coming off watch and going down to the mess deck by a metal stairway when I heard an almighty row taking place. Someone must have insulted Fluker, or been sarcastic about him, since he had literally gone berserk, and was being held by two leading seamen in a reverse elbow lock on either arm. He was roaring that he would 'fight every effing bastud in the effing mess one by one' at which point he looked up, seeing me through the red mist of his rage, and added the unforgettable words 'except him!' About eighteen months later I was in a destroyer escort at Portland, where we had a semi-professional ex-boxer on board, who used to regale us with his past fights, and he mentioned that the only man that he could not put down for keeps was a Scot about three stone lighter, who kept bouncing back. 'I suppose you're referring to Fluker,' I told him, and he looked at me in stunned amazement when I explained that he was one of my old oppoes. For most of us coming from sheltered backgrounds where we only met our own kind in boarding schools, these years were a necessary part of the University of Life to learn how the other half lived, and in some cases it was not a pretty way.

By the middle of December we were told that we were to sail for Australia to spend Christmas in Sydney. I immediately got out my address book and sent off a letter to Grandpa Sam in New Zealand, telling him the good news. By this time the Newfies, those sons of the sea, had colonised the cushiest, if warmest, job in the ship, which was to operate the laundry. The one thing we lacked was fresh food, having lived on canned meat, eggs pickled in brine and canned vegetables for about six months, since Hong Kong had not enough fresh greens to go round. The largest Newfie, a great bear of a man, covered with hair, would go up to the galley and persuade the Chinese cook to fish some large ox bones out of the soup tureen. These would then be spread out on a piece of oiled cloth on their mess table, while they smashed them open with marlin spikes or hammers, and then got down to sucking out the marrow. They were cavemen really. Our skipper set a leisurely course and said that we would drop into some interesting places. By this time we new sailors had done our six months' sea time to become able seamen, so I was the quarter-master on the bridge. First port of call was the Halmahera, or Spice Islands, of which Ternate was one of the larger ones. These had been the scene of fierce competition during the seventeenth century between the Dutch and English East India companies for the spice trade, particularly nutmeg, ending in the Amboyna Massacre, but not before the English had transferred some nutmeg seeds or bushes to Ceylon and collared the trade (I suggest reading *Nathaniel's Nutmeg* by Giles Milton). We steamed slowly into a long inlet girt with the typical rows of palm trees bowing down to the water's edge. For some while nothing happened, but when the islanders decided that we were not Japanese, a couple of catamarans, swiftly followed by others, put out from the shore and paddled over laden with tropical fruit to trade for singlets, pants and so on from 'slops'. It was straight out of Joseph Conrad. We even had an ambitious stoker, who got hold of a parakeet and put it in a wooded cage, intending to be Long John Silver when he got home, but the bird escaped and found an open porthole.

The captain's next bright idea was to steam down the inner passage of the Great Barrier Reef off Queensland, keeping a lookout for reefs. At night we would anchor and dangle the fog light, made of multiple electric bulbs in a reflector, over the stern to attract fish to catch. In the early hours of the morning the duty part of the watch would be roused to raise the anchor by walking round the capstan bars. This was much quieter than putting on steam and waking the rest of the crew! At Whitsunday Island, now a holiday resort, but then deserted, three parts of the watch went ashore in motor boats, whalers and Carley floats with a supply of food and lime juice, and played cricket on the beach. How any of us ever got back to serious life after that 'cruise' I will never know.

After a short visit to Brisbane, sailing up whatever the river is called there, we arrived in Sydney just before Christmas, a city more or less out of electricity since the coal miners in Newcastle were on strike. However, the pubs were open but only between 5–6 p.m., the so-called 'five o'clock swill'. Since beer and spirits were rationed at around ten to six, whatever was left was poured into one large vessel and served out. This was known as 'Plonk', since when the drinkers went out into the fresh air, many just went plonk, or clung to the nearest lamppost. The Aussie sailors were not particularly welcoming and referred to us as 'kippers' – that is, no guts and two-faced. This was probably as a result of the debacle at Singapore in early 1942, when everyone blamed everyone else for taking to the ships, women and children last, and also because our Navy could handle the German and Italian fleets combined, but not the Japanese. Therefore the Australians felt deserted by their 'mother' country.

Sydney was the first place where I went to the ballet, but not the last. Robert Helpman was the leading male dancer in, I think, *Swan Lake*. Forty-five years later I heard a story about him that had a double punchline. A speaker came to our local Probus Club in Beaconsfield to talk about his rural business of making walking sticks. The man giving the vote of thanks said that his favourite story on that subject related to Robert Helpman, who was playing in New York in the 1950s. One day he was walking down Fifth Avenue in the manner of male ballet dancers, clutching an alpaca cane topped with mother of pearl, when the point got jammed in one of the gratings in the sidewalk. Helpman tried to free it, but it was jammed. He made a further abortive attempt, before shrugging his shoulders and continuing on his way. He had gone but a few steps when he felt a tap on his shoulder from behind, where a large New York policeman stood holding his stick. 'Say, fairy,' drawled the policeman, 'ya lost yer wand.' Completely unfazed, Helpman took it from him, stepped back a pace, waved the stick across the policeman's face and instructed him to 'disappear'! Too bad political correctness has put an end to such exchanges.

Awaiting me in Sydney was a letter from Grandpa Sam, sounding as exited as a schoolboy at the thought of seeing a grandchild for the first time, and encouraging me to buy my way out of the Navy and join him in New Zealand, a young country where I would be getting in on the ground floor, saying he would help me get a start. Having experienced contact with three of the Dominions by this time, where life seemed to be a lot more free and easy than in the so-called mother country, and being more than semi-detached from my family, I thought it was an idea worth considering, and wrote to my parents in Calcutta accordingly. The next thing that I knew was that I was hauled up before Jimmy the One, a really decent chap. Left right, left right, halt, off cap, stand to attention! He asked me what it was all about and I told him, whereupon he advised me that since I was under twenty-one years old he was *in loco parentis*, and my parents had advised by cable that under no circumstances was I to be allowed to join my grandpa. So that was that, no reason given. However, he said that I could have two weeks' compassionate leave to see my parents and sort things out, provided I paid my own way, when we passed India on the way back to the UK.

Our skipper still had not finished with his personal tour of Indonesia and the Pacific islands. In retrospect I think that as he was about to retire for the second time, he was determined to enjoy himself as much as possible at the Admiralty's expense, so after leaving Australia we put into Kupang in the island of Timor. I did not get ashore but the captain came aboard with the young wife of a Dutch colonial officer, from whom she had become separated, and who was now on the island of Sumbawa, just north-east of Bali. This was, of course, strictly against King's Regulations and Admiralty Instructions (KR and AIs) and he turned the navigating officer, Lieut. P RNR out of his cabin for the use of the lady in question. Lieut. P was incensed, questioned the captain's motives, said that it was unlucky to have a woman on board, and refused to navigate. Stalemate, since he could have thrown the book at the skipper. To reach Sumbawa we had to sail through the Lombok Straits where there is a mountain on Lombok full of iron, which rendered our old-fashioned magnetic compass useless. Consequently we navigated that passage with the skipper taking bearings on various points on the chart, and with me at the helm steering according to his instructions. It took about two days to reach there, during which time the sailors working on the boat deck were told that if they did not watch their language they would be put on a charge, which effectively rendered the majority both speechless and frustrated. Our arrival was again out of Conrad, steaming into a large semicircular bay girt with palm trees, and the water hidden under a series of tropical rainstorms, which came and went in rapid succession. Out of this appeared a Japanese landing barge, built a bit like a pagoda with high bow and stern. When it came near, a tall European in a cape and peaked hat left the wheelhouse and walked to the bows as they lifted on the swell. Our passenger recognised him and started to jump up and down shouting, 'Dickie, Dickie!' whereupon 200-odd male voices endorsed her plea, 'For Christ's sake come and get her, Dickie.'

On arrival in Singapore towards the end of January 1946 I went to the RAF station to see if I could get a ride to Calcutta, but no joy. We then went on to Penang, a lovely old colonial town, where they could have given me a lift to Rangoon, but no further, and that held too much of a risk of being stranded. I wrote somewhat despondently to my parents. On arrival at Colombo a regulating petty officer came aboard with a chit to take me ashore. My father had contacted both the RN and Shell, and the deed was done. All my mates wished me luck and gave me a good send-off, including Fluker, who insisted on carrying my kitbag down the gangway to the launch. Embarrassing but touching. The general manager of Shell lent me 600 rupees for the fare, but a friendly draft PO told me to keep it and added my name to a list going north to Calcutta, breaking the journey in Madras, where I was told I could stay with the Johnstones, with whose sons Tim and I had gone to India on the SS *Strathmore* in 1940. Madras station was full of sailors and RAF personnel on our arrival, with just one Sikh driver standing by a large, black Wolseley 18. It just had that look of Burmah Shell about it, so I slid over and asked the driver if he was waiting for Orchard sahib, as we were called in those days. When he confirmed he was, I grabbed my kitbag and hammock and moved off as surreptitiously as I could, when a flight lieutenant approached and asked, 'Is this your car, old boy?' I have always had an innate suspicion of people addressing me as 'old boy', feeling that they are usually after a favour, so I mumbled back, 'Not really.'

'Well, if you have the use of it old boy, do you think you could give me a lift to somewhere or other, old boy?' By this time I just wanted to get away before I was spotted by the other matelots, so I told him to stuff his case inside and jump in, and off we went.

Tishy greeted me enthusiastically at Howrah Station in Calcutta a few days later. At dinner that first evening I asked what it was with Grandpa Sam that made him an apparent pariah. When I heard about his days in Kenya and his hasty departure over the ivory smuggling incident, I thought he must have been quite a character, but apparently he suffered from regrets during his last days in New Zealand, and his wife predeceased him. My elder son and nephew have since both visited the gravestone for him and his wife at Whangerei, north of Auckland. I went the rounds of Calcutta to see who was left from the New School lot. Most had dispersed by then, some to the Army in Burma, which had been pretty traumatic, but I met John Lethbridge, who turned up in Beaconsfield with his family fifteen years later.

A very considerate Naval PO in Fort William, who was to sign me in for two weeks' leave, told me to come back in four days or so and start then. All along the line I could not have asked for more from the RN, even if there was also an element of God helps those, who help themselves. Calcutta had not changed all that much in the meantime, and though independence was getting closer, the social life for which Calcutta was famed went on. With the arrival of the Attlee government they had a new Governor of Bengal, to replace the somewhat upper-crust Australian (if that is not an oxymoron) called Casey. The new one was Sir Fred Burrows, and he came up through the railway trade union ranks in the Labour party. As usual, the British memsahibs were breaking their necks to get invitations to Government House by putting their visiting cards through the letterbox, and to his credit Fred Burrows introduced himself by saying that they would find him different to his predecessor, who was a huntin', shootin' and fishin' man, while was an ex-shunting, tooting and hitching man. It went down well.

After my leave I joined a troop train for the three days and nights' rail journey to Bombay, all of the others being RAF ground staff returning from Thailand. Unfortunately for them we travelled coolie class, which meant wooden slatted seats; these can get pretty uncomfortable unless you have a hammock to sling between window frames at night. I headed for a naval barracks, where I experienced what one reads about but never quite believes – that is, successive squads going round whitewashing the ropes and stones, to be followed by others dirtying them. Got to keep the men busy, you know, else God knows what they will get up to! I was fortunate to have an introduction to an English couple, where the husband was the general manager of Castrol Oil, and also very hospitable. Bombay had what I think was the only integrated, non-racial club in any of the larger Indian cities, the Willingdon, named after a previous viceroy of more enlightened views than the average. The old Aga Khan, all twenty-two stones of him, father of Aly, was going to be weighed against rough diamonds to raise money for the members of the excellent Ishmaili community. It was a glittering party with all the Indian women wearing their sarees of Benares silk fluttering in the breeze from the sea, like swarms of spectacular butterflies. My new No. 1 suit from Hong Kong really came in useful that evening.

When it was over my hosts returned to their home and then sent me back to the barracks in their company regulation black Wolseley car. As we approached the barrack gates I had an awful premonition of acute danger, and tried to get the driver to pull up short and let me out, calling on him '*aste, aste*' (slowly, slowly) the only appropriate Hindi word that I could recall in lieu of 'stop'. The driver could not understand my wishes to stop short, so we rolled up to the gate. The barrack Commander had also been out that night, in his black Wolseley 18, and the sentry, seeing our approach, called out the guard. I stepped out like a field mouse surrounded by tomcats. I did not notice whether they saluted me, presented arms or whatever, but I just walked fast and straight away from the gate. I had got about fifteen yards when a heap of the most furious blasphemy landed slap between my shoulder blades. 'Who the [something, something] do you think you are? Name, rank and number, you horrible, horrible sailor! You'll be on a charge before the Commander first thing in the morning. Now go and don't let me see your feet touch the ground.' Needless to say, I went as instructed, possibly even faster. In the morning the Commander looked at me quizzically. 'Able Seaman Orchard, I understand that you've been trying to impersonate me?' he asked.

'Purely by accident,' I assured him, and then, before he could inquire further, produced my chit concerning compassionate leave and said I had to get back to the UK to sort things out while my parents were still in India. That did the trick; he said that he would get me on to a troopship, while the PO looked disgusted. I avoided the latter for the rest of my stay.

We came back on a liner called *Britannic*, soldiers and sailors all mixed together among the troop decks. About the only thing I remember about that trip was that a sailor would belt out 'Jerusalem' at the slightest encouragement, at the full extent of his lungs at supper each evening, while the evening entertainment was watching soldiers or 'brown jobs' trying to get into the hammocks! Our arrival in Liverpool in April 1946, sailing up the Mersey, past row upon row of back-to-back red-brick houses of the Bootle slums, was not exactly the 'land fit for heroes' that many of us imagined. Liverpool had taken quite a battering since I was last there in August 1940, and I made a mental note never to go there again. However, one feature was the same – the cheerful, friendly Salvation Army girls who would appear out of nowhere, day or night, to provide char and wads to troop trains, at whichever station they halted. After leave with Tommy and Claud in Yorkshire, I came down to earth with a bump with a three-month stay in Chatham barracks, full of sailors going nowhere, with ships being decommissioned, where the trick was to walk around carrying a file as if one was on a mission. Fortunately my god-mother's husband, Biggers, had been busy since Tishy returned to India and had got me a couple of interviews to take a degree in agriculture at Wye College, near Canterbury, Kent, which was part of London University, and Queen's College, Cambridge. Pa Holly had put the idea of a career in conservation into my head. Since Wye was the closer I went there first, hit it off with the principal, who had been a wartime wing commander, and since my group, Number 62, was not due for demob until February 1948, he would apply for me to have a Class B release in time for the 1947 academic year. His proviso was that I had to study and not get addled, so I hooked up on a biology correspondence course through Wolseley College, Oxford. A bird in the hand being worth two in the bush, I did not go for the interview at Cambridge. In addition to studying I polished 250 bayonets on a buffing machine that left one coated in cotton waste by each evening, but to my satisfaction they turned up with the naval section of the victory parade in London some time later.

Tim was at Bickley Hall just up the line from Chatham, so I could drop in on him at weekends for a talk and a meal. Bill Matthews had also left a letter at the barracks for me on his return in the *Flamborough Head*, and I spent a short leave with him and his parents on the large estate in Sussex that they managed, which was used as the setting for the Himalayas in the film *Black Narcissus*, since it had lakes and slopes covered with rhododendrons. The winter of 1947 was as bleak as anyone before or since could remember, since the coal miners, chose that moment to go on strike for £1,000 per year, effectively holding the country to ransom, when a fair middle income was £400–500 per annum. I recalled that when Mrs Thatcher decided that enough was enough and it was time to put an end to such blackmail. I served in HMS *Easton* a destroyer escort based at Portland Bill, Dorset, where we used to go out on daily anti-submarine training exercises, tossing an agreed number of hand grenades over the side to denote whether we had sonared them or not. Around that time my parents returned from India for the last time, to settle in the rented wing of 'Trewidden', a country house overlooking Mount's Bay opposite Marazion, Cornwall, the small town of Tishy's birth. Julia, another cousin, also appeared on the scene for the first time during one of my leaves, which coincided with school holidays.

In July, our ship steamed past Land's End on our way to the Fleet Review on the Clyde before the king and queen and their two daughters, probably the last of such massive reviews. My demob replacement came aboard on August Bank Holiday 1947, and the place where we were issued with our civilian kit of overcoat, suit, shoes and so on was at Southsea, near Portsmouth. I was standing in a queue waiting to see Ivor Novello's *The Dancing Years* when I heard a voice behind me that I thought I recognised. Turning round, there was Jim Wall from the Skegness initiation days. We had both been out in the Pacific together, he on the battleship HMS *Anson* which had joined us in Hong Kong.

He asked what I was doing, and I told him I was being demobbed to go to Wye College. 'So am I,' he replied, but a year later since he had not got an early release. I was best man at his wedding in 1951, and we have met up at reunions at Wye from time to time. I lost touch with Bill Matthews after I emigrated to Canada, but a few years ago he read a letter of mine to *The Times* about our time out in Hong Kong, and got in touch. He became a forester, and was awarded an OBE for services to arboriculture. John Lethbridge from the New School, Calcutta days retired from Beaconsfield to a small town in Oxfordshire, and I see and hear from him and his wife reasonably often. It is satisfying to have friendships that go back a long way, either side of sixty years in fact.

So ended my brief naval career, including one unforgettable year that money could not buy, under the benevolent auspices of that well-known naval character, Harry Tate. I cannot think that there were too many other ships with the combination of the route and the inclination of our skipper, and I hope that he enjoyed a good retirement.

Kenya, 1925.
My mother and Sam, my maternal grandfather, are second and third from left.

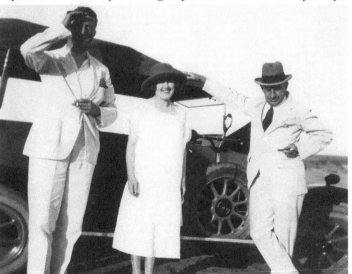

Mother and Sam, the old pirate.

Jock (my future uncle by marriage), Aunt Lucie and 'Tishy' (my father).

Me (aged five) with Granny Orchard in Hoylake, the Wirral.

Me (aged four to seven years) bonding with Miss Braithwaite in front of Meols School and kindergarten.

Miss Braithwaite and I in a haystack while on a Shropshire farm holiday.

Mr Cove, an amiable man, my guardian between the ages of seven and ten, on holiday in Coverack, Cornwall.

With Mr Cove on Llandudno pier, North Wales. I am on the right.

With Mr Fare, the Coves' driver, on the Great Orme, Llandudno.
I was aged between seven and ten years old.

A roadside picnic on one of our holidays.

'From Here to Eternity'.
My parents frolic on Madras Beach, mid 1930s.

Simple pleasures – shrimping at Rhosneigr, Anglesey, 1932.
I am on the left of the tall boy.

The three Ts: Tishy, Tony and Tim. My Father and I (aged ten) on my first holiday with my brother Tim (aged three to four years old) in Kent, 1936.

The Reverend Claud Stephenson and Aunt Tommy (my father's cousin). They were my guardians in Yorkshire between the ages of ten and fourteen years old.

Bickley Hall School, Bickley, Kent. The visit of some of the Australian XI test cricketers (wearing our school caps). I am in the front row, second from left.

Darjeeling, 1941.
The view of Mount Kanchenjunga while I studied ancient Greek.

Holly's farmhouse near Maritzburg, Natal.
South Africa, 1942–44.

Me aged seventeen at Hilton College, Natal.

The Inauguration Ceremony of the United Nations
at San Francisco Opera House, May 1945.

A reunited family.
Our first English home at Trewidden, near Newlyn, Cornwall, 1946.

8.

University and Return to Liverpool (Years 21–26)

My final contact with the RN involved an amusing little social incident of those times. A group of us, having collected our demob clothes in their cardboard boxes, boarded the train from Portsmouth to Waterloo, where we intended having a farewell drink or two at the Union Jack Club next to the station. As we were leaving the platform there was a group of young Wrens struggling with their kitbags and other luggage as they were boarding a train. So a couple of us grabbed one of those large luggage trolleys with four wheels and a handle for pulling, loaded up their stuff and handed it to them in the train. To my slight dismay and amusement one young Wren, clearly a well-brought-up gel, as Wrens tended to be (Daddy often knew someone in the Admiralty), held back from the others and was struggling to open her purse to find the coppers for a tip. Poor girl, huge embarrassment when we patted her on the head and breathed beery good wishes over her!

My parents must have retired around October 1946, having got in a couple of local much deserved holidays in India while I was in the Pacific and Chatham barracks. Such local leaves had been out of the question during the war, so they went on a pony trek through Sikkim, followed by the best of all such experiences, a stay on one of the houseboats on a lake in Kashmir, a happy place before Indian Independence kicked in the religious war between the Hindu ruler and the mainly Muslim people. So ended my parents' twenty-five-year sojourn in India, where they lived the traditional colonial life of the box *wallahs* or expatriates in the commercial world, triangulated between their bungalow, office and club with side visits to the appropriate hill station such as Ootacamund or Darjeeling, but otherwise almost totally insulated from Indian life or culture. It was a wasted opportunity really, but the spirit of the times. The only friend whom we had who took an interest in Indian life was Louise Rankin, the American wife of the head of Standard Oil, and she was regarded as rather odd in her tastes.

So Tishy headed for Cornwall, the county of his birth that he had left as a young boy to go up to Hoylake, and probably had not seen since. There must be something in homing instinct theories. I have to admit that when I used to think about England while in South Africa it was always in the context of Cornwall, never Kent or Yorkshire. I think that this was probably due to the fact that my father came from there and also that Mr Cove imprinted the uniqueness of that county on me when we visited it on holiday, walking, fishing and boating – mercifully, no golf. I can think of nowhere else in the world that has its combination of coastline with magnificent views and tolerable swimming (Maine has a similar coast, but the sea is not for dawdling in), a plethora of small harbours, which in those days were almost deserted due to wartime restrictions, a tremendous variety of flora, particularly early due to the mildness of the climate, and above all a history whose traces go back long before the Christian era. On the negative side, it has two disadvantages: a prevailing westerly wind revealed by the eastward slope of the trees, which brings in a range of wet weather from penetrating mists to storms, and a mining economy that was exploited and worked out years before, leaving very little for the surviving inhabitants but fishing and farming.

For some reason we started out in a rented cottage in Carbis Bay on the north coast just west of St Ives, at that time a healthy fishing port with a genuine artists' colony. They lived in the pastel-coloured cottages in the narrow lanes leading down to the harbour front, dominated by the Sloop Inn. It was everyone's idea of the archetypal Cornish fishing village, but it had two negatives so far as Tishy was concerned: firstly, the nearest golf course was at Hayle a few miles away, and secondly there was no transport thereto. So after a few months of this my parents found what they thought they were looking for, the wing of a country house to rent called 'Trewidden', with its own large grounds and sweeping views across the lawns to Mount's Bay, Penzance, and Marazion just beyond, opposite to St Michael's Mount. And so they thought that they had found their ideal retirement spot, a John Majorish idea of country lanes and genteel folk. Like all colonials who retired at that time, they had two challenges to meet and overcome. The wives had to learn to cook, probably for the first time in their lives, on post-war rations, while the men had to learn to walk, without benefit of company cars or golf courses, not to mention doing their share of the washing up. What a shock, what a comedown, no longer the universal cry of '*koi hai*' to bring the instant attention of our old Madrasi butler! No wonder so many colonials retired to Kenya or British Columbia, where the living was easier. But after some tears and traumatic experiences, Dorothy went on to become a very good cook, particularly with the aid of cordon bleu classes after she moved to London.

But there was still no local golf course. Trewidden, a country house that belonged to one of the members of the Bolitho family, was located about one mile above the busy harbour town of Newlyn, which in those days was still famous for its school of artists. The Bolithos were part of the Cornish squirarchy that had owned the Bolitho bank, sold to Barclays. Other large landowners had previously owned tin mines. The next fishing village along the south coast from Newlyn towards Land's End is Mousehole or 'Mowzel', which I try to visit at least once a year and feel more at home there than anywhere else but my actual home. The nearest pub to us was in Newlyn, a twenty-minute walk from the A30 downhill, but a thirty-minute walk back with a couple of pints or so in the tank for lunch at home. Our spaniel enjoyed the walks, but Tishy failed to do so. However, there was a solution to hand. The bus into Penzance stopped just outside the gate of our long drive, which was a walk in itself, so when the need arose (which it did fairly regularly), Tishy and I would bus into town, go to the local brewery and buy a thirty-two-pint barrel known as a firkin, hire a taxi and take it back home in the boot. It then had to be allowed to settle before being tapped and drunk. Thirty-two pints are not a lot of course when they stood looking at us in our kitchen, so the taxi driver got to know us quite well, and his petrol ration seemed to be adequate. This raises the point that in those truly rural parts of England there was always local food surplus to the state rations and farmers became notorious for just departing a pub with a couple of docile pigs in a trailer hitched to their cars, powered by agricultural petrol. No doubt in the Cornish economy taxi drivers and farmers were interchangeable.

This gives me the opportunity to introduce the other part of the Orchard family that had always lived in the Cornish peninsular. I am not very good at family trees, but suffice to say that 'Tommy' Thomas was a cousin of my father, and about the same age. He and his family were the people that I had only heard about from Aunt Tommy in the Yorkshire vicarage. Her real name was Florence or Flossie, but her family name was Thomas. There was a tradition in Cornwall, once tin and copper mining had virtually collapsed due to lower cost alluvial tin from Malaya and Chile, for the Cornish male workers to go across to the States to work in the summers and then return home for the winter. They were known as 'Cousin Jacks' and one has only to look at the map of New England to see the connection with Devon and Cornwall in the place names: Truro, Exeter, Falmouth and so on. Cornwall was famous for its mining skills throughout the mining world via the Camborne School of Mines, which is still flourishing. I guess that if one can get tin out of Cornish granite down a narrow seam, anything else is fairly easy.

Tommy Thomas had actually emigrated to the USA where he became a coal miner in Pennsylvania, but on the death of his father he returned home, with dual nationality and an American wife, to look after his mother. They then went to live in St Hilary near Penzance, where my paternal grandfather came from, and Tommy set himself up as a dealer in pigs and cattle, as well as a grower of anemones and early daffodils or lilies as they are called down there. Tommy was a man to whom the word 'character' fitted like a glove. Like most people in that kind of business, who had to go round the farms to collect the livestock, he knew everyone, and everyone knew him. I usually associate dealers with the consumption of a fair amount of drink in markets, but he in fact was teetotal. This could have had something to do with the strong Wesleyan tradition in Cornwall. He and his wife had two daughters, Mary Ellen, the elder, and Evelyn, whom I have seen regularly since my mother died. In fact, just after Lene and I got married I took Lene down there and we stayed a night with them, during when we were given the main bedroom to sleep in. Quite an honour! There was also another cousin called Martha, who was divorced by the time we got there. She bore an uncanny resemblance to Aunt Tommy, and if I closed my eyes I might just as well have been listening to the latter, so similar were their voices. However, she was not teetotal, appearing on occasions with a black eye. 'Just walked into a pillar, love.' Or she had 'tripped'. As Mary Ellen pointed out recently we are the last of the Mohicans. No more Orchards, but she has a daughter and grandson who, via another Thomas, is also a Thomas.

Julia appeared on the scene for the first time at Trewidden. It must have been in the spring of 1947 because my earliest photos are of her crouching in a bed of daffodils in Trewidden's garden, looking small behind a large pair of spectacles. So presumably it must have been in the Easter holidays from her convent school. The addition of another female into the family improved the sex ratio, no longer three to one in favour of the males, more like living with the Noyces than the Orchards, and it occurred to me that Tishy would have been happier with one of each. So we did a lot of walking, mostly along the coast towards Mousehole and Lamorna Cove, but not inland to the wild parts around Zennor to the north. I also viewed it all from the sea, when in July 1947 HMS *Easton* sailed with me on board for the last time past Mount's Bay on our way to the fleet review on the Clyde. August Bank holiday, 1947… Oh, happy day! That was the day when our ship was anchored off Troon and as I was on watch on the gangway, I spotted a launch coming towards us from the shore, with a spare sailor and his kit on board; he was my relief. The sheer boredom of life afloat in peacetime Navy was over. The last thing that I recall of that time down there was of Tim entering for the freestyle race over two lengths in the Penzance sea water swimming pool on the seafront, which was not heated and therefore freezing, even in the summer of 1947. Not having lived with Tim for five years or so, I had no idea that he had learned to swim so well in Calcutta, and he came in second or third against the local lads, without any training, with a steady stroke that made him look a bit like a turtle, head up with arms coming over like clubs into the water. He was made of sterner stuff than me.

Wye College, near Ashford in Kent, was part of London University, and at that time in 1947 there were about 300 students studying for general BSc degrees in agriculture and horticulture. Wye was a very small village set at the foot of the North Downs. The main college buildings were based on an old Latin school connected to Canterbury to the east, which gave it its 'old' cachet in those days before the building of the red-brick universities. The principal, Dunstan Skilbeck, was a very energetic ex-wartime wing commander, a graduate from Oxford, where of course they 'read Rural Economy', nothing as vulgar as studying a science. He must have been very highly regarded since he had been on the Groundnuts Committee in 1946–7 that looked into the possibility of growing groundnuts in what was then Tanganyika. He was the only member who recommended against going ahead with the project. The rest is history. £8 million from this bankrupt nation, which had been on a life-support machine from the USA since 1942, were poured into the African soil unsuited for mass ploughing, and the labour untrained to handle mechanised equipment. It was there that the wartime slogan 'give us the tools and we'll finish the job' was reversed to 'give us the job and we'll finish the tools'!

So after a short stay at home I headed for a job on a farm near Wye at Brabourne, to get practical experience during the harvest and to start earning some money, since the ex-Service further education grants covered the tuition but not the accommodation, or vice versa. It was a mixed farm of several hundred acres, including dairy, arable and sheep as one would expect being on the edge of Romney Marsh, where they could fatten more sheep per acre than anywhere else in the British Isles. The farmer was a young man of only thirty-two, an ex-diploma student from pre-war Wye, who had married well, as they used to say, and as a farmer had had exemption from military service. He went on to become a governor of the college and was very active in local Kent life. I lived in digs with the head cowman and his wife, in one of the tied cottages owned by the farmer, a throwback to a more feudal age when farmers 'owned' their workers. What it really meant was that a farm worker was bound to his boss, was paid the agricultural wage negotiated by his union plus overtime at peak seasons, such a spring lambing or harvest, but if he stepped out of line too far he could lose his job and the cottage with it. The same applied if he wished to change his job, either within or outside agriculture. This tied cottage system was legislated out by Parliament some time during the 1960s, presumably when a Labour government was in power. What it resulted in as, I soon found out, was that the older farm workers had learned to adjust their pace and spread out the hours, and their advice was, 'Slow down lad, just remember when you're walking, you're not working.' To supplement the labour shortages, particularly at harvest time, German prisoners of war were brought in daily from a local camp. We had four of them, a baker, a dress designer, a retail worker from a haberdashery store and the fourth whom the others said was ex-SS, and with whom they would have very little to do. But being German they had the work ethic, and they were both a pleasure to work with and more interesting company than the old farm hands, which was probably a pretty intolerant attitude on my part. Nowadays it has all changed; a farm worker is a skilled operator, who owns his own property, has sophisticated equipment to maintain, drives a heated tractor with plastic shields to protect him from the elements, no doubt with a radio to keep in touch with the outside world, has outside assistance from contractors at peak seasons and deserves every penny that he earns.

The autumn term at the college started in October and we all lived in. We were the second batch of ex-servicemen and women, who made up the majority of the students and were renowned for getting our heads into our books. There were no cars, only a few had cycles and we all arrived at Wye station by train. The train ran from Ashford to Wye, Chilham, Chartham and Canterbury. The porter on Ashford station was renowned, when the train arrived, for calling out to passengers, 'Why kill 'em and cart 'em to Canterbury,' and was rewarded usually with a laugh. Since there was no motorised transport in the village, a carter with his horse and cart met the incoming trains to collect the trunks and take them up to the college, with a few of the second or third year students, who knew the form, sitting on top. A vanished world of rural life with a strong underlay of Mrs Miniver, Wye really consisted of one village street with a loop at the top, some shops, about four pubs, a couple of tea shops, a commercial egg-packing station, and a village hall. It lay in the valley of the river Stour, which flowed on through Canterbury to the coast. For those who had had a hard time of it during the war, such as a couple of men who had been prisoners of the Japanese, it was the ideal spot to slide back into English life. But we had to make our own enjoyment, there being no local bright lights to visit, so student societies and sports clubs were probably more active and better attended than they are today. The downside was that we were completely detached from the rest of London University, a splendid isolation that was both coveted and boasted about, but lacking in stimulus from other disciplines.

We had to work on farms in the vacations both to get practical experience, and also to earn one's keep for the next term. It was really the tail end of the old way of farming and harvesting, with combine harvesters only just beginning to creep in from North America. Plenty of nineteenth century writers during the Romantic period extolled the enjoyment of harvesting in groups, picking up the bundles of grain from the binders to build into stooks or shocks, and later collecting them to build into stacks with pitchforks – stick, swing up and plonk down – an unending rhythm except for the tea and lunch breaks. Finally, there was a ride back on the trailer to the farmhouse to collect one's bike, and a general feeling of tired well-being.

Working on the threshing machine was probably the worst job in the sense that once the machine had got into its stride, there was no stopping it. One operated in a dense cloud of dust, and the machine was lethal if one slipped on the platform and one's feet went down the chute. Not too many guards in those days, and no health and safety regulations. The worst job that I ever had was a summer spent rogueing wheat on the NIAB (National Institute of Agricultural Botany) farm located on the road to Huntingdon, north of Cambridge. There were six other undergraduates from Cambridge apart from myself. The others all lived in digs in a small village off the A14 and I lodged in a pub on the main road;

it is now quite a swanky roadside pub where we have been for lunch when visiting friends south of Cambridge. At that time it was run by a young man, who also operated a truck taking vegetables down to Covent Garden market in London. He had a very young wife of nineteen, who was seven months pregnant with her first child when I arrived, and just about ready to pop when I left six weeks later. The domestic services were basic – no bath, the loo was a bucket in a wooden shack just outside the back door, not even at the end of the garden, and since it was only emptied every few days, its condition in the middle of August was not nice. They also used mostly cans of condensed milk rather than fresh milk. The former, when the tops had been opened, used to attract flies. When I remarked on this my hostess replied that such milk had the advantage of sticking the flies' wings together so that they were easier to pick out! Why did I stick it out? The main reason was that it was a two-mile cycle ride each way to the village where the Cambridge lot were in digs, and on a fixed-gear bike after a hard day's work, that is quite a long way. Besides, deep ditches below hedges on the 500-acre farm became alternative facilities, and for baths we converted a drinking trough for the cows, after a good scrub out, into a reasonable simulacrum of a tub, with the permission of the farm manager, who was dependent on our labour.

Rogueing grain for seed, in this case wheat, is an absolutely mind-blowing job. The wheat was Squarehead Master, one of the old breeds, and we had to pick out any other wheat, barley, wild oats and so on that had found their way into the crop. A sack was tied with a bit of twine in front of one's waist, we walked in a line, fingertip to fingertip, up and down the fields, stuffing the rogue heads into the sack, getting damp from the waist down in the morning dew, getting wetter when it rained, and thinking of what? After about the first two hours of desultory conversation, absolutely nothing, not even sex. In due course, the fields were harvested, and DPs (Displaced Persons) were brought in by lorry each morning from a labour camp to assist with the harvesting and building the ricks. They were mainly Poles, Ukrainians and Estonians, and as with the Germans, they were a pleasure to work with, interesting and cheerful. Gradually the Cambridge lot peeled off and returned to the comforts of their homes, when it was time to harvest the last crop, mustard seed. The farm manager pleaded with me to stay on to the end of the vacation, which I did, and that, 'oh best beloved', as Kipling would write, is how I got into skiing. From somewhere the manager rustled up an orange-coloured Allis Chalmers combine harvester, without self-drive, and a D2 Caterpillar crawler to pull it around the fair-sized fields. My job was to put the crawler into gear to set it going, jump down, hop up onto the platform of the combine to tie up the sack when it was filled, and kick it down the chute, then reverse the procedure when it was time for the crawler to make a turn at the end of the field. No health and safety regulations then meant a need to concentrate, but an opportunity for a lot of overtime wages, and the farm manager and his wife gave me supper in the evenings of a considerably higher standard than at the pub. Which goes to show that there is no such a thing as a free lunch, or supper, in this world.

At the end of the seven weeks or so I went to Cambridge to catch the train for London, and stocked up on my second- and third-year textbooks at Heffers bookshop. By this time – that is, the summer of 1948 – our parents had moved to Walmer, Kent, one of the Cinque Ports near Canterbury fortified during the Napoleonic wars against the threat from the French (who else?). There was a Royal Marine depot at Deal at that time, and a large group of returned colonials, all bewailing the fact that the Old Country was going to the dogs, the lack of gin and cars, the food rationing, the lack of servants and those frightful socialist *wallahs* in London. One of them must have got a message to Tishy in Cornwall, who by this time had had enough of the prevailing south-west winds and pervading mists of his native county during the winter.

But crossing London I happened to walk down Upper Regent Street past the old Regent Street Poly, and there in the window were pictures of snow scenes from Switzerland. A young chap about my age was also looking at them and he explained that he was getting up a party to go to Zermatt for two weeks at New Year, and he still had a couple of places to fill, so would I like to come along. We went upstairs to the booking desk, I parted with

£5 deposit, quite a lot of money then, but I reckoned that I had earned it the hard way, and he said that he would be in touch. The reception that I got from Tishy on arrival at High Trees, our rented home, was similar to that accorded to Pike by Captain Mainwaring. He did not actually call me 'you stupid boy' (aged twenty-two, ex-service and all that), but he did ask me if I had ever heard of confidence tricksters? I assured him that the other chap was just a student like myself, and so began a fifty-year love affair with skiing, 1949–99, at a cost of £25 for two weeks in Zermatt at an exchange rate of eighteen Swiss francs to the pound, and a bottle of Pinot Noir for six francs every evening in the Walliserhof Hotel, where a Jewish refugee couple from Austria played the piano and accordion for us to dance to, and loosen our aching limbs. A lot less sophisticated than nowadays, but no less enjoyable, *and* I brought Tishy back a full-length pair of quality woollen golf stockings, to show him just what they could do over there.

Working college vacations happily gave me the opportunity to return to Cornwall on a couple of occasions. The college bursar, who had been in the Army for the whole of the war, decided to retire early at the end of my first year and farm for himself. He bought Tregoose farm, about 200 acres, located on the small road from Devoran, between Truro and Falmouth, and Pil Creek at the head of the Falmouth Roads, not too far from the Fal ferry. It was a mixed farm of dairy cows and pigs, and for the latter the arable crop grown was so-called dredge corn, a mixture of barley and oats seed, which was supposed to ripen at the same time. The fields ran down to Pil Creek, and on the opposite bank was the famous Pandora Inn, which has gone from strength to strength. In that climate the evenings start to get moist around 5.30 p.m., when the grain became too damp for the binder to cut properly. So out with the dinghy and down the creek to the Falmouth Roads, where there is some of the best sailing in the world. I also began to appreciate pigs as animals. They have a habit of looking one straight in the eye as if they feel themselves to be on the same level of understanding, and I believe that since transplants came in, their hearts are interchangeable with ours, so we must have something in common. That was the summer vacation, but the move did not suit the bursar's wife, who for whatever reason decided to take her life with a bottle of aspirin behind the hay stack around Christmas, leaving a husband and a son of about fourteen years. So the following Easter vacation I returned to manage the farm for three weeks, while they went off for a break. I don't know if the farm is still intact, but the house is still there called 'Tregoose'. No doubt it is a highly desirable property with that location, and the last time that I passed it in March 2003 I talked to a South African lady walking her dog along the lane.

During our parents' stay in the Deal-Walmer area from 1948 onwards, they lived in three rented properties until Dorothy finally persuaded Tishy to buy her a house in her name. I think he was probably kicking for touch, hoping to get another job of sorts, since he was only fifty-two, or move to a warmer clime with lower income tax once Tim had finished his schooling. The first house was 'High Trees'; the second was a small bungalow on the seafront at Kingsdown, which was an extension of Walmer towards Dover. It even boasted a small golf course on the top of the chalk cliffs, which was more accessible and playable than the championship links course at Deal, and when cars became available Tishy had more flexible transport to indulge his single-minded passion for that game. A better descriptive word might have been obsession, with his wife cast in the role of the long-suffering golf widow.

We also gave up dogs temporarily and acquired a small black cat called Lucy. Having had no experience of such animals, Tishy expected it to behave like a dog when he put it outside to do its business. But of course it did not return immediately, so he went out looking for her. We later heard that some of the neighbours had remarked that a peculiar man had moved into the cottage, who from time to time would walk up and down the shingle beach calling out, 'Lucy Locket, Lucy Locket, where are you?' when there was absolutely nothing in sight!

The other visitor was Julia from her convent school. Since I worked most of the holidays I did not see much of her, but recall that she was either growing at an extreme rate, or was half-starved by the nuns on post-war rations to the point that she appeared to be permanently hungry. So she was christened 'Sophie Tuckshop' either after a young girl in a radio show, or one of the members of St Trinian's School. There was one further port of call in rented accommodation halfway up the hill from the Rising Sun pub, until Tishy was finally arm-locked into buying a four-bedroomed house, 'Windy Ridge', right on top of the hill. It was well named, exposed to the full force of the Channel gales. That was his last home, until in 1954 a lifetime's habit of sixty cigarettes a day caught up with him. That and the Shell actuaries, who calculated that the majority of those who had spent twenty-five years out in India would not see their sixty-first birthday. They were in most cases remarkably accurate, which probably accounted for the generosity of Shell pensions. The memsahibs mostly outlived them by many years, made of sterner stuff and less addicted to tobacco and 'burra pegs' (Anglo-Indian far large measures of spirits, usually whiskey) no doubt.

I graduated from Wye in the summer of 1950. In those days the main careers open for those such as us, who did not have access or inclination to farming itself, was the National Agricultural Advisory Service (NAAS), the Colonial Agricultural Service, or commercial firms in the fertiliser, feed or pest control businesses. The latter were not held in high esteem by the academics, who still held strongly to that old bias against 'trade' – even our New Zealand Professor of Agriculture. However, since my best subject had been economics, and in my final year I had been President of the Students' Union, and thus got some experience of running things, I elected for the commercial world, just as long as it was not with Shell – in which to mix metaphors, one is just a pawn in a bloody great womb. Maybe small cog in a large wheel would be more accurate. At any rate, I forgot the oath that I had sworn to myself when returning to Liverpool in the troop ship in 1946 – namely never to return to that benighted city – by accepting a job with R Silcock and Sons, manufacturers of animal and poultry feeds, with a head office close to Exchange Station, not far from the River Mersey front and the ferry terminal. It seemed like a good idea at the time; it was a medium-sized company, unlike say ICI or Unilever, the latter also being in the feed business, and the starting salary was good. I was to go into the Large Livestock (cattle and pigs) Nutrition Department as a nutritional advisor, but before that I was to be exposed to sales at the sharp end.

Silcocks had over 600 sales agents covering Great Britain, all on commission only, so that the more they sold the more they earned. Some in huge territories in Scotland lived like lairds, and earned more than the area sales managers. I drew the short straw and was sent to Norfolk for three months, a county and its people that could not be much more different from Cornwall and the Cornish, flat as a pancake and farmers as dour as unleavened bread. I was attached to a wild, red-headed Irishman, who lived somewhere near Diss. Every day we went out in his car to call on the farmers to try to get their sales according to their allowances for protein and cereal coupons, depending on the size of their dairy herds or numbers of pigs. Saturday morning was spent in Norwich market, sitting at our desk, swilling beer and following up the farmers, who had brought their animals in for auction, for payment. As far as they were concerned, ex-university graduates were the pits, all theory and no practical knowledge, the latter described as 'muck and magic'. They were probably right at that time, but since then colossal gains in agricultural productivity have been made through genetics, plant breeding, fertilisers and mechanisation, all of which came from the universities. Norwich was not a bad city, and I was reminded when she died, that Alicia Markova (born plain Alice Marks in London, but with the required Russian 'nom de ballet') came up with her partner Anton Dolin to put on *Swan Lake* at the local theatre. She did a lot for that art, and did not seem to have had the same racy private life as the famous ballerina Margot Fonteyn.

That completed, I set off for my new job in the head office in Liverpool, a city which had been badly knocked about in the Blitz, and also had lost a lot of its transatlantic trade in grain and other commodities. Acres of it were still vacant bomb sites with the rubble barely cleared away, particularly in Toxteth around the new Anglican cathedral, which took seventy years in its building. There was also a new Catholic cathedral, made mainly from concrete, that took only five years to build, and the two represented the religious split in the city, where many of the citizens were the Irish who had not made it to America. So local politics were bedevilled with the Protestant/Catholic split, even to the local football teams, where Everton players were Roman Catholics, while Liverpool's were Protestants. The same applies to Rangers and Celtic in Glasgow, of course. In those days there were no flats to rent, and young men lived in digs with the notorious northern landladies. I thought that it would be quite amusing to commute daily over the Mersey by the ferry, so I found a room on the Wirral side at New Brighton. I rapidly learned this should not be confused in any way, shape or form with the Regency town (now city) of that name on the south coast.

A bus ride in the early morning got me to the ferry landing stage, where this being November 1950 the passengers huddled in serried ranks leaning into the wind, like sheep do against a wall during foul weather, to maintain a mutual warmth. The ferry ride across the Mersey was only a few minutes, followed by a brisk walk to Edmund Street. Having sampled the charms of the ferry at the wrong time of the year, I decided to move across to Liverpool proper and found digs with about five others in one of the tall, old terraced houses near Sefton Park, not too far from Toxteth, but more 'select'. It was located on Devonshire Avenue, and the landlady who was aged about fifty, was really quite a character with some style. Her daughter was something else, a returned GI bride with a Scouse voice like a Mersey River foghorn on a very rough night. They had a full-length fur coat between them, and mother and daughter never went out together. When the mother went down the road dressed in it, she was known by the locals as the Duchess of Devonshire, and really looked the part. She was a good sort and I liked her on the whole.

However, all relationships with landladies have a shelf life, possibly due to the permanent search for something better. I had got to know a local GP, a Dr Earl and his young family, whose pride and joy was the ownership of a Bristol pilot cutter called *Spray*, the same kind of gaff-rigged yacht, with a main and mizzen masts, and the same name as the one in which Josh Slocum had made his famous solo round-the-world voyage many years before. Dr Earl kept her in Garston Docks, a suburb up the Mersey, where the Elder Dempster banana boats used to come into to unload. The Mersey has a surprisingly large rise and fall of tides, about twelve feet or more on spring tides, as I was to find out. *Spray* was manned by a volunteer crew such as myself, and we used to sail as far as the Isle of Man, once even to Dun Laoghaire in Ireland itself. For the overnight trips, particularly if we were going near the Menai Straits with the tide rips, the doctor employed a retired merchant navy skipper, who looked the part of the traditional old seadog as in Bird's Eye TV ads, as captain and navigator.

In the Isle of Man race overnight one weekend, we had to sail through some sea mist but arrived in the early morning absolutely spot on Douglas harbour. While the captain was being congratulated on his navigation, one of the crew noticed an object at the foot of the binnacle housing the compass. Reaching down, he picked up a steel marlinspike about twelve inches long that had been carelessly tossed down there after splicing rope. Since the compass was magnetic, it had probably been put out by about ten degrees, so our landfall was not all that accurate after all. Needless to say, the skipper was not amused!

When it was time to lay her up for the winter in October, it had been noted that she had sprung some leaks through her decks and it was therefore time to re-caulk her decks. Since she was fifty-one feet overall in length, which may have included the bowsprit, and also broad in the beam, it was a fair job at weekends to dig out the old oakum with a caulking hammer and chisel, replace it and pour in the boiling tar. Fortunately I had the ideal partner for the job, a young Pole in his twenties called Jan Moisheyvitch, built like a middleweight wrestler, and studying at Liverpool University for a Bachelor's degree in leather chemistry, of all subjects. Dr Earl was so pleased with the results, and knowing that my relationship with the duchess was deteriorating, offered me *Spray* as a houseboat to live in at ten bob per week, with the proviso that I kept her clean, and if ever he came down and found me eating off newspaper, he would throw me off. 'Remember the British in the jungle,' he advised, 'who always maintained standards and dressed for dinner.' He was only half-joking, but with a home like that, the last thing that I would do would be to pig it.

Spray like all those old yachts had a wonderful interior, all mahogany and brass work. The main saloon had a long bunk to port, with the polished table and L-shaped bunks around it to starboard. It could be heated very rapidly by a stove in the centre with Bakelite windows, and I laid the fire each morning before going ashore up an ordinary window cleaner's ladder. There was a single cabin forward with drawers below the bunk, a double cabin aft of the companionway down from the deck hatch, a kitchen with Calor gas and a flush loo. My fridge was an empty Peak Frean biscuit tin dangled over the stern in the dock water, which never rose much above 32°F in the winter. There was also a hand basin and shower, and twice a week Dr Earl and another man, who was the Engineering Director for Pilkington's Glass, offered me the use of their bathrooms, which was about par for the course in those days of fuel and soap rationing. I got a coal ration permit from the Town Hall for a houseboat, and supplemented the food rations by buying eggs and bacon from the Irish coasters that used the dock.

New Year's Day 1951 was memorable. High spring tides met a gale going in the opposite direction down the Mersey, so that the docks were swamped with waves coming over the sea wall. It was just a question of battening down the hatches, lighting the fire and getting out a good book. Around teatime I heard footsteps on deck above, and opened the hatch to find the doctor, his wife and the engineer, who had arrived to check on my condition. I had the necessary lubrication on board, so for me New Year was celebrated sixteen hours late.

My job in the Nutrition Department consisted mainly of recommending winter feeding rations for dairy herds, and designing Danish bacon houses, which were just becoming the thing. Farmers would write in for advice, giving details of their milking herds and followers, the amount of protein and carbo-hydrate rations they were allocated from the Ministry of Agriculture, their acreage of kale and root crops, tonnage of silage and hay in the stacks, for us to recommend feeding regimes. It was not the most exciting work to churn out day after day, but it had its lighter moments. A farmer from Wales wrote in on a scrap of lined school notepaper to advise that he was being investigated by the inspector for possibly adulterating his milk with water to increase the volume sent to the milk collector, for which, if true, he could be prosecuted. I therefore gave him the standard reply to the effect that butterfat content varied by breeds, and since his herd was mixed Shorthorns and Friesians, he could boost the fat content by adding a couple of Jersey or Guernsey cows. Another possibility was that he was not giving his herd enough roughage such as hay or straw in their diet, or there could even be a leak in the milk cooler, allowing water to enter the milk unwittingly. About two weeks later, I got a reply from him on a similar scrap of paper, expressing his fulsome thanks as follows (more or less): 'Dear Mr Orchard, Thank you for your letter. I have shown it to the inspector and he has agreed not to prosecute me. I am very grateful for your help.' It was signed Dai Jones, or whatever his name was. 'P.S. There is now a hole in my cooler!'

I shared the office with the departmental manager. To describe us as oil and water would be the understatement of the year. He was a Glaswegian, who lived on a smallholding outside the city where he kept pigs. Let's just say we were completely incompatible.

However, help was at hand, when in February 1952 I was told to collect a Morris Minor car and go down to Biggleswade, Beds. There I was told to take over and restore the sales territory, where the salesman had absconded with tons of uncollected ration coupons, £70 and somebody else's wife. I was told to recover these in that order, and I achieved the first two, but not the third. It gave me the chance to take stock and look around. Under no circumstances was I going to return to Liverpool in any capacity. In those days, commercial firms got their staff in so-called key positions of knowledge, to sign an agreement that they would not move to a similar firm for two years – probably an illegal requirement, but hard for a junior employee to buck then. So the only alternative was to emigrate, and since Canada was in its up phase at that time, with its currency riding high above the American dollar on the back of its mineral wealth, I decided to have another look at what I had only passed through in the RN in 1945. Ontario House in London, to which province most of the British emigrants headed, gave me a visa on the strength of my qualifications, and the addresses of some companies that I could contact for employment after arrival. I even nearly got a lift across the pond. I had met John Jordan, who has since built up the sizeable and successful Jordans Foods, when playing rugby for the local Biggleswade team. He was an ex-RAF pilot, who was ferrying planes across to Newfoundland, and offered to give me a lift that far. But the onward journey was problematic, so I elected to take an emigrant ship, £58 from Southampton to Quebec City.

I returned to Liverpool to work out my month's notice, and that was a good location to take my leave of all those up there who had stood in as parents from the age of four to fourteen Miss Braithwaite from 1930–33, Mr Cove in West Kirby (1933–36) now a widower, who remembered my interest in history, and gave me the six volumes of Churchill's *History of the Second World War*; and Aunt Tommy and Uncle Claud in Yorkshire (1936–40), with whom I had had a very special relationship. I owe more than I can say to all of them, who gave me a home as well as giving me parental guidance and experiences of many parts of England, from Yorkshire to Land's End. The most difficult part of that sort of upbringing was to keep up with all of them as well as one should, while being shunted around the world, distracted by new experiences and people. Regretfully Aunt Tommy died of cancer while I was in Canada; she was the last person whom I would have thought would have succumbed to that illness, since she never smoked and did not appear to have a stressful life. Last but not least, I went down to Shrewsbury for a weekend to visit Tim, who was doing the first part of his National Service in a training camp there. Despite the six years' difference in our ages, and the short intervals that we spent together, we always had a reasonable relationship.

I suppose the one historical event that influenced my life, and that of many other children with parents in India, was Dunkirk. Without it I would have gone on to an English public school, studied in the classics stream, and ended up as a solicitor or some such, as did many of my peers from those days. But the voyage on the *Strathmore* and arrival in India opened the door to a lifetime of travel, which the stay in South Africa, where itchy feet was an endemic condition, also contributed to. There were hundreds of thousands of us during those four years, who saw or experienced the free and easy life in the Dominions, so different from the stratified, deferential structure in Britain. So I reminded Tishy that he always used to say that every young man should get out of the UK for a few years to gain experience, and while Liverpool had caused him to go east in 1921, I reckoned that the Empire was a busted flush by then, and it was a case of 'go west, young man', to a country where one could live a family life. Being the cautious person that he was, the thought of my pushing off without a job was completely alien to my father, and probably worse for someone who liked to be in control. But there was no turning back; I simply had to get out of England for what I thought would be the rest of my life, and the last time that I saw him was waving farewell as the boat train steamed out of Waterloo for Southampton on 13 June 1952, my twenty-sixth birthday, which I took as a good omen.

9.

Go West, Young Man (Years 26–28)

It is always a considerable step to emigrate from one's country, except that by 1952 I did not really consider England a place where I wished to spend my immediate future. Seven years after the end of the European war Britain was still largely a socialist state, with rationing in food and other commodities as bad as it had been in 1945. Within that whole, Liverpool was particularly dreary and is only belatedly climbing out of its predicament this year, sixty years on, when it has been declared to be the cultural city of Europe. The loss of its transatlantic trade and the destruction by the bombing of its docks and housing played a considerable part in this, but so did its religious sectarian divide as in Glasgow.

So, having experienced the freedom of a job in sales in the unlikely town of Biggleswade, there was no way that I was going to return north. Another hindrance to job changes in those days was that, as already mentioned, large companies made new employees sign a document that they would not join a company in a similar field of activity within two years of leaving. This probably had no validity and has since been declared illegal as a restraint to an individual's freedom of employment, but I never heard of anyone deciding to take on their employer in this way, and probably alternative employers followed the same rules. In the animal feed business, it transpired in 1957, when Unilever applied to have their stock listed on the New York exchange and had to declare their subsidiary interests, that they owned BOCM, Lever Feeds and had a controlling interest in my employer Silcocks. Thus any dash for freedom would have been a jump from the frying pan into the fire.

Where to go then? The Australian £10 emigration scheme was starting up, but that country was a long way away. To the west

Canada was surfing the explosion in commodity prices, particularly those minerals connected with atomic power, military or civil, such as uranium, and their currency was riding high at a premium to the US dollar, one Canadian dollar being worth US $1.05. Since then the balance has been sharply reduced because while Canada had the mineral ore, the USA had the GNP based on its significantly larger population. Thus the saying arose that Canada had a great future ahead of it: it always had had, and always would have! One only has to look at its geographical location with all that tundra and ice across its northern half. But while I spent the last few weeks with my parents in Kingsdown, I was fortunate to be taken aside by a family friend, Sir John Nixon, a retired secretary to the treasury of the government of India, who held what were regarded as very left-wing ideas for those times, and was known as the local communist. In short he was open minded, and he had the endearing habit at those dreadful cocktail parties in the Walmer area of settling down on a chair in a corner away from the general hubbub of people shouting at one another, on the assumption that anyone who had anything worthwhile to say to him would seek him out, and the rest weren't worth talking to! He encouraged me, since I had enjoyed my recent time in sales, to go for that in Canada. He had noticed that there was not the prejudice against selling in North America that existed in the UK and continental Europe (Fuller brush salesmen with foot in the door, and all that) and that American sales people that he had met in India were highly qualified and trained with degrees. Some years later I had experience of what he meant, as I will relate in due course.

I cannot recall the name of the ship, but the cost of the one-way ticket to Quebec City was about £58, and the trip took six days in a four-berth cabin, with the last half day or so proceeding up the St Lawrence River with small villages on either shore. There were a fair number on board seeking a new life after yet another collapse of the textile industry, others just putting distance between themselves and the dreariness of post-war Britain, and of course the inevitable group of DPs, Balts, Poles and Ukrainians, who had been in camps here and had decided to move on. In some ways I feel that those of us who had a disjointed colonial upbringing also fall somewhat into that category, and for a description of such alienation and semi-detachment I can recommend a recent book titled *Children of the Raj* by Vyvyen Brendon, an ex-history teacher, who has done her research both through written sources and personal interviews. Her observations apply to anyone raised in the varied parts of the old British Empire. Quebec City was an attractive old place dominated by the Hotel Frontenac with its gables and curly wurly bits. My worldly goods were contained in one of those green trunks with wooden bands, a tin trunk containing my books collected from childhood, and a set of wooden-shafted second-hand golf clubs. For some reason the female customs officer decided to go through my possessions with a fine toothcomb, turning everything over and asking what it was. This continued until she came to my schoolboy stamp collection, which contained a few envelopes with first day stamps from places such as the Federated Malay States. 'Gee, they're nice,' she advised me. 'My son would sure like to have one of those.'

'Take your pick of any one, just as long as you sign off with that piece of chalk on the rest of your search,' I replied. And so it happened. Welcome to French Canada, where the Roman Catholic Church still ruled the roost as in Eire, and a 3% tax on all sales in the province went to help maintain its comfortable position.

After a brief stopover in Montreal, where someone had given me an introduction to Alcan or the Aluminium Company of Canada, I continued by train to Toronto, Ontario. Alcan offered me a job managing their poultry farm in what was then British Guiana, where they had huge bauxite mining interests. This did not seem to be a very good idea, but I little guessed that some three years later I would be selling Quaker Oats to their employees there. In 1952 Toronto was the growing business centre of Canada to which the majority of Brits and other non-French immigrants headed, while Montreal was the commercial centre of French Canada. Their relationship was similar to that which exists between Sydney and Melbourne. To carry the comparison further, both Canada and Australia had artificial federal capitals like Ottawa, where civil and military servants lived in their own little worlds, but the engine of the economy was elsewhere, including Alberta, where the vast oil and natural gas deposits were being opened up. There was the usual rivalry and intolerance between the British and French Canadians, which at times was a drag on the progress of the country. I say British Canadians since of course thousands of Scots were pushed out there during the Highland clearances and Toronto was a very buttoned-up city, known locally as Toronto the Good. Canadian casual shirts and other clothes reflected the designs of Scottish plaids; square dancing was all the rage and ice hockey and curling the national sports. On some occasions when an Ontario Canadian was explaining something to me and I asked, 'But what about Quebec?' the invariable reply was, 'That's not Canada, that's Quebec.' Oil and water.

The climate of southern Ontario, surrounded as it is by Lakes Ontario, Eyrie and Huron, is not the best; it was hot, humid and sticky in the summer, and cold and at times damp with ice storms in the winter, which coated and pulled down the telephone and hydroelectric lines. This was before air conditioning ameliorated the effects of their climate. Thus at the end of June I found myself a berth in the Hotel Ford in west Toronto, a $2.50-a-night flea pit, but affordable. Shortly after my arrival the World Middleweight title fight took place somewhere in the USA between Sugar Ray Robinson and, I think, Randolph Turpin. It was relayed over TV in the hotel bar, heaving with punters, and with the temperature around 100°F and humidity in the 90s, even though it was the evening. About thirty years on when watching the young man from the country entering the big city by bus in the film *Midnight Cowboy*, I thought back to that night. If it was Randolph Turpin, he lost, but it was a bruising contest of sheer survival.

I had about £100 in savings from Liverpool, courtesy of living on the yacht in Garston docks, so opened an account in one of the local banks, got a list of the companies in the animal feeds and other cereal businesses and started doing the rounds to find a job. After a week or ten days I began to experience the genuine helpfulness of Canadians in all walks of life which continued for the rest of my stay. As I went into the bank one day the young female teller asked me if I had got a firm job yet. I thought she might be worried at the rate that my funds were running out, but she pointed me in the direction of the Maple Leaf Milling Co. whom, she had heard, were looking for a sales rep to cover northern Ontario, where they had difficulty in getting young Canadians to stay for long, due to the distance from the bright lights of the big city. That is how I got my first job, but before I took it I went to see a local businessman, to whom I had been given an introduction from someone in Liverpool. He advised me to take it; Maple Leaf were not the best, but nevertheless were good employers, and such a job would immerse me in local Canadian life and culture. He told me to avoid any group of British immigrants who had a tendency to sit around and grumble about their new host country instead of joining it, warts and all. So apparently whingeing Poms were not restricted to Australia.

The deal was $65 per week as a 'combination salesman' – that is, one selling flour, cereals, cake mixes and animal feeds, with travelling expenses when 'on the road'. I needed to buy my own car to cover a sales territory about the size of Wales geographically, starting about ninety miles north of Toronto at a place called Orillia on Lake Simcoe, going due north via the Muskoka Lakes holiday area to North Bay, and then due west to Sault Ste Marie, commonly known as the Soo. The car was a pale green Chevrolet coupe, the first that I had owned for myself, and it immediately put me $1,900 in debt to the company, a hold that they had on me, and an incentive to work it off my back just as soon as possible. Everyone had a car in North America in order to live a normal life outside the towns or cities, and this was the way to get one.

The first part, the Muskoka Lakes, was a region of many small freshwater lakes immediately to the east of Georgian Bay on Lake Huron, and it was really the summer and winter holiday region for Torontonians. Canada was on a roll at that time with the boom in mineral commodities, and with their expanding incomes, families were investing in the so-called cottages that they all aspired to, probably the majority being built by their owners over the weekends, since they all seemed to marry young and to be good working with their hands. I was constantly asked when I was going to get married, and did not have the heart to tell them that I had no intention of getting tied down until I had seen a lot more of the world, since they were on the whole home bodies contented with their lot. And why not, since it was a pretty good lot? Fifty years on I read in the colour supplements of the better weekend press in England that the Muskoka Lakes are being touted as the new playground for the American old money from the Hamptons on Long Island and Martha's Vineyard, who want to get away from the influx of new money from New York City. More planes criss-crossing the ether, and when they get up there they will still have to deal with the black flies in August plus the somewhat hostile feelings of the established Canadians, who may resent their American invasion. Anti-Americanism is what drives a significant number of Canadians to varying degrees, just as it does the Scots towards the English today, now that the latter are stuck in their rut and no longer sharing in the spoils of Empire.

The north of the territory stopped at North Bay, a fairly large town that had probably been planted there in the first instance as a stopping point for the Canadian Pacific Railway system, the means by which folk in the 1950s travelled from coast to coast. To clear the line or announce their arrival their engines would make that haunting, long-drawn-out 'whooo whooo' sound, just like a RN destroyer would let out a cheerful, shorter 'whup, whup, whup' sound on leaving harbour. One forgets that at that time it was still the age of the automobile and trains, with business people commuting from New York to Chicago on the so-called 'Twentieth-century Express', while those with a greater wander-lust took to the road west to California by Route 66. Four-lane highways were only just being built between fairly close large cities like Toronto and Hamilton. I could have gone further north to Timmins, the archetypal tough mining town for uranium and other heavy metals, where it was said on a weekend night one could hear twenty or more different languages spoken as miners were sucked in from all over the world. It was a tough place, there were no farmers up there, and local wholesalers could service it. To the west of North Bay the trans-Canada Highway was being constructed, the road that was to link Canada from the eastern

Maritime Provinces to Vancouver, a distance of 4,860 miles. All that area was geologically an extension of the Laurentian Shield of old, hard, igneous rocks and there were all sorts of enthusiastic amateur prospectors running around with their hammers, chipping away at the rock, mostly unrequited I am sure.

The construction of the highway necessitated the removal of any hills that were too high, with the contents dumped in the ensuing valley, so the road was lined with vast, bright yellow insect-like earth removers, mainly made by the Caterpillar Corporation, the likes of which I had never seen before. By now it is probably just a local highway connecting towns, its original purpose rendered obsolete by air travel. Part-way along this to the Soo was the mining town of Sudbury, the home of International Nickel, or INCO, and it was a good example of that North American phenomenon company town. Everything was based on the extraction of nickel and the associated service industries, and it demonstrated that aspect that was not supposed to exist, namely 'the wrong side of the tracks'. Sudbury had a nice lake and one of the tallest factory chimneys in the world, if not the tallest, which belched out day and night a sulphurous yellow green smoke. The prevailing wind came from the west, so all the management houses with their trim gardens were clustered around the western lake shore, while the homes for the miners or operators were to the east, blighted by the sulphur deposits, giving the appearance of a moonscape.

Sault Ste Marie was another company town based on the Algoma Steel works, which were owned by one of those emigrant Scottish families along the lines of the Murdochs or the late Kerry Packer in Australia. It was located at the junction of the three Great Lakes: Michigan, Huron and Superior. Vessels would come up from Chicago, the grain market centre of the world, to the top of Lake Michigan, make a right into the top of Huron and then a left into Superior and so west to the major grain ports of the Head of the Lakes and Duluth. The passage interconnecting the lakes was via a series of giant locks and canals. Wealthy Americans from Chicago would also sail up in their fancy motor vessels on their way to Minnesota, to be commented on enviously by the local, less affluent Canadian onlookers. So much water off a duck's back. I arrived in this town with my new car and worldly possessions, and was sent by the resident sales rep, to digs in someone's house, since those still existed in those days. I then went to meet him in one of the local bars full of steel workers and lumber men.

Paul George, for that was his name, was a short, trim, fifty-year-old Canadian of Australian origin, bald headed and with a face screwed up like a sour apple. He was the nearest thing that I have seen to Mr Magoo, the American cartoon character, and had an uncheerful nature to match. Life apparently had dealt him some lousy hands, he did not seem ever to have been married, and he carried his grudges and bitterness on his sleeve. He would introduce himself to anyone by thrusting out his hand and barking 'Paul George' in the manner of some 'how to get on' sales manual. He seemed to do most of his business over the phone. I rapidly learned that he regarded my arrival as the equivalent of another personal cross to bear, and within a matter of days he introduced me to all and sundry as the young Limey who had been sent up to show him how to do his job. Thus I had travelled 3,000 miles to replace an incompatible Scot in Liverpool with an embittered Australian-Canadian hybrid, who would make any whingeing Pom seem like a twenty-four-carat optimist. He clearly thought that I had been sent up to do him out of his job, or close down the office, and since I had no intention of being stuck in the Canadian sticks, I decided to turn his business around without delay and then get out.

It took me about a week to work my way east and south to cover the whole territory, and then a similar time to return taking in the alternate towns that I had missed on the way out. On the section from the Soo to North Bay there were not too many small towns apart from Blind River, which was to expand with an atomic power plant from the locally mined uranium, but to the north off the highway were lush small valleys settled and farmed for the most part by immigrant Finns. I came across them quite by accident when someone suggested I went in to find out what was going on. They were very hospitable, often insisting that I stay for a meal, and were obviously delighted to have someone new to talk to from the outside world. One got the impression that their parents or grandparents had emigrated from the home country along with the Swedes during some agricultural depression, and had simply stayed on the same line of latitude, the Swedes going further west to Minnesota, where the lakes and woods reminded them of home. As they got to know me they dropped their existing suppliers and passed their orders over to our products. Paul George was impressed, and after I left he might just have got off the phone and on to the road to keep those orders coming in. Mixed product of animal feeds, domestic or bakery flour and cake and cereal mixes were shipped up by rail from the plant in the south in so-called carload lots of twenty-four to forty tons each, so one had to scramble around for the last tons to make a load. Some of the bulk flour in 50 lb cotton sacks had decorated patterns printed on them, so that they could be washed and used for making up children's summer clothes or ladies' dresses. They were known as Pretty Prints and were mainly for sale in Quebec Province, where relative poverty and large families went together. But this was not the idea of Canada as the land of milk and honey that people had at that time.

In the top right-hand corner of Georgian Bay was Manitoulin Island, which one reached after a short ferry ride from the mainland. Thus it had become the place where vast numbers of turkeys were raised, since it would have been free of the various poultry diseases, and the surrounding water would have kept it a little bit warmer in the winter. It was also a tourist summer resort and they needed to stock up with supplies, and once again my competitors did not unduly visit it. It was a nice spot to spend a weekend with excellent walking and swimming in Lake Huron, although I never got used to those vast expanses of fresh water that had no salt nor ozone. Motels were only just coming in on the highways, and up in those parts there were groups of small wooden cabins clustered around the lakeshore charging $1.75 to $2.50 per night for something a bit fancier. As far as I can recall there were separate shower and washrooms for men and women. It was a good way to live cheaply and save to pay off the car. Food was pretty unsophisticated taken mainly in the local or roadside small cafés or soda fountains. There were various soups with crackers, there was the whole gamut of sandwiches up to the triple-decker club with tomato ketchup liberally sloshed over it, and then there were the 'afters'. The routine was always the same; the young waitress would ask what you wanted, and in reply to questioning her as to what she was offering, the same reply came: 'Waal, we got apple pie, pumpkin pie, apple an' raisin pie, or pie à la mode.'

'Pie à la mode, what's that?'

'That's pie with a scoop of ice cream on top.'

'Right I'll have apple and raisin à la mode please.'

'What flavour of ice cream would you like, sur?' And so on. All these places had one thing in common, which was that they all sported a nickelodeon that played that endless, whining country music from dawn to dusk, as the diners fed their quarters into the machine. A dislike of this was about the only thing that Paul George and I had in common. However, in one such eating joint there was temporary relief, in that the machine had a record called 'Two Minutes' Silence' for a nickel, so a quarter coin bought one ten minutes' peace and quiet.

Small-town life in rural North America is of course very, very small, particularly when the hick town is miles from any large city. People were born, raised and died there, contented with their parochial lot. This was also before the age of TV. However, the folk were not without a porky sense of humour. Many years later when Trudeau was Premier, he with the flower-power wife whose favours he was reported to have shared with one of the Beatles, he and his Liberal party had come in promising all the usual things such as new hospitals, schools and aid to this and that group of supporters. After about three years of this expenditure, the coffers were beginning to run dry and his party could not afford to spend more without putting up taxes, which would have been a vote loser. So he went on coast-to-coast TV and told the nation that the Liberals had come into power promising to do this, that and the other. They had done all of that, but expenditure was running in advance of income, so for the rest of the parliament only those people living in dire straits could expect to receive any financial help from the federal government. At that time the Ontario provincial government was Conservative, and when the mayor of one of the small towns in northern Ontario heard this broadcast, he immediately called an extraordinary meeting of his council, who voted nem con (that is, unanimously) to rename their town from Clearwater Lake (or whatever it was) to Dire Straits, and applied for a federal loan to improve their ice-hockey centre! The next day the *Toronto Globe and Mail* had a photo of them all standing there holding a wide banner stretched out in front of them with the new name 'Dire Straits'! I somehow doubt if they got their grant.

At the end of October, just as the snow was beginning to fall and I was looking forward to getting some skiing in the Huntsville area of the Muskoka Lakes, where there were some reasonable hills and lifts for my beginner's standard at that time, I was told by the Toronto office that I had confirmed what they thought about there being enough business to go after up there, providing Paul George got out of his office, and I was to be transferred to Guelph, about sixty miles west of Toronto. So Paul and I parted not exactly as friends ('you're not such a bad young Limey after all') but at least with an understanding on his part as to how he could go about keeping his job – and Canada was not a good country in which to be let go, as the euphemism went, at the onset of winter. But before I left I was able to see for the first time Ontario's famous fall colours as the leaves of their national tree, the maple, changed from greens to reds, oranges, yellows and all the combinations thereof. Altogether better than one would see in New England, since this part of Ontario was full of small lakes, with the colours visible twice, both on the trees and in their watery reflections.

Guelph was one of three medium-sized towns forming the apex of a triangle, whose base was the Toronto–Hamilton axis along the shore of Lake Ontario. The other two were Galt, which had been settled mainly by Scots immigrants and had architecture in stone to match, and Kitchener, whose inhabitants were mainly of German stock, with a reputation for hard work to match, next to a large colony of Amish and Mennonites about whom I was to learn much more the following year. Kitchener's original name had been Berlin, but in 1916 for obvious reasons they had changed it to the name of the current British military hero, then shortly to perish in a watery grave. Guelph must have had a population at that time of about 40,000 folk, basically of English extraction, but with a colony of Italians who lived literally on the other side of the tracks, just as Boston, Massachusetts has an Italian colony separate from the prevailing Irish and Anglos. How the Italians got there and what they did for a living I never really found out. Guelph was a minor university town since it was the home of the Ontario Agriculture College (OAC) and the Ontario Veterinary College (OVC), both affiliated to the University of Toronto. They have since expanded markedly with the size of the city into the full-blown University of Guelph. I lived on College Avenue and got to know many of the lecturers and professors, and they were very welcoming, open minded and hospitable. The college dining hall was open to outsiders such as me, so I was able to meet a variety of people during the mealtimes there.

Many of the other people that I met had been in the Canadian Armed Services during WW2 and thus had seen more of the world than the people in the north of the province, and could be described as being loyal to the British ethos. Undoubtedly some of this feeling was probably due to their need to combine their identity with a greater whole, the better to resist some of the overpowering influences from south of their border that they did not always want to emulate or be overwhelmed by. Outside the provincial parliament buildings in Toronto there is a memorial to those Canadians who fell fighting for the mother country in the South African war. How they got mixed up in that, other than through blind loyalty to a national cause, I cannot think.

Shortly after I retired in 1986 I helped organise for a friend a group visit of Canadians to London to see the sights, as part of some company reward system. One of them told me that he was going to visit some cousins whose address he had in the Midlands. He had been born and bred in Canada, so I asked him how he had acquired those relatives. Apparently his father had been the black sheep of the family, in the days when such younger male members were packed off to one of the colonies with a small income, known as 'remittance men'. However, when WW2 was declared he heard from his relatives to say that the Old Country needed him and that it was his duty to return to fight for the mother country from which he had been so unceremoniously ejected. So back he came, had a 'good war' that redeemed him, and returned to Canada. As I said, Ontario Canadians were loyal to the British cause.

When I was in northern Ontario I did not really have the need to acquire a liquor licence for my personal consumption, since there were bars, or beer parlours, in some of the towns where I could get a drink. But now that I was living a more stable and social life I needed to be able to return hospitality and have access to the local rye whisky, Canadian Club. The Temperance League seemed to have a very strong hold on Canadian life at that time. In Australia they are referred to by the drinking classes as 'the Wowsers' – except, of course, Australia is supposed to be classless. But in Canada, whether a town was wet or dry depended on a local vote of its adult residents. If they voted for beer parlours they got a pub divided into two. The one section was for men only and it had no traditional bar but was full of metal tables with four chairs per table at which the drinkers sat, to be served by a waitress. The theory, and indeed maybe the practice, was that if a man was sitting down he was less able to get into an argument or start a fight. The adjoining section was for 'ladies and escorts' where a lady could only enter accompanied by a male partner. This was to prevent prostitutes entering for the purposes of soliciting. All very Calvinistic. To get hard booze one needed a personal liquor licence, since spirits were sold only in stores owned and managed by the Ontario Liquor Commission, and whatever one bought was entered up in one's little book. Thank goodness Guelph was wet.

My new sales territory stretched north from Guelph through a hilly area up to the shore of Lake Huron and Georgian Bay. A big surprise was the size of the farms, mainly 100-acre, lots laid out on a grid system off unmade roads designated as 'rural routes', which had been allocated to the immigrants as they came in. They were mainly mixed farms with cattle, pigs and cereal crops, although broiler chicken raising was starting to take off. The farms in East Anglia had been much larger by comparison. In addition to the house each farm had a large wooden barn, built on a mound of earth to raise it above ground level, or into a hillside, so that the upper part could be used for the storage of grain or hay and machinery, with a cellar below to keep the livestock in the cold weather. Many of them were painted a red colour, and at the time I simply accepted that as the local design. However, when I went to Norway for the first time in the 1970s I saw similar ones on their farms, confirming the source of their design. Similar climates, similar solutions for storage. So it occurs to me that Ontario is not so much Anglo-Scottish but rather Scandinavian – the same design as the Norwegian barns, the same ridiculous laws that still exist in Sweden with its government liquor stores, so that Swedes head for Copenhagen to throw up over the weekend, and the same obsession among the more affluent population for securing their small piece of lake shore not too far from where they lived, to build a summer cottage, where the wife and kids could go for the long school summer holidays, closed up for the winter after the Canadian Thanksgiving holiday in October.

Once the winter set in after November, the main roads were kept clear by their efficient highways system used to such conditions, and the easiest way to visit the farms strung along the rural roads was by ski, so I bought myself a pair of wooden ones. Once again it was a case that what was a novelty to a new immigrant was a bore to the locals, for whom the winter was for watching ice hockey. However, the farmers were pleased to see a new face and rewarded it with their business. By the end of 1953 I had paid off my car, decided that Maple Leaf Milling Company was not for the long haul, and started to look for pastures new. Such word gets around and one day as I was sitting having my sandwich lunch, another salesman, about a year younger than I was, sat himself down next to me. He introduced himself as George Gray, and asked me what I was doing? As he well knew, I was looking through the job ads in the *Toronto Globe and Mail*, and he asked me if I had thought of the Quaker Oats Company, who had a vacancy in the sales area next to his. I had not, since their head office was in Peterborough, ninety miles east of Toronto, and if I had been caught wandering off like that, it would have been the chop and I could not afford the risk.

That is how I came to join the Quaker Oats Company of Chicago, with whom I spent the next thirty-three years based in three countries, with a wealth of travel to others, some good long-term friendships and on the whole, despite the usual frustrations from time to time, happy memories. Last, but not least, I gained the wife whom I met at work. I kept in close touch with George until his untimely death about seven years ago. He did me a good turn.

I was put to work in the German part of southern Ontario based on Kitchener. For the first couple of days I went round the farms, mainly owned by Amish and Mennonites, with my new boss and the representative of our largest feed dealer, at the end of which I was taken to their office and told, 'You'll do.' When I asked what they meant, I was advised that this had been a proving round to see if the farmers would accept me as 'simpatico'. Apparently the two previous sales reps had been local men, who had showed some of the prejudice against these sects that was pretty common, despite the fact that Canada was a country of immigrants, but not so much as it has become today.

The Amish, known in the USA as Pennsylvania Dutch (meaning Deutsch or German) were the old order of this Protestant sect that had fled religious persecution in Germany many years previously. They lived in towns with names like Elmira and Schomberg, refusing to accept the trappings of modern life, wearing black clothes, the women having head-scarves and no make-up or jewellery, driving into market with a black horse and buggy, reading only the Bible and having nothing to do with modern entertainment or communications like radio. TV was only just starting then. They numbered about 40,000 and married their own kind, so that there was progressive inbreeding since 'outsiders' who converted to their ways were rare. Like the Pakistanis and other Muslims, who marry their cousins, their stock was degenerating, and I often observed on their farms a child that was mentally backward doing some menial job. Doubtless incest entered the equation somewhere too, as it does in such rural, closed communities. The big beef that the true Canadians had against them was that they wanted their own schools and would not serve their country in time of war. Some of them had accepted a part of the Canadian way of life and had advanced to being the New Order Mennonites that I worked with. They had cars, but with dull colours and all the chrome painted over black. They would read other books and even listen to the radio, but they would still not marry out of the sect. However, one could carry on a normal conversation with them about current affairs, and they did not object to one asking questions about themselves, which the Old Order did.

An even more way-out sect were the Dukhobors, a Russian non-conformist sect, who after rejecting Orthodoxy and attaching little importance to the Bible, were banished by Alexander I. In the 1840s some of them immigrated into Transcaucasia, where the Russian ruler had territorial designs, but the only sign that remains of their presence is a neglected cemetery outside Urgensch by Lake Aral, later turned into a wasteland by Soviet economic policies. Leo Tolstoy and the English Quakers helped them to immigrate to Saskatchewan, where the winter climate is enough to freeze the balls off a brass monkey, so they pushed on over the Rockies into British Columbia. There in the 1950s they continued their anarchic life, accepting the benefits of the Canadian state, while refusing to integrate or send their children to local schools. Eventually the provincial government came down on them hard, and there were photos in the papers of elderly Dukhobors gentlemen protesting by parading through the towns in the altogether, with their long bushy beards reaching down to, but not quite covering, their reproductive tackle, of which an Aberdeen Angus bull would have been proud. Finally the provincial government had had enough, and told them either to shape up or ship out, which latter they did, to Mexico. Goodness knows what its Catholic hierarchy made of them, and I think they continued south into one of the Central American countries that were looking for agricultural immigrants.

Summers in Ontario were short and hot, roughly from the beginning of May to October, so people took every opportunity to get out of doors, either at their cottages, fishing in the lakes, playing baseball and so on. But in 1953 the town of Stratford, about thirty miles south of Guelph, was encouraged by the English Shakespearean director Tyrone Guthrie, to take a leaf out of the American phenomenon, particularly in New England, of 'Summer Seasons' or some such name. But he was more ambitious and he persuaded the local people, governmental and artistic, to set up a theatre in the round under a marquee for a season of Shakespearean plays, which in due course became permanent as the Stratford Summer Festival. At the time of that first one an English vet, who had taken a post-graduate degree in Guelph, and now worked at Ibadan University in Nigeria, was in Guelph for part of his 'home' leave, and we met up. *Richard the Third* was playing, with Alec Guinness in the lead role, and despite the fact that the world and his wife were heading in that direction, we decided to take a chance on picking up tickets. We were standing in a very long queue on the open grass, when we noticed a middle-aged couple looking our way, who beckoned us over. They asked, 'Would you boys like a couple of seats?' – and simply passed the tickets to us, saying that some of their friends had had to cancel, and absolutely refused payment. Second row from the front of the circular stage. One cannot but appreciate North American generosity, and it would not have happened in London in those days.

I had no inkling of it, but by the summer of 1954 my stay in Canada was coming to a close. Quaker Oats porridge is a remarkable product; the people who built the business did an extraordinary job in getting it accepted around the world, in a huge variety of climates and consumed in a variety of different ways. I guess one can put it down to old-fashioned missionary zeal shared with the founding fathers of companies such as Kellogg's, also based in the American Mid-west, whom the bien pensant Europeans think of as being parochial. The company export office was in New York City, divided into two, the one for the subsidiaries and exports in the Caribbean and Latin America, and the other dealing with the rest of the world. Since WW2 they had not had any sales representation covering the Caribbean islands, where they had good markets, and they concluded that it would be better to have Canadians going into that area, with their British connection, rather than Americans. The exports were mainly for human cereal products and bread flour, handled by the cereals division, rather than animal feeds, which were something of a subsidiary. I thought this was an ideal way to see the world and get paid at the same time, and asked my supervisor to put my name forward. He was a bit stuffy and refused to do so on the grounds that he had spent a year training me, and just as I was getting productive he would have to start all over again with someone else. So that was that until I called for the first time on a man called Ray Blair, who had built up the largest business for day-old chicks in Ontario. He was an ebullient character, asked me what I was being paid and told me he would increase it by fifty per cent for me to go and sell his chicks in Quebec with my schoolboy French. I told him that French Canada was not for me and that what I really wanted to do was to get into the export division of my present employers. The next thing I received was a phone call from my supervisor on the lines of, 'You're in big trouble, who the hell have you been talking to?' I was told to meet the company president in Toronto in a couple of days when he flew back from the corporate office in Chicago.

Jim Wharry was a giant of a man, 6'4" in his socks and with a girth and weight to match. A graduate of the Ontario Agricultural College in Guelph, he had risen to become the President of the Canadian company, which had been the vehicle for expansion around the Anglo-Saxon export markets, including the UK from 1896. He listened to what I had to say and confirmed that he would do all that he could to get me an interview, although they were only looking for one candidate at that time. Within a matter of days I was on my first flight to be interviewed in New York, which took a couple of days. On my return there was a letter awaiting me from John Nixon in Walmer, couched in the usual circumlocutions of those days when anyone was telling anyone else that that someone was dying of cancer. Briefly, my father had been diagnosed with having the disease in an advanced stage in January 1954 and this was June. Despite the fact that the connection with smoking and cancer had not been clinically proven at that time, this came as no surprise to me since he had smoked sixty cigarettes per day for over thirty years and had had a bad smoker's cough that used to wake the household up for years. I arranged to fly back 'home' immediately, and with aircraft range at that time we made stops at Goose Bay in Labrador and Prestwick in Scotland, from where I phoned my mother to learn that Tishy had died that night. Thus, aged fifty-eight, like most of his male Indian peers he did not make it into his sixties.

Tim was out in Malaya planting rubber, my mother had collapsed into the care of a daily nurse and John Nixon made all the funeral arrangements. He and I set off in his car for Charing Crematorium near Ashford, a few of Tishy's pals who had cars came along and joined us in a pub afterwards, and that was that. I am eternally grateful to John Nixon and a few years later when I visited Australia to look for acquisitions in 1957, the year of Sputnik, I realised his motivation apart from his innate helpfulness. The Nixons had one son, who, after wartime in the Army where he was an officer in the Commandos, had blown an inheritance of £30,000 from his grandmother on some wild scheme where he bought an ex-Landing Ship Tanks to trade between Tangier and Gibraltar. Goodness knows what they were trading in – smuggled goods before the drugs trade I assume – but he lost the lot. When I looked him up at his father's request he was working as a wharfie in Sydney, those blokes who wielded large metal hooks to handle cargo sacks in the docks. He was basically a nice chap who had lost direction, and when I met him in a bar he was with a group of those ghastly ex-public school Brits, male and female, who had dropped out in Australia, that sat around bitching about the natives while thinking the world owed them a living. John's son died of drink a few years later. I can only conclude that he had decided to give me the benefit of his advice and experience as a surrogate relative. It was well received.

I took Dorothy off touring the West Country for a week or ten days, and when we returned to Kent, there was a cable advising me that the job for which I had been interviewed was mine if I cared to return. I also called in at my alma mater Wye College on their Commemoration Day at the end of June. The professor of horticulture recognised me and asked what I was doing. I replied that I was in Canada. 'Oh really, at McGill?' (This is the famous university in Montreal.)

'Er no, Quaker Oats.'

'What, growing them?' he asked.

'No, selling them.'

There followed a pause while the sheer horror of this information was absorbed into his academic mind, ending with, 'Oh well, I suppose that someone has to do that sort of thing!'

Evidently attitudes had not changed and since 'needs must when the devil drives' I was off to be given six weeks training in the Peterborough, Ontario mill, all seven floors of it, in flour milling and cereal manufacturing, so that one had a knowledge of the products that one would be selling. I was warned by George Gray's wife, who hailed from there, that the town had the reputation for being very cliquey, due to being originally settled by Scots, and now the Canadian home of two large companies, Quaker Oats and General Electric of Canada.

Whatever the reason, of the four towns where I lived in Ontario, it was the least hospitable, and I must have read more books and gone to more lousy MGM blockbuster films there than anywhere else in my life, mainly with a biblical or Roman plot at that time (does *The Ten Commandments* ring a bell?). I was put up in the McGinnis hotel, where the proprietress of that name was a small woman of middle age, her grey hair pulled back into a severe bun, looking like some disapproving seventeenth century Puritan lady. She sat in her rocking chair and peered over her spectacles at anyone entering *her* lobby of whom she disapproved. Eventually, desperate for some home cooking, I volunteered to help someone that I had met, who was redecorating his house over the weekends, and saw how at least one of the local families lived. They were just very reserved.

I took Lene back there in 1985, and it was still in a time warp, with the clothing stores selling lumberjack patterned shirts for men and frumpy stuff for the ladies. This at a time when Toronto, ninety miles to the west, had had a complete makeover, architectural as well as cultural, with the influx of continental Europeans like the Ukrainians and Balts, and some Chinese, who introduced a cuisine and atmosphere that is now compared in the travel pages of our press with Boston, Mass. All of which only goes to show that one should not judge a country and its people from one's experience in a single town.

That then was my two-and-a-half-year stay in one province of Canada, where from everything that happened to me, including the welcoming help that I received from all sorts of people along the line, I concluded that I had made the correct choice in 'going west', like all young men were advised to do. Nevertheless I could not have settled there permanently; it had too cold a climate, was too far from the sea, and ice hockey and baseball don't appeal. My next move was to New York City with a certain amount of trepidation, since I had never lived in such a place before, and it had a tough, unfriendly reputation.

10.

New York: Gateway to the Caribbean (Years 28–29)

Early in November 1954 Tom de Bloeme and I were transferred from the Canadian company to join Quaker Oats Pan-American Inc., the export division for all the company's products sold into Latin American and the Caribbean markets, except those countries where there was a subsidiary company, such as Brazil or Columbia. I think we must have been the first two individuals at our level (that is, excepting Americans who had been sent out mainly to European subs as chief executives) to have been transferred. Tom was a Canadian of Dutch origin, as his name implies, aged forty-two years, with a wife and two daughters, and had been a bomber pilot in Britain during WW2, while I was twenty-eight. Securing a permanent resident's visa to work in the USA in those days was a pretty lengthy business, and one had to sign a list to the effect that one had never been a member of a communist party, nor had indulged in the most lengthy and extraordinary list of misdemeanours and sexual and social practices. So rather than wait to go through the whole rigmarole, we were sent down on student visas. I set off first by train from Toronto to New York city with my green trunk, tin box of books and set of golf clubs, while Tom followed by plane a few days later, since his family were remaining in Ontario.

The immigration officer at the US border control took one look at this visa and asked me where my mother resided. I replied that she in fact lived in England, but I could not understand the relevance of his question to my entry. He went on to say that if my mother lived in England that it was my home, and I countered that I had emigrated to Canada some years previously and that was my new home. He was pretty local in his thinking, but despite his doubts agreed to let me in, and that is how I entered the Land of the Free, with a sigh of relief.

The company office was at 120 Wall Street, at the east end where it bordered the old Fulton fish market, now gentrified as a tourist area. The building must have been about fifteen floors or so high, and we were on the fifth. I reported in and was told that I could have a few days in a hotel at company expense while looking for somewhere to live, but not to find anything too permanent, since after a few weeks' training and familiarisation with the markets we would visit, Tom and I were to set off early in December. It must have been mid-week and I found a hotel just to the east of Washington Square at $3.50 per night, and awaited Tom's arrival. On Saturday I woke up reasonably early, and drew the curtains of my room to see smoke billowing out of the roof of the large building across the street. I had no idea what it was but called reception to send for the fire brigade, which arrived almost immediately, so it must have been on its way. And what a fire that was! It was Wanamaker's store going up, one of the big department stores at a medium-price level with Macy's and Gimbles, but not up with Saks Fifth Avenue, all basically Jewish owned, I guess. Fortunately the wind was in the right direction so that I had a grandstand view of it over the weekend. That was the end of their store, and I don't think that it was ever rebuilt. However, creating things clearly ran strong in that family, and twenty years or so later London was the recipient of their imagination and generosity when Sam Wanamaker, driven out of the USA by McCarthyism conceived the idea of rebuilding the old Shakespearean Globe Theatre on the South Bank of the Thames.

On $115 per week the price of that hotel, whatever it was called, was a bit too rich for our blood, so we looked around until we found the Hotel Earl on Sixth Street just off the west side of Washington Square, where we were offered a two-bedroom apartment with a shared bathroom at $2.75 per night each, and that became our home from home while in New York. It was a typical old-fashioned small hotel with a front desk and a rickety lift with metal gates going up the five floors or so. It offered no food and we had no cooking area, so we had to go out to eat all meals. But it was 'home' and they very kindly agreed to store my gear in their basement while I was away on long trips which ran into months. So as far as I was concerned, New York had a soft centre after all. About three years ago, when Concorde was going on some of its last flights to the USA, my son Peter took one of BA's weekend offers and looked the hotel up for me. It has reoriented its front door ninety degrees to the east and the old Hotel Earl chrysalis has metamorphosed into a butterfly named No. 1 Washington Square, and charges accordingly at $58 per night, which is still pretty cheap by New York standards. A good marketing move.

We took the subway, which was a hot, uncomfortable mode of travel in those days, down to the Wall Street office. It sounds pretty exotic, but in fact it was a fairly basic building, not air conditioned nor up to the swanky standards of the banks and brokers such as Merrill Lynch nearer the famous church at the top end – a case of God and Mammon in close association. You could say that we were at the wrong end, since Quaker Oats was not known for throwing its money around. The office staff was like something out of a B movie. The first thing that I learned was that the USA was not exactly the meritocracy claimed at the time, since companies such as Ford, Heinz, Swifts, the meat packers, Campbell's Soups and Quaker Oats were essentially run by the scions of the founding families and their relatives.

There were three dark Italians who stuck together and were inevitably referred to by the others as the Mafia. Smithy, aka Doris Smith, was a lady in her forties with a heart of gold, who soothed the young secretaries and kept the ship on an even keel. Hank was a big German, in charge of the shipping department dispatching our products overseas from plants in Canada and the USA, and was clearly motivated by the hospitality that the shipping companies laid on after work on Fridays. This, I should make clear, involved booze, not broads. Teddy Steul was a delightful, typical, small New Yorker around sixty years of age, who was extremely hospitable and took Tom and me out to Jones Beach to swim when we returned from our trips the following summer. He retired to Florida; we kept in touch with Christmas cards, and years later when we had a business conference near Clearwater, Florida. I persuaded whoever was in charge to invite Teddy up for a meal after the work sessions to meet old friends, which he certainly appreciated.

At one stage I was with a group chatting in the office, and one of them asked me where I came from, since I did not sound like a Canadian. I explained that I was English, and had been brought up in various parts of the world since my father had worked for an oil company in the Far East, 'Where did I mean by the Far East?' someone asked. 'Oh, countries like India, Pakistan, Singapore, Malaysia and so on,' I replied.

'So that's what you regard as the Far East', he replied. 'For us in New York the Far East is Saudi Arabia, the Lebanon is the Near East, and Brooklyn is the Very Near East!'

Before we were turned loose on to the company's import agents in the Caribbean markets, we had to be introduced to the grocery products that we would be selling, and we were assigned for a few days each to the domestic district sales managers in Harlem and Brooklyn for product induction. I drew Harlem first, which in those days, sixty years ago, was still mainly white. The Puerto Ricans were starting to come in, but not as yet the African Americans from the south. Which reminds me that some time in the 1970s when foreign travel began to open up, a little old lady wrote in our local *Beaconsfield Advertiser* that she had been on a trip to America, but that she did not meet any Americans. They had all introduced themselves as being, for example, from Sweden, or 'I'm Italian but my husband's from Germany', and now the Puerto Ricans and African Americans have been added to the salad bowl with ingredients that keep their distinct backgrounds.

At any rate the grocery stores were mainly so-called mom-and-pop small self-service units, owned by Italians or Jews. They probably knew that they were about to be squeezed out, so it was a dog-eat-dog situation to get distribution of one's products. The district manager simply carried in a case of breakfast cereals and began to squeeze them on to the shelves, throwing out the competition if necessary. This understandably upset one store owner called Louis (pronounced Loo-ey), to the point where I thought that they would lock horns physically. I stood back and tried not to look part of the scene. Eventually our salesman pleaded 'Aw c'mon, Louis, for Chrissake gimme an order, that's my borse.' Louis's face took on a look of utter contempt as he spat out, 'Piss off, I hate borses!' and I think he probably meant it.

When I got back to the hotel I found Tom flaked out flat on his bed, after his introduction to the Brooklyn trade. When I asked if he was ill, he replied that he was just tired, everyone that they had met had been so *rude*. I replied that that was New York for you, and to wait until he went up to Harlem! One could see where Arthur Miller found his material for *Death of a Salesman*.

We had one more stop to make before we set off and that was to buy tropical clothing – not the easiest thing to find in those days at the beginning of a North American winter. Eventually we were pointed to that crème de la crème of men's clothing stores, Brooks Brothers on Fifth Avenue, with prices to match. Tropical and man-made fibre suits were stacked in neat piles according to the chest measurement of the jackets. The jackets fitted well enough, but the trousers hung on us like those of stage clowns. Eventually the salesman enquired, 'You gen'lemen are not from the USA, are you?' When we confirmed that we were not he continued, 'I thought not, we cater for American seat measurements.' He ended up by mixing and matching jackets and trousers at no extra cost.

At last we were ready to set off. Since I was British I was assigned to our then colonies of Jamaica, Trinidad and Tobago, Barbados and British Guiana, ending up in Venezuela. The whole trip was to take from December 1954 until April in the following year – not hard to take, when the population of the UK were still restricted to £25 foreign exchange per annum. Tom de Bloeme, with his 'foreign' name drew the short straw and was assigned to Haiti (Papa Doc, Ton Ton M'coute and all that), the Dominican Republic, Curacao, Aruba and Surinam or Dutch Guiana, next to Venezuela. I don't think that he was all that impressed, but at least the climate was better than that of a Canadian winter. My last request to my boss, Harold, was to sort out my permanent resident's visa and send me the necessary paperwork, so that I could return to the Land of the Free, and he assured me that he would. Some hope.

Jamaica was still a British colony at that time, with the governor at the top of the pyramid and the poor Jamaicans living in west Kingston at the bottom. It has always been a somewhat violent place, fought over by the British, French and Spanish, and home to pirates, such as Captain Morgan. Nevertheless like most colonies it was well run, the roads were paved, there was a reasonable amount of so-called law and order, and most people were fairly well off. Its economy depended on sugar, bananas (sent across the world in Fyffes banana boats), alumina mined from bauxite by the two American and Canadian companies, Alcoa and Alcan, and last but not least Jamaican rum, which is much darker than those from the other Caribbean islands, and provided the rum ration for the sailors of the Royal Navy.

Tourism was in its infancy, mainly for Canadians who came down to Montego Bay on the north coast and the odd wealthy expatriate Brit freed from the restraints of currency restrictions by virtue of their overseas earnings, such as Noel Coward, who built his small house on a headland east of Ocho Rios. This had its large open window looking out to sea, the famous 'Room with a View'. The centre of the island with the Blue Mountains ascending up to several thousand feet was as beautiful as the coastline, and gave the name to the eponymous brand of coffee exported worldwide. Last but not least, as we did in many colonial countries, we had established excellent botanical gardens outside Kingston, to which parents would come with their children dressed in their colourful best on Sunday afternoons, a sight for sore eyes, and a source of great social pride for the parents. Nevertheless the post-war rumblings for independence from colonial rule had started, and within a few years charismatic leaders or self-serving demagogues (according to one's political interpretation) like Bustamente and Manly had taken power for the islanders. Harry Belafonte played it in *Island in the Sun*, the Marxists took over and the middle-income people with money fled to Canada and the UK.

Quaker had not had a representative visit there since the 1930s, so I was to investigate how our main oats product was consumed. It has many uses in the tropics apart from as a porridge, such as a weaning food, for invalids, or even to make a cooling oat drink by soaking the oats in water, straining the liquid off and adding squeezed lime and ice. I therefore went up to the university to see if they had a statistical department, and was in luck. They had recently completed a social survey of the island,

and the departmental head, one John Oliver, who had a Master's degree in statistics from Ames University, Iowa, agreed to help me. We devised a questionnaire regarding breakfast eating habits, divided the map of Kingston, where the bulk of the population lived, into a so-called Latin square to randomise the visits, and decided to make 500 calls, with the aid of four cheerful Jamaican lady interviewers. I packed them into a Ford Zephyr car, and we set off.

All went fairly straightforwardly until about the third day when we drove down Hanover Street, and stopped outside a tall building with balconies, decorated by a few of the local girls leaning out for a breath of air. Ten minutes later my lot emerged giggling together, and when I pressed them for what was so amusing, they explained that all the girls claimed to have had porridge for breakfast, Quaker porridge specifically, because 'Madame says it gives us vigour!' Well, well, who would have thought that about such a mundane product? It opened up new avenues for advertising... After tabulating the results and writing up the report, with major assistance from John Oliver, I took him out for a meal. He was in his late twenties, as black as the ace of spades, and part-way through our meal remarked that he would never receive hospitality like that from anyone in the management of our local agent, where the management and staff were Jamaicans of various hues. When I asked him how many Jamaicans were black or coloured (mixed race), he replied, '98% and the other 2% won't admit it.'

So there was not just a colonial colour bar, but a Jamaican one too. I thought about this in 1993 when my mother was in a nursing home in London, where most of the nursing staff were either from Caribbean or West African countries, most of which I had visited. Naturally I used to talk to them about their home countries when they came into the room, since we had something in common, to put them at their ease, but after a while two of the West African girls, who came from Ghana and Sierra Leone, remarked separately that they enjoyed chatting with me because I did not talk down to them. When I asked them who might talk down to them, they replied, 'Oh, the other nurses from the Caribbean. They think they are a cut above us, and tell us that we are just bush Africans.' Meanwhile Caucasian people beat their breasts, thinking that they are the only ones harbouring racial prejudices!

I spent Christmas and New Year in Jamaica, which was a bit lonely and of course unseasonal, but it was enlivened by beach parties and the horseracing season. Before I left, the dates coincided with the Chinese New Year, and we made a rapid circuit of the Chinese wholesalers to collect the money that they owed, since they were noted for gambling at that time, to the point of losing their life savings. I had also been warned by someone in the New York office that the Chinese were very hospitable and were wont to press a glass of whisky on visiting overseas representatives, which could add up to a bad case of the DTs over several days. The only way out without losing face, was to clutch one's stomach and with a wry smile claim that one was the victim of a stomach ulcer, which in the 1950s was quite common, particularly among advertising executives, who sank too many dry martinis with a twist of lemon peel. Times change; now apparently they snort cocaine.

Trinidad and Tobago were not on the direct sequential route for the markets that I had to visit, but it was pointed out to me that Ash Wednesday was towards the end of February 1955, and under no circumstances should I lose the opportunity of seeing Carnival in Port of Spain, at the end of a couple of weeks' work there. The people were utterly different to Jamaicans, whom they did not like one bit. Trinidad is quite mountainous with ranges of hills going up to 940 metres, covered with forests. The people were a mixture of about forty per cent each of African and East Indian descent, one per cent each of whites and Chinese, and the rest a happy blend of all races. Columbus had discovered it in 1498 so the Spanish colonised first, followed by French refugees from Haiti and St Domingo during the French Revolution, with the inevitable British acquisition after the Napoleonic wars, so the Europeans themselves were pretty mixed and mainly Catholic. The economy was strong, based on sugar, oil and asphalt exports, but Trinidad was not a tourist objective, since the beaches were on the north side of the coast, with strong surf. The School of Tropical Agriculture was located there as part of the university affiliated to London, and a great deal of research was undertaken on behalf of many tropical crops grown in the British Commonwealth.

The Port of Spain's main claim to fame is undoubtedly Carnival, associated with steel bands, now exported to Notting Hill in August. During WW2 when the American forces were based there, oil was stored in steel drums, and the locals discovered that by cutting them down to different depths according to whether they were making a base or treble drum, they would then tune the ends with a hammer and chisel to get the notes they wanted. For days before Carnival one heard them up in the hills going bang, bang, bang with their hammers, followed by ping, ping, ping or bong, bong bong as they tested the notes. Finally it all came together in a great three day bacchanalian festival, where the whole population took to the streets of the city, linked arms and shuffled forward behind each band with their imaginative costumes, doing the so-called 'jump up', fuelled mainly by rum. Doubtless the birth rate exploded nine months later.

I had a friend from Wye working there at the agricultural school, and when carnival ended he and his Canadian wife took me over to Tobago, a mere twenty-minute flight away, but a world away from its big sister: rural coconut groves, a mountain covered with original rain forest in the centre, and the most wonderful beaches lapped by the turquoise Caribbean to the west and the blue-green Atlantic to the east. They made a claim to being Robinson Crusoe's island, despite being thousands of miles from the Pacific island where Alexander Selkirk was shipwrecked, but never mind, one's imagination could make the required step. The people were nearly all of African stock, completely laid back, and the story was that when the first American cruise ship dropped anchor offshore there, they ran up the yellow flag from a large masthead to indicate that yellow fever had broken out among the locals in order to deter the tourists! Almost the first thing that I did when I retired was to return there with Lene, and it really had not changed at all.

Barbados was the next stop, that most British of Caribbean islands jutting out into the Atlantic to the east of the Windward Islands. The story goes that when Britain declared war on

Germany on 3 September 1939, the local government assembly sent a cable to the British Prime Minister reading, 'Carry on, Britain, Barbados is right with you!' And they were – hundreds, if not thousands, sailed for London and joined mainly the RAF where they served both as pilots and ground crew, and found a minimal colour bar compared to the Army and RN (see *Bloody Foreigners* by Robert Winder, 2006). The island depended almost entirely on its sugar crop, with tourism growing from North America and wealthy expatriate Brits, who used to go out by sea for the winter. Their population was almost entirely of African descent, well educated and with a passion for cricket.

I was put into a small hotel at Accra Beach near Bridgetown, so I assume there was a slave trade connection with Ghana, which would account for their being such pleasant people. A small proportion of whites with permanent residence lived the usual colonial life. The exceptions were the so-called red legs, poor whites living in the Scotland district of the island to the north, who had originally been sent out there as indentured labour as punishment for the Monmouth rebellion by Judge Jeffreys after his Bloody Assizes in 1685. I returned to Barbados with Lene in September 2004, just in time for Hurricane Ivan to strike. By this time they had put many of their eggs into the tourism basket at the two ends – package tours from the UK and apartments on overpriced golf courses for the nouveau riche. On the day before the hurricane when they were battening down the shop fronts, we drove up to Scotland district and visited an old sugar estate mansion, of which there are a few left as museums. When our guide asked us if this was our first visit, I replied that I had visited the island once before in 1955. 'Ah,' she replied, 'that was the last time that we were hit by a hurricane!' Oh well, you can't please them all, and by midnight it had been downgraded to a tropical storm; it did damage, but not on a hurricane scale.

The last British colony was British Guiana, on the top north-east shoulder of South America next to Brazil, Venezuela and Suriname or Dutch Guiana. All the way down I was told, 'You wait until you get to Guiana, they are really hospitable down there!' It was true, partly because they were a very cheerful mixture of races – at least until independence when it all fell apart

– and partly because there was very little else to do but party and gossip, and they were hungry for outside news. The Dutch nation must go around looking for places where they can exercise their expertise in throwing up sea dikes, since they occupied the coastal areas, which are below sea level, between 1616 and 1621. The British took it over with an expedition from Barbados during the French Revolution, and after a couple more quick exchanges of ownership, it became British in 1814. The country at that time was suffering from the almost classic case of absentee land-lordism, with owners in another country. The British company Booker Bros. owned most of the sugar and rice estates, while the Canadians owned the bauxite mines, producing alumina. The people were about forty per cent of African origin (slaves) and forty per cent East Indians brought in as indentured labour for the rice and sugar plantations after the end of the slave trade. Each group more or less kept themselves to themselves. The balance was a small percentage of whites, like our agent de Caries, who came in from Brazil, the inevitable Chinese wholesalers, and people of mixed blood. As all over the world, including India, the light skinned were at the top and the dark at the bottom.

It must have been one of the unhealthiest places on earth. Elephantiasis was present enough to be noticeable among the population. It is caused by the Filaria roundworm that gets into the lymphatic glands and blocks the channels down the legs and to the scrotum. Not pleasant. Out at the airport called Robert's Field for the capital Georgetown, there were fairly large hydro-ponic gardens for growing fresh vegetables. Again they had been built during WW2 when American planes were being flown across the narrower part of the Atlantic to Dakar in West Africa, before going on to the UK. This was safer than by sea during the Battle of the Atlantic. When I visited, the gardens were managed by a local couple, where the lady had elephantiasis in one leg. She told me that the only cure was to move to a cool climate, where the worm would die off. Doubtless, when after independence in 1966 the country degenerated into civil war between the blacks and the Indians, they took their chance of moving to Canada, as did many others, brown, black and white. The country was then renamed Guyana.

The other disease that dare not speak its name was leprosy. I was told that our agent's family had a daughter with that illness, who had been sent off to a Catholic home somewhere; she was not referred to, just banished out of sight. One day our agent's sales manager took me to the other main town, New Amsterdam, some distance along the coast. When leaving one wholesaler, we shook hands and I thought his grip was rather odd, so I asked the sales manager if they had freemasonry in Guyana, explaining the reason for my question. He replied, 'Oh no, that man has had leprosy in that hand, but you're all right, he is cured now.' It seems that he was, or at least not contagious!

The great hobby was flying all manner of kites on a Saturday evening, with dozens of aficionados standing on the Dutch sea wall outside Georgetown, working their strings in the sea breeze. The other really memorable trip was by Grumman Goose seaplane, when about six of us from the agency flew across the dense rain forest to the head of the Kaiteur Falls, on the Essequibo River, as it flows out of Brazil. In from the coast there is the densest of rain forests with hard woods like greenheart from which the piles for the Liverpool piers were made to last (as in 'piles for piers, not haemorrhoids for the haristocracy'). The seaplane landed on the river about 300 metres above the falls, which are 365 feet in height, twice that of Niagara, and we taxied to a small wooded landing stage on the river bank, where a local Amerindian lived with his wife and small child. It was an incredible sight with the foaming brown water full of soil and vegetable matter plunging into the dark green jungle below. There was even a convenient solid rock jutting out from the side, where one could stand and take it all in. The take-off was equally memorable. The pilot took the seaplane further up river, turned it round and roared downstream, lifting off about 200 metres short of the lip, so that the plane dropped as it met only air beyond the edge of the falls. This was also the location where one of those way-out American sects, led by a man called Jones, decamped from California in the 1960s or so, and fearing the end of the world committed mass suicide with some poisonous drink. A terrible job for the people who went to investigate what had happened to them, but it should have been fairly simple to dispose of their bodies locally.

Down in the jungle below there were gold, diamonds and other mineral deposits that prospectors used to risk their lives to find in extreme conditions of heat and wet. I learned that in those parts Quaker was the generic term for food, tea being referred to as green Quaker, bacon as bacon Quaker, and Quaker Oats as porridge Quaker. I can only surmise that the metal, reusable cans with screw lids in which our export products were packed, became the airtight containers for commodities in the local stores, and so assumed the name.

The final stop in April 1955 was a short flight to Caracas, the capital of Venezuela which was at the start of its oil boom based on the offshore fields at Maracaibo. Americans, or some of them at any rate, described the locals as monkeys who had fallen out of trees and landed in Cadillacs. So it was not just the Brits who thought up derogatory terms for lesser breeds. As I submitted my report to New York on leaving each market, I had reminded desk-bound Harold, who had never been out in the export field nor lived out of a suitcase for several months, that I needed a proper visa to get back into the States. Promises, promises, but nothing awaited me at the US embassy in Caracas. I checked into the Hotel Tamanaco at $17 per night, which was a pretty fancy price for those days, explained by the fact that Aly Khan, accompanied by his then wife, Rita Hayworth, had checked out the previous day after a short stay. The place was agog. Quaker were selling in a new oat-based refreshing drink called Frescavena, a compendium word for '*refresco de avena*', or refreshment of oats, similar to one of the uses revealed in the Jamaican survey. This involved going out with local sales teams under an American manager to the surrounding towns and villages in order to sell in the initial stocks and put up the point-of-sale advertising. In the evenings we met to compare notes, before eating together at a late hour as is done in Latin countries. At some point I bumped into an Englishman, who recognised my accent and invited me to visit the British club. I explained that I was working for an American company and we had a full schedule with the local staff, and therefore I would not have the opportunity. A few days later I met him again and he got quite stuffy, asking why I had not come round to his club, and I politely gave him the same reason. About six years later I was queuing to board a plane on the tarmac at Düsseldorf, which was taking its time. I got into conversation with another businessman as we waited, who told me that he was finding it difficult to find good export representatives for his company. In answer to my question as to what qualities he was looking for in such individuals he replied, 'Oh, I want the sort of chap that can hold his own in any British club around the world.' And we wonder why we lost export markets to the Germans and Japanese!

The day of departure came, still with only a student's visa, and I went to the airport and presented what I had to emigration, only to be told that this was not good enough even though it had got me into the USA from Canada. So I sat and stewed while the rest of the passengers filed through. When there was no one else there I returned to the desk, and this time the officer waved me through without even the need of a bribe. So far, so good. But at what was then called Idlewild Airport in New York, it was another matter. The immigration officer was polite but firm: 'Sir, I am afraid that this is not a correct visa, I can't think how they ever let you on to that flight.' I then went through the original arguments that the visa had been good enough to come in from Canada, and my company had assured me that it would get me home again. No chance. He spelled out the alternatives, either to be sent to Ellis Island, or to catch another plane back to Canada. For a moment I considered Ellis Island. I could have called up Harold on the phone, and in reply to his query as to where I was advised him, 'Harold, I'm in a cell on Ellis Island, one of your "give me your huddled masses", now please get me out of here.' I could have dined out on that for years, but given Harold's record to date, I might still have been there, and even if I had got out it would not have looked at all good on my passport. So sanity prevailed and I returned to Peterborough, Canada, and set about getting a resident's visa. Since the quota for Kenya was three persons per year, I had to cable Burmah Shell in London requesting a letter from them to the US authorities, advising that my father was British and had only been on a three-year temporary posting to that country. In that way I could enter under the British quota.

Thus Tom and I were reunited at our modest pad at the Hotel

Earl, Washington Square until the autumn, for what proved to be the hottest and most uncomfortable summer in terms of heat and smog that New York had experienced for eighteen years. On at least two days it was bad enough for all the offices to send their staff home at lunchtime. Our routine on emerging from the subway nearest to Washington Square was always the same. Alternately one of us would head back to the apartment for a shower or cold bath, while the other went to the deli to buy a large punnet of ice cubes. This would be placed in the bottom of a metal waste-paper bin with a towel soaked in cold water over the top, thus providing an approximation to an ice box, in which we could cool down our tonic water for an evening of steady reading and G and Ts, after a meal in a local restaurant or diner. Being so close to Greenwich Village there was plenty of choice in that respect. Across the street there was also a small bar with a long polished counter, frequented by its own group of habitués. The bartender was an old Scot called Mac complete with his spoken burr, and it was the habit to tip barmen in those days before leaving. Sometimes one offered them a drink in lieu. On the only occasion that I did the latter, Mac looked embarrassed, as if he did not wish the other drinkers to hear, so we moved to the end of the bar on our own, where he leaned forward and in a low, hoarse voice advised me, 'I'm sorry, sir, I canna accept. You see, I signed the Pledge twenty-three years ago, and I ha'nae touched a drop since!' Clearly a man of principle.

Unless one was affluent and could afford to live in the apartments on the Upper East Side near Central Park, Washington Square was as good a place to live on Manhattan Island or even in the rest of New York City, since it was the centre of a varied and interesting hub. In the middle of the square was the circle with grassy areas that folk used to walk around, benches to sit on to read the voluminous Sunday papers, and a group of stone chequerboard tables with dark- and light-shaded squares on the surface, where the Italian men would come in to play draughts, locally called checkers.

Fifth Avenue ran north out of the square, and in those days the buses went both ways, whereas now it has become one-way, south only. It was lined with very expensive, swanky apartments, each having its own covered walkway from the side entrance of the block to the edge of the kerb. Each was staffed by a doorman in resplendent uniform, whose job was to see residents in and out, call a cab as necessary and see them into it with a parting salute. On one occasion when Tom and I were going uptown we boarded a bus, paid our fare into the glass container, and then walked down to the back seats set fore and aft. Already sitting there was a very pretty, dark, youngish woman, wearing the summer dress with multiple petticoats underneath that were fashionable that season. A couple of stops on, a similar young woman boarded, paid her fare and then as the vehicle drove off, teetered down on her high heels to where we were sitting, and sat herself down opposite the first one. It took a few moments, but then recognition came between the two, who had clearly known one another well in the past, but had not been in touch for quite a while.

'Hi, aren't you Maisie Cohen from so and so?'

'Yes, and you're Martha Loman, ain't ya, how ya bin?' (I do not recall their actual names).

'Oh, I'm fine,' replies the first. 'Are you married yet?'

'Oh sure,' replies the second in a somewhat blasé way, 'I've been married twice!'

'Clever gal,' gasps the first. 'How d'ya manage to do that?'

Martha: 'Well, the first one was a bit of a dope, so I bugged him until he gave me a divorce and some US steel stock, and I used that to get the second!'

All this at the top of their voices for anyone listening in, as we definitely were, to hear in full. They were clearly out of our league, known colloquially in that big city as JAPs, or Jewish American Princesses. In the current PC world it is worth recalling that Americans had a habit of labelling national or ethnic groups as Wasps, Nips, Krauts, Limeys, Polaks and Big Swedes, to name the less offensive.

To the east of the square was Third Avenue or the Bowery at its lower end, a pretty run-down, shabby area, where the winos used to sit in the doorways of the old buildings, blotting out their predicament with meths or cheap wine, and begging from passers-by. So far as I know there were no drugs floating round in the 1950s, and there was no violence, it was quite safe to walk down there – which we did, from time to time. Just off Seventh Street and Third was McSorley's saloon, an Irish pub founded in 1854, with sawdust on the floor, and as I recall for men only, with the exception of a female descendant of the original owner, who was running it. It made an interesting change, a different clientele ready to compare notes and sort out the problems of the world, providing both variety and spice to city life.

South was Greenwich Village with all its small restaurants, art cinemas for mainly imported movies (often Japanese at that time), and buildings connected with a New York university. So there was always plenty of life. To the west was Sixth Avenue, neither one thing nor another, and the only incident that sticks in my mind relating to that is of a small Austrian restaurant run by a nice old Austrian gentleman from Vienna. I had been given an introduction to the son of a professor from an Ivy League university, who was about my age, and we agreed to meet there for supper. I arrived first, stood at the bar and ordered a beer. Shortly after, my acquaintance walked in and joined me in a beer, standing on my left. After we had talked for a few minutes, a black American came in the door behind us, visible to me but not to Chuck (as I will call him), moved to our left and ordered a beer in that deep voice that many black people have. Chuck simply picked up his glass, moved behind me to my right, and said, 'I'll carry on our conversation from this side if you don't mind. I don't like to stand next to one of them.' This was no 'good ole boy' southern redneck, as I have said, so it wasn't just south of the Mason–Dixon line where race relations were still bad, ninety years after their Civil War.

In fact, the black or African Americans had only just begun to move north at that time, in search of jobs. One evening I was walking from the office to the subway at the top of Wall Street with Frank Forrestal, my next boss and the nephew of the previous Secretary for the Navy, when a very smartly dressed black girl passed us going home in the opposite direction. Frank remarked, 'One sees more of them coming down here to work nowadays,' so that area was still a Caucasian and Jewish area. Most of the secretaries seemed to be in their thirties and forties, and it occurred to me that they had gone there to find a husband without success, and then got into a rut. They used to spend their lunch hours sitting on the stools of the sandwich bars, having a gossip, a club sandwich, a dry martini and a couple of cigarettes, more or less in that order. After lunch one day I was strolling back to the office, and caught up one of our young secretaries tripping along, and got into conversation with her. 'You're from Canada, ain't ya,' she enquired in that nasal New York accent. When I confirmed that I was, she went on to explain that on their honeymoon she and her husband had gone to Niagara Falls and then crossed the border into Canada and the St Catherine's Peninsular. When I enquired as to how they had liked that, she replied that it was great and that her husband had remarked that 'the restaurants in Canada were the best in the whole of the United States of America!'. New Yorkers can be pretty parochial in their geographical knowledge, and I guess that Canadians have reason sometimes for that well-known chip on their shoulders.

The new people who were moving in by the thousands were the Puerto Ricans, mostly in Harlem. While I was living there I decided to do all the sights and places to try to find out what made the inhabitants tick, and on a couple of occasions went up to the Yankee stadium, which then was at the north end of Harlem. I can't say that I felt all that comfortable moving around on my own in that area. At any rate I decided to go the whole hog and sit among the bleachers or hard benches, open to the summer sun and therefore very hot, a lone Wasp among the Puerto Ricans. It was good entertaining stuff, and I had seen it before on TV in Canada, where Yogi Berra and Pee Wee Rees had impressed me, although they may have played for the Brooklyn Dodgers rather than the Yankees.

What one really misses in Manhattan with its narrow canyons, traffic, twenty-four-hour activity and bustle is anything remotely connected with the natural world – with the exception of Central Park, but that was a long way from Washington Square. It does not have a series of parks like Boston or London (Hyde, Green, St James, Regent's, Hampstead Heath and so on), which I think resemble one another more closely. But when I really needed it I would take the subway up to Fifty-sixth Street or so, and emerge to the blissful smell of horse manure from the horse-drawn carriages or surreys at the south end of the park, followed by acres of walking and fresh air. My real getaway was Everett Rankin's small farm just outside Ithaca on Lake Cayuga in upper New York State. He was an old friend of my parents with Standard Oil in Calcutta during the 1940s and had retired to the Finger Lakes, a gorgeous part of New England south of Rochester. He had a farm manager and his wife to run a small herd of cows, a large flock of laying hens and some acres on which they grew soya beans, so that his concerns had shifted from oil futures during his career to the price of beans (not to mention the rain) in his retirement. The way there from NYC was by a small airline from Newark, New Jersey to a country airport at Ithaca with a grassy country strip. The airport bus to Newark went via a road on stilts above some foul-smelling marsh land that reeked of pigs, since it was not fit for any other agricultural activity. It was also said that the bodies of the victims that the mafia wished to dispose of were buried in that land (except where they became part of the concrete supports for a new bridge). Some years later I was told that the mafia bosses that made it to retirement settled in Princeton, New Jersey, and as a result that town had the best crime record for miles around, since they did not want any two-bit, low-down hoodlum coming in and messing up their rest and recreation, and put out the word accordingly. At the opposite end of the social scale, Princeton was also the home of the university from which, in those days, many of the Quaker Oats company directors of Scottish descent had graduated.

Over that summer I completed the work connected with the Caribbean markets, appointing advertising agencies, working up advertising campaigns and so on, at which point they decided to switch me to the African markets, which were run out of another paper subsidiary in the same office called Quaker Oats International Inc. This I think was on the flimsy basis that they had noted from my CV that I had been born in Kenya (although spent no time there) and had had my secondary education in South Africa. So far as most New Yorkers were concerned, Africa was still regarded as something of the 'dark continent' and they would rather someone else go there. Thus I was helped along by the location of my birth. The president of the Canadian company had toured the west coast African countries briefly a year previously, where they had good flour exports to what was then the Gold Coast, Nigeria and so on. Once again all the local markets from the Belgian Congo northwards had to be appraised, local representatives assessed and changed if necessary, and all the other information gathered, since no one had spent real time there since the 1930s, all the control being exercised by correspondence.

Hank was also the office joker, and when he heard that I was heading for the Congo, he took me aside and asked if I had heard of the journalist whom the *New York Times* had sent there by sea, early in the twentieth century, to investigate if the inhabitants were still cannibals, and report back accordingly. Nothing was heard from him for at least three months, and even allowing for the duration of the sea voyage, they feared the worst in head office and thought poor old Charlie, he's ended up in a cooking pot! However, out of the blue a cable arrived, which read: 'CONFIRM THAT CANNIBALISM DOES INDEED STILL EXIST IN THIS COUNTRY STOP HAVE DISCOVERED THE REASON WHY THEY EAT ONE ANOTHER STOP THEY'RE DELICIOUS! – CHARLIE'

Again the Hotel Earl came up trumps and agreed to store my main baggage for free until my return some time in the spring of 1956. As I paid my bill to the man on the reception, who was more or less a fixture, he paid Tom and me the hotelier's compliment: 'You two have been a pair of real good boys, never tried to take any girls up to your rooms all the time ya bin here!' On such esoteric grounds are judgements made in the New York hotel world. So early in October I set off for London, first class in a Boeing Stratocruiser with a bar/lounge in its belly, which was a lot better than the immigrant ship to Canada three and a bit years earlier.

11.

Return to Africa (Years 29–30)

For some reason, I can remember the date that I set out from New York by air to London in order to make a complete survey of the African markets for the company's products, which until then had been handled by correspondence. It was 4 October 1955 and the trip was supposed to last for about four months. In the event it was extended to May 1956 with a couple of weeks off halfway through, so that proved to be fairly strenuous. However, to be able to travel so extensively and be paid for it in those days of currency restrictions, and to see those countries before their independence (and in most cases subsequent decline), was an opportunity not to be missed.

The Quaker Oats Company was established towards the end of the nineteenth century by a couple of Scots Canadians, who immigrated to Akron, Ohio in America and built a rolled oats mill. After various trials and near bankruptcies, they and their successors got the company up and running and launched their eponymous, mundane porridge product into the world's markets with what can only be described as commercial missionary zeal. It was the time of the big trusts in the USA, covering steel mills, railways, oil and banking, which were subsequently broken up due to their unreasonable power, so it was probably all part of the same nationalist syndrome. Quaker Oats were not just exported to such markets for consumption by expatriate minorities, but became what were known as trade lines for the consumption of the local populations. Undoubtedly such expansion was assisted by the Dutch and the British, since busy Dutch traders took the product to the islands of Indonesia, while the British took it to their colonies throughout the Far East, Africa and the Caribbean. By the start of World War Two these markets had been well established, but for obvious reasons had not been visited since, except by the president of the Canadian company, Jim Wharry, which company, along with all the other north American millers, had huge export markets for hard wheat flour. He had gone to the old Gold Coast in 1953 for a short look, and recommended that a representative be sent out on an extended tour. He was 6'4" tall, weighed twenty stone, and when I arrived two years later the African market 'mammies' were still talking about him, since he was their idea of a white chief, the equivalent of the King of Ashanti!

Dollar exports to most of the markets had been curtailed due to exchange controls, so alternative arrangements had been made for production facilities with the Dutch company at Rotterdam and the UK Company at Southall, west of London. I had to call in on them first to be briefed on their agents. Before leaving New York, in response to my poor handwriting, which had deteriorated over the five months of twice-weekly reports from the Caribbean markets, I had diffidently asked if I could buy a portable typewriter on expenses, only to suffer a lecture to questioning whether I thought the company was made of money, and did I not realise that the shareholders' dividends paid out of profits were sacrosanct, and so on. So when I sent in my first couple of reports I made sure that there was no improvement in legibility. The Dutch company controlled the Benelux markets, and since the first market to be visited was the then Belgian Congo, our largest market in tropical Africa, I had to make some calls on head offices there. This included the doyen of the Dutch East Indies companies, the Borneo Sumatra Trading Company or Borsumy, which had been kicked out of Indonesia and was now making a play to be our distributors in the Belgian Congo, where we were weakly represented. I was to learn later from other Dutch businessmen that Borsumy personnel, along with those from Royal Dutch Shell and Phillips Electrical, had a reputation for arrogance and could be recognised by the way that they walked around like the Lord's anointed.

I don't recall how long the flight to Leopoldville took, but it was certainly not direct, with a break in Cairo or Lagos. Those were the days of conventional engines for planes such as the Constellation, with the fleets of ex-World War Two Dakotas as the workhorses around individual countries. For the sake of clarity I will stay with the old names such as Leopoldville, or Leo, and Elizabethville, or E-ville, rather than Kinshasa or Lumumbashi. Leo was a real surprise, a modern city in central Africa, set in the middle of the bush, along the banks of the vast Congo River, which with its tributaries constitutes the third-largest river in the world after the Amazon and the Mekong. It was clearly very prosperous with wide streets lined with stores for European goods, modern hotels, pavement cafés as in Brussels, and was the capital of about the only hard currency African colony. This was due to its vast mineral riches in the south-eastern Katanga province, the source of the uranium for the first atomic bombs dropped on Japanese cities, as well as other metals such as copper, cobalt, tungsten and manganese essential for the Allied war effort. Thus it was riding high with living standards that simply did not exist in post-war European countries.

But there was an 'apartheid' there, before that term was invented, that did not exist in other European colonies to the same extent. Leo consisted of two cities, the 'cité Européenne' where the Europeans and Americans lived, and the 'cité indigène', where the Congolese lived. There was a daily curfew at 6 p.m. (the sun sets early in Central Africa) by which time the locals had to be out of the European part until 6 a.m. the following morning – except for the ladies of the night, that is. Not that the 'indigène' part was a mess (like Lagos for instance); it was kept in good order, *but* they were kept separate from the rest. This was the only colony that Belgium had. They failed miserably to educate any of the locals to degree standard (unlike in Rhodesia, for example) and most other Westerners did not have too high an opinion of them. I was once sitting having a beer with a Dutchman, and asked him what the population of the Congo was. He replied, 'There are 7 million blacks and 100,000 whites, and some of the blacks should be white, and some of the whites black,' politically incorrect in this day and age, but easily understood sixty years ago.

I should say something on the history of the Belgian Congo. According to the Encyclopaedia Britannica, during the nineteenth century King Leopold I of Belgium had tried to found enterprises in Spanish America, which failed. His son, Leopold II of Saxe-

Coburg-Gotha (a German state), on assuming the throne, founded the Congo Free State owned by himself, to develop agricultural trade for humanitarian reasons as an alternative to slavery and liquor. He leased vast tracts the size of other countries to trading companies, including his own Crown Domain, to develop rubber plantations from which they were expected to make profits and pay him dividends as the owner of the land. He never actually visited the country itself, and when rubber tapping proved to be less profitable than ivory or slaves, the trading companies forced the natives off their agricultural land into the forests, where they were maltreated and worked to death, the population falling from 10 to 5 million. The scandal was brought to public attention by Roger Casement, who was the British consul, as well as by the Christian missionaries. The net result was that the Belgian state confiscated their king's company and formed the colony. Joseph Conrad, the Anglo-Polish author, based his story *Heart of Darkness* on this, and a few years ago Adam Hochshield described it in *King Leopold's Ghost*. The actual details of that part of Belgian history are still not available for academics or writers to access at the public records office in Brussels.

The native city of Leo was also clean, modern and the colonial government had made an attempt to improve the local market by building a new one a short distance from the old, with concrete buildings, drains, lighting and so on, and they moved all the market traders into it. The trouble was that it did not have any trees for shade, so within weeks the traders started to move back to their old-style market, more higgledy-piggledy, less regimented, but what they were used to and therefore preferred. On arriving in any new market one was expected first of all to check at least fifty and preferably a hundred shops or stalls for distribution of one's product, rather than believe what the local agent told one, because the two versions did not always tally. Thus one indulged one of the pleasures of life – to walk around native markets, each stall or small shop managed by the local women clothed in the brightest of cotton cloths, with headties to match in primary colours of reds, yellows, blues or gold. This material had originated through the Manchester cotton trade, and I notice from the current news reports of the massacres in Darfur, in the western Sudan by the Janjawid, that even there the poorest Bantu women still wear these bright cottons. Since protein is in short supply in central Africa from root crops like yams, cassava, plantain and so on, Quaker Oats in hermetically sealed cans had become a trade line to be used as an invalid or post-weaning food, as well as products such as Ovaltine, Ostermilk, Klim (milk spelled backwards), Gillette razor blades, Aspro, tinned biscuits and bread flour in sacks, Dettol for hygiene and scores of other brands. It all made for a colourful, lively scene that I recorded on 35 mm Kodak slides, as clear now as the day they were taken. Having done this I mailed off my first trip report from that market, to be rewarded about a week later with a cable that read: 'FOR GOD'S SAKE, BUY YOURSELF A TYPEWRITER.' One small victory against the forces of inertia by a humble foot soldier, so an Olivetti Lettera 22 in its plastic case it was, from the local dealer.

Before leaving Leo I decided to go across the river for the day to visit Brazzaville, the capital of the French Congo, where we had an agent, but did a minuscule business. The Scramble for Africa, as it was called, started after the Treaty of Berlin in 1885, called to try to rationalise the European national quest for colonies on the mistaken belief that they would provide new markets for manufactured goods. The problem was that the British had got the best bits, first in central and southern Africa, followed by the Germans in east Africa, so the French went for quantity rather than quality, and ended up with some vast, useless spaces. In 1982 the Congo Peoples' Republic, as it was named after independence, still only had a population of 1.8 million. That story was well written up in *The Scramble for Africa* about fifteen years ago by Frank Pakenham, the son of the liberal but unworldly Lord Longford. Small steam-driven ferryboats left the quayside at Leo daily for Brazzaville to cross the Congo, full of locals with their head loads, crates of chickens, produce and manufactured goods. The river was *vast*. It must have been about a mile wide at that point, a great mass of brown-green water rolling inexorably towards the coast at Matadi, with huge rafts of matted water hyacinths floating down, having choked navigation in the upper reaches. These were from plants sown by the earlier missionaries to decorate their gardens, and had expanded to the point where they were known as *la Peste du Nile*, having originated on that river. Now they are all over the world, on the Irrawaddy, Brahmaputra and anywhere else the missionaries went to save souls. Just below Leo the 13,000 km of navigable river ended in a series of rapids, before tumbling down to the sea. As we were crossing I wondered to myself what kind of rescue tug might be available should the engine conk out, how soon could it get to us, and even if they would consider us worth saving, or just another bit of flotsam on the unending expanse.

Our local representation was simply a young Pole with one of those old Citroën cars with splayed wheels, who worked for an old British agency called Walter Clarke, which was clearly inadequate. So I did the rounds of alternatives including Borsumy, who gave the impression that they only had to ask to get it, and set off to fly to E-ville in the Katanga province. Internal flights were by a Dakota, noisy and slow, and it flew hour after hour over dense, green jungle with occasional clearings below, but no major towns. Katanga, as I recall, consisted of a high, dry plateau above 1,000 feet in altitude, directly north of the copper belt of the colony of northern Rhodesia, now Zambia. Elizabeth-ville was called the Paris of central Africa, with wide streets lined with Jacaranda trees, sophisticated shops, the best hotel called the Leo Deux (no evidence of Belgian shame in that name) having oysters on the menu on Wednesday evenings, courtesy of Sabena Airways (whose initials, for the cynical, spelled 'such a bloody experience, never again'), and no curfew between the expatriates and the locals. It was all very civilised and Europeans made their homes there in a dry, healthy climate.

The mining towns were to the west and I thought that I should visit our distributor in one of them since they bought a lot of flour in bulk for their staff and workforce. The nearest one was Jadotville, which could be visited by a train ride of one and a half hours or so, one class, so it was a bit like travelling third class on Indian railways (which I did in the RN in 1946) with everyone piled in including their head loads, families, chickens in crates, sacks of this and that, but when in Rome, do as the Romans – not as A P Herbert said of the English abroad, 'When in Rome, do exactly as you would do at home!' African ladies, particularly after they have had a couple of kids, are not exactly anorexic, so it was a snug fit, but noisily jolly. The sight of the hills from which the copper and other minerals are extracted was extraordinary, almost as green as grass with a sheen glinting in the sunlight. Whether they were mined by hand by the African locals before the Western mining companies came along I know not, but they are now the quarries for Europe and America, with China coming on to the scene.

From Elizabethville I was due to go on to Stanleyville, named after the eponymous journalist and explorer, but I was beginning to home in on a Dutch trading company as our best choice for representatives. They were called L. E. Tels, and were based in Enschede in the east of the Netherlands, again repositioning themselves after forced withdrawal from Indonesia. Unilever were in fact by far the largest trading company in the Congo via United Agencies, but they were so dominant that if one gave them the account, other companies were reluctant to handle your line. Mr Mellink cabled me from Leo asking me to stay in Stan (as it was called) to meet one of their directors from Holland, who would be there in the second week of November. This was a fortunate turn of events, since someone pointed out to me that the first Tuesday of that month was a holiday for All Saints' Day, and I should take the long weekend to visit the Kivu, the so-called Pearl of Africa. How right he was! One flew from a town called Bukavu up to Goma, the border town with Rwanda in a small three-seater plane, landing at an altitude of about 6,000 feet on a small grass runaway overlooking Lake Kivu, just north and west of Lake Tanganyika, all part of the Great Rift Valley chain of lakes. Belgian settlers actually lived up there with their coffee estates as in Kenya, and there was a beautiful hotel on a hillside, called the Hotel des Volcans, overlooking the lake with its beach, sailboats and picnic areas. Just north of what was a typical, small east African town in the highlands were the three more or less extinct volcanoes of the Virunga Mountains, whose slopes are the home of the great apes. One of the peaks had a pronounced, visible crater, and in fact it erupted about ten years or so ago, burying part of Goma and flowing into the lake. As a result the water was bilharzia-free and safe for swimming, unlike many similar ones in central Africa.

I met a Belgian in the hotel, who had been liberated by the Canadian Army. When I said that I was representing a Canadian flour company he insisted on lending me his Chevrolet car and driver for the long weekend, so that I could see the country north to Lake Edward at the foot of the Ruwenzori or Mountains of the Moon in Uganda. Kenya is beautiful, but this was just stunning – lush green rolling hills like Uganda, with the purple haze that vistas of African hills often have, the locals farming the land apparently in peace and harmony with one another, even though they were divided between the tall Nilotic Tutsis and the more numerous Bantu Hutus. The Belgians always favoured the Tutsis as being the more 'aristocratic', and therefore born to rule, but no one could have foreseen the uncontrolled savagery that the two groups descended into in the mid 1990s, with a bit of help from President Mitterand, his egregious son and the French Army, while the UN troops looked on. (Read *Silent Accomplice* by Andrew Wallis, 2006.) The journey north took most of a day, and led to a large plain where Lake Edward lay, the home to an estimated 20,000 hippos, plus free-ranging elephants and other game on the banks. There is something to be said for working one's way around the world. There was a small campsite there with a few rondavels and staff for the expatriates who spent short leaves there before the days of mass tourism. The Ruwenzori were, of course, sheathed in mist as I understand they are from shortly after daybreak onwards as the sun generates heat. Too late to visit them now!

Stanleyville was the main trading town in the north-east Congo, named after Henry Morton Stanley (1841–1904) of Dr Livingstone fame. He made several journeys under the harshest of conditions through that country, one of them funded by the London *Daily Telegraph*, which was founded by the forbearers of the Lords Burnham of this town of Beaconsfield. Apparently they were Jewish immigrants of French origin, who anglicised their name from Levi to Lawson before they were ennobled, had bought a printing business and founded the *Daily Telegraph* newspaper. The Congo River becomes unnavigable for riverboats just above that town at the Stanley Falls. There were also some lesser falls called the Wagenia Rapids, where the still-wide river was broken up into a series of cataracts by islands in the middle of the flow. The local fishermen had driven wooden posts into these to which were attached cone-shaped baskets made from bamboo, which were lowered into the water to catch fish. Their boats were made from huge cottonwood trees, whose centres were chopped out by axe and must have been about forty feet long. Mr Polak, the local manager of Tels, took me out in one after work. It was real *Sanders of the River* stuff. A crew of about ten paddlers wearing only cotton lungis applied their paddles with a rhythmic sweep and looked like human ebony. In my enthusiasm I suggested to Polak that for an advertising promotion we could sponsor a Quaker Oats cup for which such crews could compete. He gave me an amused look, asked if I had ever seen how those boys got worked up when they did compete, and wouldn't the crocs have a lovely feast when they were tipped over? A non-starter.

Mr Cohen, their director from Amsterdam, arrived and we got down to business. He was a really pleasant Dutchman, old enough to be my father with a lot of experience running inter-national agencies, but his idea and the company's of a reasonable rate for the job were somewhat apart. This was born of our having a ninety per cent plus share of most markets despite fierce price competition from other brands. It took a few exchanges of cables with our office in New York, who needed convincing that Tels were better set up there than Borsumy, before we agreed, and took the plane back to Leo. It was hot and humid as it usually is there, and hotels did not have air conditioning in those days, and I had to submit a full report before I left for Angola for a few days. They were not the best conditions in which to learn to type reasonably accurately, with each mistake corrected with one of those strips of paper put over the offending letter, and then struck again. But there was a solution. Most reasonable hotel rooms had a bidet and one of those stools with a cork top in their bathrooms. So the trick to keeping as cool as a cucumber while under stress was to run the cold water in the bidet at such a flow that it only just did not overflow, strip off and use it as a seat, while hammering away at the typewriter on the stool. A lot of water must have flowed past my backside during the course of my travels, before word processors or laptops made typing and corrections easy.

The flight from Leo to Luanda, the capital of what was then Portuguese West Africa, now Angola, was only about one and a half hours or so, but a world of difference in atmosphere. Originally that area plus the Congo basin had been *the* entrepôt for the Portuguese slave trade to Brazil, which over the next few centuries accounted for about thirty per cent of the total European trade involving 11 to 12 million slaves. In 2007, we had the 200th anniversary of the bill by William Wilberforce to abolish the carrying of slaves by British ships, and much attention was paid to that in the various sectors of the media. Less attention, however, was given to a recent report by the agency that monitors such practices, to the effect that there are currently estimated to be 12 million slaves living today in countries as Chad, Mauretania, Niger, the Sudan and the Middle Eastern states, mostly Muslim. By the mid-1950s, Angola was a typical laid-back Portuguese territory, and Luanda seemed to be like the mirror image of Rio on the opposite shores of the Atlantic, with the wide sweep of a sandy bay around which the town was built. Based on a very short visit, they seemed to have much less of a colour bar there than in the colonies of other nations, with staff such as hotel waiters or taxi drivers being of all pigments from black to white and shades in between, working alongside one another. On the basis of this brief and very superficial visit it came as a surprise to me that the locals rose so violently against the Portuguese in the 1970s.

Four or five months later, at the end of the tour, I went to Portuguese East Africa, or Mozambique as it became after independence. That was quite another kettle of fish, and seemed to be a coastal tourist resort for South Africans and Rhodesians who did not wish to go as far south as Durban. Being an admirer of Somerset Maugham's stories about the manifold failings within the human condition (he it was who described Monte Carlo as a sunny place for shady people!), I had read *Gigolo and Gigolette* about the couple that worked the hotels in the south of France, but I had never seen the phenomenon in action. The Polano hotel in Laurenco Marques was very smart, and clearly the favoured destination for the wealthy tourists from Johannesburg. There were these four ladies in their forties or so, their skins tanned the colour of well-done beef, before the days of skin cancer worries, who were adorned with gold jewellery that could be weighed not so much in carats as in kilos. Each evening they dined together at the same table, after which they took up station at separate small tables in the marble tiled foyer and ordered coffees. After a short interval the young Portuguese gigolos walked in, selected one of the ladies, made a little bow and were invited to sit down for a coffee or a cognac. That introduction completed, the pair walked out through the lobby past their dinner companions without a flicker of recognition, into the nightclubs or boîtes. No doubt notes were compared at dinner the following evening.

In Beira, the old capital to the north, there was a vast new hotel, which had just been completed for the Rhodesian tourist trade, with an Olympic-size swimming pool and a casino. The problem was that no one had got permission for the latter from the Roman Catholic hierarchy before it was built, and such permission had been refused, with the net result that where it had beds for 150 guests or so, during my visit there were barely a dozen. These, however, were an exotic lot, being scrap metal merchants – not any old scrap metal merchant like Steptoe and Son, I hasten to add, but central European Slavs or those from the Balkan states, with their ladies floating like silk butterflies. The scrap metal that they were after was big stuff from vessels sunk during WW2 in the Mozambique Channel, which runs for 1,000 km in length and between 400 and 1,000 km in width from the Mozambique coast to Madagascar. It must have been a happy hunting ground for German and Japanese subs attacking convoys going up the coast from Durban to the Egyptian battlefields, down which I came in MV *Inchanga* in January 1942 without mishap. The doyenne of this interesting group was actually not a Slav but a somewhat stout Portuguese lady in her thirties, who paraded in the lobby with a three-month-old lion cub on a dog's lead, plus her German boyfriend. All of this for me came as a welcome relaxation after about seven months living out of a suitcase in Africa hotels.

My last memory of Mozambique was more recent. A few years ago, they had experienced disastrous floods that almost wrecked that country, already devastated by civil war. A TV news bulletin showed a native woman, who had either given birth to her baby in the branches of a tree above the swirling floods, or had got up there somehow after being rescued by a helicopter crew. A few days later she was shown again on the news screen, immaculately dressed in bright cotton, squatting down with her child on her back, lighting a fire to prepare her meal. She seemed to typify the resilience and cheerfulness of African women. Perhaps the new lady president of Liberia, who must be as tough as old boots to have got where she is, will set a new trend in the rule of African countries.

After central Africa I headed for the then British colonies strung out along the west coast from the Bight of Benin. Lagos in Nigeria was the first port of call – every expatriate's nightmare since it is built on a swamp, and has a sweltering, humid climate only alleviated by the harmattan wind that sweeps out of the Sahara from the north-east between December and March. Then there are the people themselves – or the men, more specifically. Nigeria was always known as the land of 'dash' or bribery, which over the past fifty years has expanded into worldwide money scams that the financially innocent or stupid continue to fall for.

I arrived there on a Saturday and can honestly say that it was the biggest culture shock that I have ever experienced, much worse than the slums of Calcutta in the 1940s. I have a slide from an upper floor of the new 'Mainland' hotel looking down on mud, overflowing drains, and the new road leading to the business centre on Ikoyi Island. Expatriates on the west coast used to go out on fifteen-month tours, followed by three months' home leave, compared to the three-year tours in the Far East countries such as India, and it was easy to see why. There was no respite from the climate, disease and working conditions that expatriates could retreat to in hill stations such as Darjeeling or the Nilgiri Hills, and if they stayed too long there was a tendency to 'go bush'. The Europeans there, mainly British, but also with a fair number of Asian, Lebanese and Syrian traders, were there only for the trade or as part of the colonial administration. Non-

Africans were not allowed to own property, so it was essentially an imperial as opposed to a colonial situation. The earliest trade must have been in coloured cotton prints from Manchester, slaves and guns – not necessarily in that order. The guns were traded to the dominant tribes to enable them to continue what they had done for centuries, namely conquer weaker tribes for slaves. Bright cotton clothing and African women with their dark skin pigmentation were made for one another. It is one aspect of life that one misses when visiting the Muslim countries of North Africa, where the women are kept in the background. By contrast northern European women, who now and then dressed up in bright cottons to identify more closely with their African sisters, looked, with their pale skins and lank hair, like washed-out cabbage leaves. The early trade started from English ports such as Liverpool and Bristol with shipping companies such as John Holt, who then founded trading stations on 'the coast' as it was called. The old pre-WW2 traders who had made their careers there were known as 'old coasters', providing they had survived the rigours of tropical diseases, booze, boredom and loneliness that went with living in the 'white man's grave'.

Nigeria was created by the British and consists of three regions. The north is vast, bordering the Sahara desert, populated by the Hausa people, who controlled seven states where Kano and Zaria were the largest towns. In the eighteenth century, the Fulani, a nomadic, pastoralist people, Negroid with Caucasian features, declared a jihad against the Hausas and proceeded to rule them through an emirate based at Kano. They built a large mosque there and in their market had deep pits where they dyed their cloths a deep indigo colour. The other feature of that area was the huge conical stacks of groundnuts in sacks, awaiting shipment to the coast after harvest. Those nuts were indigenous to Brazil but the seed was introduced to Nigeria, so that colonial trade was not all in one direction. In the southern part of that area was a high, dry plateau based on the town of Jos, where there were tin mines worked more or less up to the time of independence. The people there were pagans, and the women went around topless with grass skirts. How they got there in the first place and survived the squeeze from north and south, I know not.

Then there were the Hausa traders, tall men in long single-coloured shifts, with conical hats, who traded all over Africa in Moroccan leather products such as bags and cushions, and wooden carved birds and animals for the Western tourist trade. They were amazing travellers. One sat outside my rondavel in a government rest house in Jos until I bought a group of figures of Nigerian people carved out of thorn wood from him. A couple of years later I was back in Elizabethville in the market and saw this chap. I was racking my brains as to where we had met before, when he spotted me and explained that we had met in Jos. This time he was speaking to the locals in French!

The main commercial area of Nigeria is in the south-west, based on Lagos, Ibadan and Abeokuta. A modern new hospital had just been built on a hillside near Ibadan, fully staffed with the latest equipment, when hospitals were virtually falling apart in the post-war UK. So it was not all take. The greatest trading women or 'market mammies' in West Africa were from the Yoruba tribe, forceful, boisterous and colourful in their trademark dress of bright blue cloth with matching headties. They sat in the African trade-line markets each to her own table or small stall, with the goods stacked up, dispensing their sales pitch, back chat (the broader the better) and humour. Invariably each one had a baby fast asleep tied to her back with a cloth, and if it woke up and whimpered for food, the mother simply swung it round to her front and stuck her nipple into its mouth. The more successful mammies were almost wholesalers in their own right. They bought goods in bulk from the large importing companies such as the United Africa Company (UAC), a Unilever subsidiary that dominated the market, and all such business was done by word of mouth and a handshake since they were illiterate in English. Some of them in the 1950s would run an account of up to £5,000 per month with a trading house, kept all the records in their heads, and could be relied on to pay up. Quite different from their menfolk and they were probably effectively heads of their families, economically at least.

The eastern part of the country was based on Port Harcourt, near where the Niger River finally debouched after its long course from the north-west into the Bight of Benin. Shell Darcy was just beginning to drill for oil, now one of the world's largest oil fields. This was terrible for the expatriates working there, good for the country's successive leaders, their wives and Swiss bankers to whom the loot flows, but not very good for your average Nigerian citizen. The main tribe were the Ibos, who unlike the western Yorubas had been converted to Christianity. For some reason that I never found the answer to, the market traders were men, and not nearly so amusing. On about my third visit to Nigeria, our sales in that region were down significantly, and I asked the wholesale buyer in the local branch of United Africa Co. the reason. He explained that it was all the fault of 'the bloody missionaries, who were preaching against polygamy and shutting down the fatting houses'. Fatting houses? Well, apparently a young mother would be pregnant with her first child, and would breastfeed it for eighteen months until it could toddle around, a form of contraception. Then she would be in the family way again for another cycle of twenty-seven months, or a total of four and a half years either pregnant or nursing, at which point she needed a rest. So a few such mothers would be given a hut to share by themselves while they were built up with a diet of Quaker Oats and Ovaltine, a very sensible practice that fitted in with their tribal customs but not, unfortunately, the new religion. *Kwashiorkor*, or so-called second child illness, was prevalent in West Africa at that time, due to malnutrition, since the native root crops such as yams, cassava and sorghum, which were pounded into a flour, were very low in protein, hence the adoption of rolled oats gruel with 12% protein as a post-weaning food.

I cannot leave the subject of Nigeria without referring to the favourite expatriate meal known as a 'palm oil chop' or palm oil curry with all the trimmings, usually eaten for Saturday lunch over a couple of hours. It would be washed down with a litre bottle or two of Star Lager beer (brewed locally), and then slept off for the rest of the afternoon. Something good has to come out of Nigeria, apart from the Yoruba traders. But come out of Nigeria the latter did, to dominate the main markets in the Gold Coast, as Ghana was then called, the next British colony to the west. But they were just too aggressive and successful for their own good, and a couple of years or so after Ghanian independence, the Yorubas were sent packing back to Nigeria, causing a West African 'international incident'.

The Gold Coast was an entirely different place to visit. For a start the people are cheerful, friendly and unaggressive. Again the country is divided into three parts. There seems to be something in that, since Caesar wrote the same about Gaul. The coastal region from the capital Accra in the east to Takoradi and Sekondi in the west is the part where most people visit, since it is where commercial life was centred during the slave trade. It may not be something to boast about but Ghana has some of the best-preserved slaving posts on the west coast of Africa. The most impressive was Christiansborg Castle in Accra, built by the Danes as its name indicates, and which during the colonial times was the place where the governor resided, to be followed swiftly after independence by the new president, Kwame Nkruma, or the Great Redeemer. In 1666, Denmark occupied the Virgin Islands in the Caribbean, where they produced indigo, sugar and cotton for their home market, and needed the imported West African labour to work the estates, something that they keep quiet about when fingers are pointed at the more obvious 'usual suspects'. To the west of Accra was Cape Coast Castle, beautifully preserved and whitewashed, used as a police barracks, and now open to slave trade tourists. West of that was Elmina Castle, whose connection was either Arab or Portuguese.

The whole of that coast faces south onto the beaches with the Atlantic surf surging in. Until the Second World War there was no port at Accra where merchant ships could tie up alongside a quay, so cargo, passengers and their baggage came ashore from ships by surfboats. These were long canoes with teams of paddlers, who paddled from the vessels to just short of the shore, where the helmsman in control brought it to a stop while he looked over his shoulder for a suitable wave to carry them in. Once on the crest they all paddled like hell and the canoe was swept up the beach for unloading – unless the helmsman got it wrong, whereby the canoe broached to and they were all tipped into the surf. Great hilarity from the onlookers! It was said that before the war a new governor arrived with a Rolls Royce. It was swung out on derricks from the ship on to a plank raft lashed between two surfboats, which then had the task of paddling inshore in tandem and sweeping up the beach together. Apparently they made it! By the 1950s a port had been developed in the west at Takoradi, and to bring everything closer to the commercial hub of Accra, a new port was being constructed at Tema, where the Volta River flowed into the sea, all connected with the Volta River hydroelectric power project.

In the centre of the country was the old kingdom of Ashanti ruled, until he was overthrown by the British, by the Asantehene or king of all the tribes in that area, and whose throne was referred to as the Stool. There he sat receiving homage until someone stronger came along and pitched him off. He must have been one of Africa's first 'big men' with which we have become familiar, who once they get power assume that it is for life. He was also an enthusiastic slaver, selling off any other tribesmen that he conquered, keeping alive the practice that goes back to fifth century BC Athens, where we only talk about the democracy that we inherited. That area gave its name to the country, the Gold Coast, since there were and are gold mines that go back into the mists of time. Bauxite to produce alumina was also mined, but it was equally strong in timber and agricultural products, hard woods such as sapele and the cash crop of cocoa, where the Gold Coast was a world leader. As with groundnuts, this was also introduced to that country and Nigeria by the British traders in 1879 when they were the world's greatest producers. Unhappily, their economy did not survive the financial administration of the Great Redeemer, and much of the cocoa market was lost to other countries – a tragic loss of income for the small farmers.

The capital of this state was Kumasi, a sprawling town with a huge market for everything under the sun, and the largest in West Africa as I recall. There was a car park as large as a football field, where all the mammy wagons, brightly painted and sporting religious and other texts on the meaning of life, assembled. The concrete buildings of the wholesalers and retail shops surrounded the main market, where the Yorubas were very obviously bunched together in their bright blue clothing. There were also herdsmen down from the north in their loose-fitting clothes, looking almost like Pathan tribesmen, with their flocks of sheep and goats to be sold on the hoof. Their capital town was Tamale, but much to my regret I could not think of a good enough excuse to go up there. To go to Kumasi from Accra took most of a day so one had to stay overnight there, and to stay in the Kumasi hotel was definitely an experience to be avoided.

Thus pre-warned, I secured a room in the UAC rest house, and the following day I was in the office of the wholesale manager of that company, when a very tall mammy came in, all dressed in black. As a potential customer she had priority and asked for the price of pork feet, or pigs' trotters in brine, and she wanted eight barrels. The buyer told her that his price was £4 10s in old money. 'What's your best price – I give you four pounds?' she shot back. After being told that four ten was his best price she went on, 'All right, I'll go to C K and get them for four pounds.'

'OK, Mrs Appiah,' replied the buyer, 'C K only has three barrels because I let him have them. When you want the rest, come back and I'll sell them to you for four pounds ten.'

So she went out in a huff, and I asked the buyer, 'Was that *the* Mrs Appiah?' to which he replied, 'Yes, that was Peggy Cripps's mother-in-law.'

I read years later that their son had a difficult time at school there since he was considerably paler, being of mixed blood. C K, to whom Mrs Appiah referred, was C K Chellaram, an Indian trading company with branches along the coast and a head office in London. The trading houses and importers were often referred to as an oligopoly, with Unilever at the top through the wholesale UAC, their agricultural and forestry divisions, and their retail Kingsway stores, self-service, they were way ahead of the UK equivalents of that time. Then there were several British and French trading houses, even a Swiss one, and at the bottom of the expatriate heap, the Lebanese and Syrians, born survivors, of whom more later.

I was fortunate to be able to spend Christmas in Accra with an Englishman and his wife and friends whom I met somewhere, and they were kind enough to gather me in, as always happened in those colonial situations. It was the usual northern Christmas in a tropical climate that Brits used to go for, but very enjoyable and relaxing. The one place not to spend it was in Liberia, the next market along the coast, which all agencies covered by visits from Accra for a few days at a time, rather than living there. I was shortly to find out the reason why.

Liberia was founded in 1847 with the aid of freed American slaves, presumably those from the north who were emancipated, since the southern states still indulged in their 'peculiar institution' until the end of the Civil War. (To put this into further perspective, the *Encyclopaedia Britannica* claims that 18 million slaves were transferred across the Sahara to the Muslim countries of the Middle East, including the Ottoman Empire, between the years 700–1905) The capital of the new country was named Monrovia after President Monroe, and the new settlers proceeded to form an elite that treated the indigenous population in the same way that they had been treated by their plantation masters. By the 1950s Liberia was essentially an American neo-colony, based upon the rubber plantations of the Firestone Rubber Company, who dominated the trade in the same way that the United Fruit Company dominated Central American banana republics such as Honduras. The airport was called Robert's Field, and close to that was the Firestone compound called Harbel, a little bit of America in the wilds of Africa with residences, a golf course, swimming pools, stores with American food and other brands, and green manicured lawns – the complete suburban scene. A few years later I was to observe a similar situation at Dhahran in eastern Saudi Arabia, where the Aramco employees were cosseted from the surrounding Arabs and desert. In both cases, Quaker had never sent a representative to check, so those companies had got representation basically for the consumption of their own expatriate staff. Knowing nothing about all this, I was assigned a room at Harbel and left to kick my heels in comfort. On the second night there was a commotion in the corridor outside my room, and when I asked the reason for it the next morning, I was told that the Dutch consul had 'gone bush' and had been flown back to Amsterdam by a couple of gentlemen in white coats. When I asked what the symptoms of his malaise were, I was told that he had gone around at cocktail parties pinching ladies' bottoms, and would not desist. That didn't seem too way-out for West Africa, but maybe Americans were more puritanical about such matters.

However, that alerted me to the existence of the Dutch West African Trading Company, who had moved in to trade with the whole population. I rented a three-seater air taxi to fly the fifteen minutes into Monrovia with a Czech Bata shoe representative, thus avoiding about a three-hour car ride over bone-jolting, potholed roads. Monrovia was where the president of the country lived in a palace, and it had a reasonable hotel. It also had its share of odd expatriates, who had arrived there and got stranded for one reason or another. There was a smaller hostelry called the French Hotel, run by a pair of French ladies from Marseilles, which had a bar that was a popular watering hole. Into this spot some years previously had wandered a tall, thin Englishman with a military moustache, wearing a khaki bush jacket and Eighth Army shorts flapping around, or rather below, his bony knees, who could only have been an ex-Army officer. He had come to Liberia from Lagos on a short business trip, lost his money at some form of gambling, and had been advised that if he did not pay up he would be slung into gaol – not funny in Liberia. However, help was at hand in the form of one of the French ladies, who did not have a man to call her own at that time, and she agreed to bail him out if he would marry her. He agreed and, true to his word as an officer and a gentleman, sent for her when he returned to Lagos. They married and had one son. A few years later the family was pointed out to me. The husband could still not speak French, nor his wife English, so the poor child acted as interpreter between the two parents.

A happier gambling story was related to me by an Englishman from our agents in Ghana. He was a keen poker player and had gone to Monrovia to make a pitch for the contract to supply new beds to the hospital. He was staying in the better hotel, when a well-dressed African asked him he would like to join a game of poker, and he accepted. I know nothing about poker, but the stakes were one unit per whatever, which he assumed to be one US cent. The African turned out to be the country's vice president under President Tubman, and my friend came out on top with quite a lot of points. To his surprise, but also his infinite relief, his winnings were in dollars, hundreds if not more, and if he had lost a similar amount he would have been in dire straits.

Since that time, of course, Liberia imploded when the other colonies got their independence from the British, or became French 'departments', and the indigenous population rose up against the American African elite, followed by a bloodbath. After countless deaths and mutilations an American-educated lady has been elected president, so the continent of Africa can see if a woman can put a country on to the straight and narrow after years of male misrule.

Next and last stop was the small British colony of Sierra Leone, generally regarded as the unhealthiest of all, and the location of Graham Greene's novel *The Heart of the Matter* in which a Lebanese entangles and compromises a British police officer. Being Graham Greene, no doubt Catholic angst also came into it somewhere too. Sierra Leone had also been founded as the home for freed slaves from the British Caribbean and homeless Africans in Britain as early as 1788. It was also said that the latter were accompanied by fifty Plymouth prostitutes, who were told to go forth and multiply, but that could easily have been just one of the coast tales. It was a well-endowed little country with bauxite and diamond mines in the north, cocoa, coffee, rice and palm oil agricultural production. The capital Freetown was a dump, and the pits were the rooms in the annexe of the City Hotel, one of which was to be my lodging place for a few days. The rooms were sparsely furnished with a bed, some sort of a locker for possessions and one of those wooden chairs with a round seat and a semicircular cane back. One wore ties for business calls, and when I turned in I threw my tie loosely over the back of the chair. It must have slipped on to the floor, where I found it in the morning with most of one end chewed off by some of the largest cockroaches that I have ever seen.

We sold quite a lot of Canadian flour in that market, and I went to call on a large bakery, which was owned by a couple of men with Scottish names. When I arrived I was shown their picture on the wall on some occasion, revealing two pure African gentlemen. Only one was present for my visit, who advised me that Mr McKay was on 'home leave' in the UK. This came as something of a surprise at that time before large-scale immigration to this country, but demonstrated what the ambitious Africans aspired to all along that coast. There was a saying that the full hand was to be 'houseful, fridgeful, been-to, Jagwah', which can be interpreted as having a nice house and family, full of modern devices, having been to or visited the UK, and being the proud owner of a Jaguar car. Since independence, all that was dropped in the rush to get to the top of the ruling pinnacle, to become one of the Wa Benz tribe, and stuff the rest of the population.

There were diamond mines in the north, alluvial, not deep as in South Africa. Some years later we noticed that sales of Quaker Oats in tins to that market were climbing rapidly for no apparent reason. When the next person from my department was going out I told him to go upcountry to Bo to find out what was going on. It seems that the Lebanese and Syrian traders were opening the cans, whose contents were packed under pressure, and removing the top couple of inches to insert rough diamonds, before repacking and re-soldering the lid. These were smuggled over the colonial border into Liberia. Since then, as we now know from the recent film *Blood Diamonds*, that trade and the whole country have degenerated into the most appalling savagery, every bit as bad as what went on in the bad old days of the Belgian Congo.

I had every intention of returning to New York via London, when I received a cable from my boss that he was coming to London to meet me. The plane service around the bulge of Africa was in small aircraft belonging to the Hunting Clan Airways that gave a stopping service at all the intermediate places. The first was at Bathurst, capital of the Gambia, a narrow strip of land, which featured in the American film *Roots* about an African American seeking his ancestry. Now it has gained a less wholesome reputation as the place where European ladies of a certain age go to seek not just casual sex with young Africans, but even marriage, which inevitably ends in emotional and financial disaster. Las Palmas in the Canary Islands was just that and nothing more, until the package tour industry boomed and they were swamped with Europeans. Now they are in danger of being swamped with economic refugees fleeing from the poor west African states, looking for entrée into the EU via the Spanish mother country.

To a considerable extent the EU has shot itself in the foot via the selfish practices of the Common Fisheries Policy, whereby industrial fishing boats from Europe have brought poverty to small African fisherman. The last port of call was Tangier, which then passed for the nearest spot that qualified as the mysterious east after that French actor, Charles Boyer, uttered the immortal words, 'Come wiz me into ze casbah.'

After going over my trip in depth with Frank Forrestal and confirming some of the changes in our representation, he came up with the bright idea that I should now get on to the next plane and repeat the exercise down the east coast of Africa. I replied that I had an even better idea, it being February, which was to go for a couple of weeks skiing in Austria. Thus I found myself at short notice at the relatively low resort of Seefeld near Innsbruck, where such post-war holidays were taking off, with Slivovitch at six old pence per glass, a hot bath at 1s/- provided one gave forty-eight hours notice, and lumbering around at après-ski tea dances wearing lace-up boots. A friendly, boozy bunch of Aussies adopted me as a semi-fellow colonial, and I forgot about Africa.

Ethiopia was the first country to be visited down the east coast. Of all the African countries, it was the only one not to come under European control during the Scramble in the late nineteenth century. It parcelled out development responsibilities to various countries, so that the hospital in Addis Ababa had been run by the Tsarist Russians. Addis, like Rome, was built on seven hills, at an altitude of 6,000 feet by King Menelik II around 1890. It was in a wonderful location, surrounded by green hills at that time of the year. Haile Selassie, inevitably referred to as 'Highly Salacious' by the British and South African troops that liberated the country from the Italians in 1941, had been restored to his throne as the absolute ruler. The Ethiopians are a good-looking race, tall with Nilotic as opposed to Bantu features. The upper-class ladies walking around Addis carried parasols to prevent the strong sunlight from burning their skins even darker, which shows that Africans aspire to colour social grading, as indeed northern Indians do too. Our agent was the inevitable Dutchman, who lived there with his wife, and was well established in the market.

Outside Addis there was an extinct volcano, whose crater had become a lake, which was a favourite weekend picnic spot for expatriates. At dinner on Saturday night the agent and his wife told me that we would have lunch there the next day. But it was not to be. Either the Dutchman was an alcoholic or he decided to drink this visiting Englishman under the table. I stuck with my usual defence, brandy and ginger ale, which for some reason is, or was, just water off a duck's back to me. The following morning, there was no sign of my host until his apologetic wife phoned to say that he was unwell and could not come out. Disappointing, but a small consolation in putting one over the Dutch.

At some point in going south our four-engine propeller plane, flying at a much lower altitude than modern jets do, was approaching the lip of the Rift Valley, when the pilot told us to fasten our seat belts, particularly since it was mealtime. I have a vision of the man immediately in front of me, who failed to follow instructions, rising feet out of his seat as the plane dropped like a stone, before he returned complete with what was left of his food in his lap.

East Africa after the west coast is like entering the Garden of Eden after escaping from the Slough of Despond, and is familiar to members of the Watkins tribe. Uganda never had European settlers in it, but its lush, rolling, green land tempted the Asian traders to move up there before Idi Amin threw them out. When I was in the Royal Free Hospital in Hampstead in May 2003 there was a Philippino nurse, who was working her way across the world to pay for a block of flats for her retirement. Her last stop before the UK had been in Jeddah, and when I asked her if she had had any interesting patients, such as the Saudi princes, she replied that she had looked after Idi Amin, whom she described as looking like 'the Incredible Hulk'.

Kenya was just recovering from the Mau Mau rebellion in March 1956. Nairobi was another medium-sized colonial town, and one would not have known what had gone on in the immediate past. The Omani traders still lived in and ran the port of Mombasa, and the old harbour was full of their beautiful Arab dhows with their elaborately carved sterns.

I spent Easter that year in Nairobi, where the agent was not particularly hospitable and I had no contacts. While I had been travelling my salary had been accumulating in my account in a New York bank. I had a friend my own age, who worked as a broker for Merrill Lynch on Wall Street, and I sent him a cable asking him to recommend a share for income and one for growth. For the latter he replied that he liked the look of a small, new company in Rochester, New York, called the Haloid Company, which had an interesting new process. Thus I put it all into that stock. Five years later, married, with two kids, highly taxed as everyone was in the UK in 1961 I saw an available plot of land to die for, facing south, backing on to public woodland, but apparently way out of my financial reach. On the odd chance I asked my bank manager what the shares were worth by then, since being in US dollars they were held by banks under exchange control regulations. He came back a day later to say that the Haloid chrysalis had metamorphosed into a butterfly called the Xerox Corporation, worth considerably more, and much to everyone's surprise we have been here for the past forty-eight years. Rolling stones apparently can gather moss after all.

12.

East, West, Home's Best (Years 30–31)

Nairobi in March 1956 was a clean colonial town recovering from the Mau Mau rebellion, where the actions of the rebels had been reported in lurid detail, and the reactions of the British Forces opposing them somewhat sanitised. There were a few so-called Kenyan cowboys strolling around town with revolver holsters at their hips, but the New Stanley Hotel in the centre, with its famed long bar, was full of visitors and businessmen. It had a vast dining room with tables set for four persons each, and the wildlife safari or photography business must have started up again since there was a Belgian couple called Michaela and Denis Arnand (or something close to that) who held court there. They could not be missed since Michaela wore a suntan face pack that was so artificial-looking it became a standing joke. It was not matched until the New Labour MP Peter Hain appeared in the House of Commons with his permatan in the depths of an English winter some fifty years later, which also became a standing joke. He was also Kenya-born come to think of it, but raised in South Africa. Conditions must have settled down in the country at large, since I decided to see if I could find any of my old Hilton and Holly farm school friends. I traced down Angus Clay about an hour's drive out of Nairobi on his prosperous Jersey dairy farm.

There was also something nagging in the back of my mind. Recalling how the New York office had let me down regarding the return emigrant's visa from the Caribbean, I began to fret about the matter of a tax return to the US revenue, which would be due sometime during April. I recalled how seriously they seemed to take these matters in the USA, since Al Capone had been sent to Sing Sing not for his activities in Murder Incorporated, but for his tax evasion proclivities. Therefore, before I flew down to Mombasa, I sent in a second request to head office to send me whatever I had to fill in and submit to the tax office. Mombasa at that time was still essentially a Swahili town, with the Omani traders dominating the colourful old harbour under the gaze of the Mombasa Club, past which Grandpa Sam had left Kenya in a hurry, courtesy of belonging to the same lodge as the judge downing his drink on the veranda as Sam floated by. The harbour was full of Arab dhows, with beautifully carved stern pieces, that would sail between there and the Persian Gulf. The Islamic presence of the Omanis, who owed their loyalty to the Sultan of Zanzibar, was very discreet, just small mosques here and there with small whitewashed pepper pot minarets to indicate where they were. All that was swept away after Kenya's independence, when the Omanis were squeezed out, and Mombasa began to degenerate in a way that African towns seem to do.

However, it was my birthplace, and since this was the first time that I had properly set foot in it, I took time off to have a look around. The port was dominated by Fort Jesus, built by the Portuguese traders when they first came up this coast on their way to India and Indonesia in the sixteenth century. There must have been trade with China even in those times as, when an old Chinese vessel was discovered and lifted from the silt, it was found to contain quantities of porcelain ware. The fort must later have been taken over by the Sultan of Zanzibar and turned into one of those entrepôts for channelling African slaves from the interior to the countries surrounding the Persian Gulf. There is also a Roman Catholic cathedral built by the Portuguese, as well as the Anglican one where my parents were married, as were Lucie and Jock, and where I was christened.

So this is where it all really began to take shape for those two dysfunctional families of that generation, the Watkins and the Orchards. They were not really true colonials, in the sense of the people who had settled and made their permanent homes in Kenya, or those in India who served in the administration, be it the ICS, forestry, medical or other services over succeeding generations. They had been taken out there by the restlessness of their father Sam, and then joined up with the available talent of marriageable age, my parents to go off to India after one tour, the various Watkins heading into what was then Tanganyika. There seemed to have been very little sibling affection handed down to them in their genes – in fact, quite the reverse. Fortunately this was not passed on to their children. They were simply one-generation only, temporary colonials.

There was not much business to be had in Tanganyika, but it was too good an opportunity to miss to revisit where I had first met Mac as a schoolboy in January 1942 off the MV *Inchanga*, and to pay a visit to the spice island of Zanzibar. Dar-es-Salaam had not changed at all, and as I was passing, by taxi, the club that overlooked the harbour, I spotted a familiar figure drive in by car, jump out and enter the building. This was an Irishman when I had been in digs with in Liverpool with the Duchess of Devonshire before I emigrated to Canada. I recalled that before I set off he had accepted a job in East Africa somewhere, and his bulky shape could not have altered that much in the intervening four years. I stopped my taxi and followed him into the club, and found him in the bar. When I 'fingered' him on the shoulder he nearly jumped out of his skin. He had been good company, but he had one weakness, which was that when we took the tram together at any time, he never had any small change on him to pay the fare when the conductor came along. Thus I ended up paying for both. It was probably only 3d each in those days, but there was a principle involved. There was also another unwritten convention that in a club, members paid for the drinks; visitors were not allowed to pay. We stayed there for the rest of the evening yarning about the intervening years, and I think he was quite surprised by how much my drinking habits had come on in that time!

Before the independence of Tanganyika and the creation of the new state of Tanzania, Zanzibar was still under the rule of its sultan, whose red flag flew over his palace. It was but a short flight from Dar-es-Salaam in that old workhorse the Dakota, and as soon as the plane door opened after landing the senses were assailed with the wonderful smell of cloves. The source of this was obvious when we reached the town, where a fleet of maybe twenty to thirty dhows lay at anchor in the harbour. Their Omani captains, colourful characters often bearded and with curved dagger tucked into their belts, were supervising the loading. My hotel overlooked the palace, and early the following morning as I rose and went out onto the balcony to get a breath of air, I was favoured with the sight of the dhow fleet, their triangular sails spread to a gentle south-west breeze, sailing out to the Persian Gulf. Zanzibar, of course, had a wicked history, being the main port to which Arab slavers brought their wretched captives from central east Africa, attached by their necks to one another with wooden poles. David Livingstone had gone out there on behalf of the Church Missionary Society in the mid-nineteenth century, and while it was said that he only made one convert to Christianity, he played his part in the ending of the African slave trade. Nevertheless, when independence came to Tanganyika, it was payback time and many Arabs were either slaughtered or driven out. Its main town is essentially Arab in design, with narrow streets to shut out the sunlight for cool. Among its more attractive features were the beautiful carved ebony doors, studded with brass decorative pieces, of which the one at the British Residency was an excellent example. The island is made up of coconut groves and clove farms, and early one evening I went to the west coast to have a swim and watch the early setting sun in those equatorial latitudes, while out in the shallows a couple of Swahili men went about scrubbing their donkey clean in the water. It seemed to enjoy the experience, judging by the forward set of its ears.

From there I had to get back to the Belgian Congo and the best route was via what was then northern Rhodesia, so I found myself in the copper mining town of Ndola. This was not all that far south of Elizabethville in Katanga province, but aesthetically on another planet. While I have previously described Elizabeth-ville as a civilised European city constructed in the middle of Africa, Ndola was a rough, tough mining town with no preten-sions to being anything else, with British and Afrikaner staff, and no doubt from many from other countries. On long trips such as these, there comes a time when one begins to run out of puff or self-motivation, and one needs an example as a reminder. One of my favourite stories related to how Kolynos toothpaste was introduced into the South African market. Muller and Phipps, the import agency and distributors, were given the account and Harry Hertz decided to take personal charge. This was in the 1930s and he got the company to supply him with a portmanteau full of sample toothpaste tubes, and set sail for South Africa. Once there, he set about booking himself for one night into a different hotel across the country over a period of three months. Presumably in the larger cities he stayed in several hotels, so that he was not travelling all the time. In those days, as anyone of a certain age will recall, people used to put their shoes outside their bedroom doors for cleaning and polishing. When they were collected in the morning and taken away, Harry would get up, wash and shave, and await their return, at which point he would sally forth and put a Kolynos sample tube into each pair of shoes. It must have been reasonably successful, otherwise it would not have gone into salesmen's folklore, but I have no idea how that brand stands in that market today.

I was instructed to go back into the Belgian Congo and then north to the then British West African markets to follow up on the various changes that I had made on the earlier visits. To a certain extent it was too soon to make a proper evaluation, and by the time that I got to the Gold Coast, I was afflicted with a cluster of boils on my leg that made walking quite painful. This was pretty minor stuff compared to what the African explorers had to endure during their nineteenth-century travels, but since Liberia was the next stop, I thought that I could do without that, and got permission to jump on a plane and return to London, where I holed up in a B&B run by old India friends of my parents, who had been forced into early retirement with Indian independence. As soon as I was fit, I was told to return to New York to learn about my next assignment, and that would have been about May 1956.

My first port of call, since no one had sent me a form for an income tax return, was to head for the Inland Revenue office, which was located at quite a swanky address (for such a mundane office) on Park Avenue. One associated that part of Manhattan with more upmarket activities, like advertising agencies, but maybe the revenue went where the most money was to be collected – like the American cowboy, who when arrested for the umpteenth time for holding up a bank in the Wild West, and on being asked by the judge why he always chose to raid them, replied, 'Well, Your Honour, that's where the money is!' It was a large open-plan office with desks; one was given a number on entry, and then answered the call to whichever desk was free. I explained to the inspector that I had been travelling since the previous October, the basic tax had been deducted at source, but I had been advised that I still had to make a return, which was difficult from Africa. He replied that that was correct, and that if he went by the book he should fine me something in excess of $100, but he did not see why he should, since I had come in of my own volition. He told me to sit there while he went in and had a word with his boss. A couple of minutes later he came back, shaking his head and apologising that he had been told not to make an exception. Then, looking me straight in the eye he asked, 'You work for a large company, don't you?' I nodded. 'And you have an expense account when you are out in those markets, don't you?' Another nod. 'Well, you know what to do then, don't you?' Fair advice. Looking back on those days it is quite extraordinary how cheap it was to travel through African countries, staying at decent hotels (Freetown excepted), since I managed to do it on an average of just under £5 per day.

Once settled back in the office, I was told that the decision had been taken to decentralise control of the export markets due to the cost of the trans-Atlantic flights and the time lag, and I was offered the chance to return to the UK and start up a so-called International Division within the English subsidiary at Southall, which would handle all exports supplied from whatever source to the markets from Portugal through the Mediterranean countries to India, and the African continent. It did not take long to accept. Big city life as in New York was always anathema to me. I had always wanted to work within reach of London, whose charms were summed up by Dr Samuel Johnson's famous aphorism. And last but not least, since my father's early death a couple of years earlier, my mother had been on her own in England with my brother out in Malaya planting rubber, and therefore somewhat lonely. This, of course, was how we had been brought up since my father had headed east in the early 1920s, leaving his ageing parents behind for three-year intervals. So I was told to take my leave of the few friends that I had made, and write up an appraisal of all the future markets and my objectives for them. One has to say that Americans can be nothing if not thorough. Until fairly recently American companies gave exceptionally short annual holiday or vacation allowances amounting to two weeks per annum, until one had completed twenty-five years' service with the company, or achieved higher seniority. But I got permission to go up and stay with my old family friend Everett Rankin on his farm just north of Ithaca, New York on the Finger Lakes. This was, and probably continues to be a glorious area on the fringe of New England, and I regret that I have not been back there. I did, however, later visit Massachusetts and Maine extensively with my wife.

There was an incident that happened during my last weekend in New York when I was installed back in the care of good old Hotel Earl which could only have happened in that city. I had had the usual Sunday brunch and was sitting up in my bedroom typing up my last report on the faithful Olivetti, when I heard the metal gates of the rickety lift slam shut a couple of floors below, and then it rose to my floor. The exit was immediately opposite my bedroom door, and I heard a man and a woman leave it and then enter another room that was diagonally across the landing from mine. Very soon it became apparent from their raised voices that they were having something of an argument. She was complaining in no uncertain terms that in her opinion his friends, or 'johns' as she called them, were just a bunch of... well, she used a good old New York descriptive term. He replied by asking could she not just be polite to them, instead of always hostile. I concluded that she was not a prostitute with her ponce, but perhaps a mafia moll with a small-time member of that fraternity. Soon shouts turned to blows, amid the sounds of furniture being overturned, and I was just at the point of weighing up whether I should go to the assistance of a damsel in distress, when I realised that judging from the male voice oh-ing and ah-ing, he was definitely taking a beating. 'Wass wrong wid ya?' she snarled. 'Oh! Oh! It's my thumb, I think you've broke it,' he wailed.

'Aw well then, just stick it—' in the same anatomical region referred to above, came her unsympathetic reply. There were then sounds of the furniture and beds being restored to their usual positions, before they decided to go on to meet his 'johns'. By this time I was bent double with my eye to the keyhole, but could only see that they were both fairly short in stature. A feisty lady, nevertheless.

The company literally pushed the boat out for me to cross the Atlantic to Southampton by booking me on to the original *Queen Elizabeth*, first class no less, when the arrival and departure of one of the Cunard *Queens* at the piers in the Hudson River was still an event that attracted crowds of folk seeing them and their friends off. It was on one of these departures that Sam Goldwyn was supposed to have made his famous Goldwynism from the deck as the ship departed by wishing those on shore 'bon voyage'! During World War Two, the *Elizabeth* and her sister ship, the *Queen Mary*, had of course been used to ferry thousands of American service personnel across the Atlantic unescorted, relying on their speed in excess of thirty knots to avoid any German U-boats lying in wait. I was assigned to cabin number E14 which, my steward assured me, had been occupied by General Eisenhower on one such crossing. It was no great suite, fairly close to the water line, so even generals must have been in relatively cramped quarters when the ship had thousands of troops on board, hot-bedding in shifts.

The ship was divided up into the familiar classes of those times, first, tourist and steerage in the stern over the propellers. First class had the best boat deck for walking round to get some exercise, or lying in a lounge chair wrapped in a rug, since even in June the north Atlantic is not particularly warm, and not very interesting to look out on for that matter. Nor were ships fitted with stabilisers at that time, so there was a certain roll to our progress. World news bulletins received over the radiotelegraph were posted up daily on a notice board. Probably stock exchange printouts, too, in first class. This is how it was in such large passenger ships until the *Canberra* was launched with a single class for the Australian run. This belatedly came into our family life when, during the first days of action in the Falklands War, our son Peter served in HMS *Antrim*, which was the guard ship for the *Canberra* in San Carlos Water, a great target for attacking Argentinean planes.

The greatest manifestation of exclusivity in such liners was, of course, the first-class dining saloon. It was de rigueur to dress for dinner in the full outfit, and the more ambitious passengers would risk physical injury in the scrum to secure an invitation to the captain's table. I shared a table of either six or eight where all the others were either British or American millionaires. But I had been told by the vice president of the New York office that when in Rome I was to behave as the Romans, and put it down on expenses. I have to say that the conversation of millionaires is pretty tedious if they were anything to go by, being mainly descriptions of how much they spent on this or that, here and there. Maybe the ultra rich don't talk about it so much, as when a Rockefeller or some such was asked by another up-and-coming member of that set how much it cost to run an ocean yacht replied, 'If you have to ask that question, you can't afford to run one!' Or the other one, when asked if he knew the Vanderbilts he replied, 'Yes, I've known the Vanderbilts since they first started Vander building!'

The crunch came on the last evening at dinner, when it was time to pass out the tips to the surrounding staff. In these egalitarian times, tips are usually included in the total price of the voyage or cruise, but then among the crew members one was expected to reward the cabin steward, swimming pool attendant and the bar steward if one had spent some time there. In the first-class dining saloon there was the head waiter, the table waiter and the wine waiter, hovering around their individual tables like jackals at the end of the meal. There was a series of generally accepted going rates on such ships, £5 or whatever for the head waiter, and so on down the ranks. To my acute embarrassment our table began to discuss and argue in stage whispers, fully within the hearing of the staff, how much the various amounts should be, and where they might even be shaved by ten bob or so. So I baled out, wished them all happy landings, and did the rounds on my own. In their defence, it was probably their own money they were shelling out, rather than from an expense account, but I guess that's how they became rich.

Thus, four years to the month since I had left the UK in June 1952, I found myself in the office of the British subsidiary attached to the main manufacturing plant located in Southall, a suburb about seven miles as the crow flies west of Marble Arch. It had originally been a railway town, when Welsh immigrants came in to construct the Great Western Railway, complete with iconic all-wooden railway sheds. During World War Two, the Poles moved into Ealing and Southall, and earned their own distinctive Polish war memorial on the A40, a couple of miles to the north. Last, but certainly not least, Asian immigrants were brought in during the late 1960s and early '70s to do the dirty work in the Wolff Rubber Company, which produced heavy-duty conveyor belts and suchlike. The immigrants were mainly Gujeratis from north of Bombay, Punjabis and Sikhs, so there were a lot of Patels and Singhs in the town, which took on an entirely different appearance with the inevitable Indian bazaars, jewellery and silk shops. There were some Muslims also. All this gave rise to an apocryphal story concerning the firmly all-white London bus manufacturing plant just to the east of the town. Supposedly the workers came out on strike, complaining of racial discrimination towards them, emanating from the local town hall. When asked to be more specific, they replied that they all knew what OHMS (On Her Majesty's Service) stood for in Southall: 'Only Hindus, Muslims and Sikhs'! But just to the west was the beginning of open countryside in Berkshire and Bucks within easy commuting distance by car, so one avoided the dreaded daily grind of catching a train into London.

I was glad to be back in England once more, within striking distance of London, but the country had not changed all that much. There was still the class divide between management and labour, with the Conservative party dedicated to managing decline with the least pain, and the shop stewards having apparently a free hand to dominate the massed workforces in the vehicle and other large industries. I recall going to a meeting of the Federation of British Industry (renamed Confederation of British Industry in order not to be confused with the American FBI), where the chairman proposed that in future the public schools should be considered as the seed bed to produce the managers for British industry. No mention as to how the other 94% of the population were to realise their aspirations and climb the ladder, and absolutely no questions asked from the floor to challenge this. With taxation at the top rate above 80% there was a disincentive to work harder, and it was noticeable when attending an afternoon meeting in London how attendees would start to sneak out, doubled up, to catch their trains from about 4.30 p.m. onwards, while the speaker struggled gamely on to 5 p.m. Fast forward fifty years or so to the beginning of this century, and commuter trains out of London are packed with City workers going home up to 10 p.m., with tax levels limited to 40%.

By this time I was thirty years of age and had never lived anywhere longer than for three years. This is probably also the typical life cycle for Service families. And like many Brits of those times, while I had travelled extensively around the world, I had only been to continental Europe a couple of times, to ski. But it was all about to end. A Danish girl, whose father had worked for the company in various Scandinavian countries, had come over to England to improve her proficiency in English, and was assigned to me as a secretary. At that time I just about knew where Denmark was, since we all learned about the Vikings from our history books, as well as the stories of Hans Christian Andersen. Danny Kaye had recently made a film with his song extolling the virtues of wonderful Copenhagen, and I recalled a photo in a newspaper of a Danish girl during the German occupation wearing a beret into which she had woven the red, white and blue rings of the RAF roundels as her protest. I also knew that the country was flat, unlike Norway, so I decided to show this girl how hilly England could be and took her down to Broadway in the Cotswolds on a Sunday. The local scrumpy must have had a kick that day, because to cut a long story short, we got engaged within a few months, and married one year later in Copenhagen, with the full works. The wedding service was in a Danish Lutheran church, with the essentials in Danish, repeated in English so I understood what was happening. Her middle name, presciently, was Anker, which means in English what it sounds like in Danish. A carriage pulled by a white horse took us from the church to the reception in a restaurant in Tivoli Gardens, whose design was based on the old Vauxhall Gardens in London. A couple of tour buses full of Americans came alongside at the traffic lights and photographed us, so we may still be in someone's album. Since then, I have lived fifty-two years in only two houses, the first for five years and the second, which we had built for us, for forty-eight years, both in south Bucks.

I have therefore come to the end of my description of what it was like being brought up in the last days of the old British Empire, an experience that, for better or worse, must have been repeated in literally millions of other cases. In an earlier chapter I quoted Tommy Trinder's jocular remark, 'Here's to our far-flung empire... [followed by pause for effect]... that wasn't flung far enough!' Someone has written that the British Empire was built on the tears of the children. That was probably true not so much for the children in settler colonies like the Rhodesias, but rather for those with parents in the Indian subcontinent and the Far East countries like Malaya, before air travel. In contrast to other European nations with empires, such as the Dutch or the French, many of the British elected to have their children brought up separately at 'home' in a quasi orphan status, with reunions every three years or so. When one was old enough to understand what was happening, these were undoubtedly gut-wrenching partings for the majority. Parental home leaves were of four–six months' duration, but all too soon months changed to weeks, weeks to days, before *slam*! The door was closed on another three years of grin and bear it. My worst experience was at aged ten, when I left what had been the parental care of the Coves in Cheshire to be transferred at a few weeks' notice into the complete newness of Bickley Hall in Kent, with not a single familiar face or landmark in sight.

However, one significant event came to the rescue of my generation, the miracle of Dunkirk, that allowed 300,000-plus British and French soldiers to escape from those beaches, and enabled the children of the Raj to experience the hackneyed phrase 'with one bound he [or she] was free!'. It was life chang-ing, and probably engendered a semi-detachment from one's peers whom we left behind, for the rest of our lives. We remained English, but not completely of England. Every now and then I have met someone who has said how satisfying it was to be able to talk with someone on the same wavelength. The Dutch whom I met during my African travels said much the same thing that the

Dutch were two nations, those brought up in the Netherlands, and those in their colonies. It certainly did not make for felicitous family relationships – not in my experience, at any rate. I have read the biography of J G Ballard, the English boy who lived with and was then interned with his parents in Shanghai by the Japanese during the 1940s, an experience that was made into the film *The Empire of the Sun*. He explained how the typical colonial social life of his parents, with clubs, bridge and social gossip in a limited community, was so alien to his own interests that when they were freed and returned to England, they simply drifted apart and he determined to set his own course. Maybe girls under such circumstances tended to be closer to their parents? I don't know. But I can think of a couple of exceptions!

I regarded it as a sink or swim experience. Quite unintentionally, I am sure, my father opened up new, interesting horizons for me by tipping me out of the nest on a couple of occasions, the first at the age of four when I was left behind, and the second at fifteen and a half when I was moved on to South Africa. As a result I experienced the warm substitute parentage of Miss Braithwaite as well as Aunt Tommy and Claud. Mr Cove (and his driver Mr Fare) provided me with an unrivalled introduction for those days to the coasts, countryside and historical sites of Wales and England, from Cheshire to Land's End. The Noyces in Durban were an example of how every family should be, but probably is not.

But what of my sibling, Tim? He was out in India with our parents until the age of seven in 1939, and goodness knows what early schooling he had there. No one could describe him as academic, but he had an easygoing approach to life. After a year at Bickley Hall he went out to India with me and stayed at the New School for four years as a boarder in Darjeeling before returning to Bickley in 1944. A couple of years later he went on to a public school in Dorset, where he was regularly beaten by those from the headmaster down for lack of academic ability, which still rankles with him. In those days, middle-class parents did not send their children to the local school. After completing his military service our father sent Tim off to a rubber plantation in Malaya for four years, and when this was terminated after the civil war by their independence, he was moved on a tea estate in south India. So there was something of the old treatment of the remittance man for him, sent out of sight and out of mind. It must have been perfectly obvious to everyone but the most purblind that after the fall of Singapore and Indian independence in 1947, future colonial life in the 1950s was a busted flush. So as far as Tim was concerned, the second part of Trinder's comment applied – the empire was not flung far enough, and he may have been better not to have experienced it.

How then does one sum up the previous chapters? Such an upbringing, so far as I experienced it at any rate, was out of the ordinary. It contained some lows, some long plateaux and many more highs, and if, as they say, variety is the spice of life, then mine had it in spades.

The End

ND - #0089 - 270225 - C0 - 203/127/14 - PB - 9781909020252 - Matt Lamination